WOMEN AND THEIR POLITICAL EXPLOITATIONS

Abused and Misused

WOMEN AND THEIR POLITICAL EXPLOITATIONS

Abused and Misused

K N Choudhary

MD PUBLICATIONS PVT LTD
NEW DELHI
www.mdppl.com

Published by :

MD Publications Pvt Ltd
"MD House", 11, Darya Ganj,
New Delhi - 110 002
Phone : +91-11-45355555
E-mail : contact@mdppl.com
Website: www.mdppl.com

ISBN: 978-81-7533-313-0

Published and Printed by Mr. Pranav Gupta on behalf of **MD Publications Pvt Ltd** at Times Press, Delhi.

PREFACE

Throughout the world, women still suffer from discrimination and oppression, for no reason other than their gender. In essence, the plight and suffering of women is the same for all of us. Today, major issues such as peace, social and economic development, and the spread of democracy have become unavoidably entangled with the issues of women.

At the end of the twentieth century, local and international forces have merged to escalate the sexual exploitation of women and girls. Policies, practices and crises are combining to increase both the supply of women and girls vulnerable to exploitation and the demand by men for women and girls to be used for their profit and sexual gratification. Sexual exploitation takes many forms, such as sexual harassment, incest, rape, child marriages, temporary marriages, female genital mutilation, pornography, bride trafficking, battering, sexual torture and prostitution. All of these practices violate women's dignity and autonomy.

Women from every world region report that the sexual exploitation of women and girls is increasing. All over the world, brothels and prostitution rings exist underground on a small scale, and on an increasingly larger scale, entire sections of cities are informally zoned into brothels, bars and club that house, and often enslave, women for the purposes of prostitution. The magnitude and violence of these practices of sexual exploitation constitutes an international human rights crisis of contemporary slavery. Globally, one form of sexual exploitation, prostitution, is becoming more normalized and industrialized, with some powerful agents and institutions advocating for its widespread legitimization and legalization.

As prostitution has increased, the demand for women and girls has resulted in widespread recruitment and trafficking to fill the brothels, bars and street corners.

Political changes combined with economic crises have devastated entire world regions, increasing the supply of vulnerable women willing to risk their lives to earn money for themselves and their families. Social problems such as sexual and physical abuse within families force girls and women to leave in search of safety and a better life, but often they find more exploitation and violence. Physical and sexual abuse of girls and women in their families and by intimate partners destroys girls' and women's sense of self and resiliency, making them easy targets for pimps and traffickers who prey on those who have few options left to them.

Global media and communication tools, such as the Internet, make access to pornography, catalogs of mail order brides, advertisements for prostitution tours, and information on where and how to buy women and girls in prostitution widely available. This open advertisement normalizes and increases the demand by men for women and girls to use in these different forms of exploitation.

I am very grateful to Mr. Pranav Gupta, Director of MD Publications Pvt Ltd, New Delhi, for his kind cooperation and support for this book.

K N Choudhary

Contents

1

Women's Negotiations with Democracy

Women are vulnerable, because whether it is Burundi, Afghanistan, Kosovo, Algeria or Jerusalem, internal conflicts are not fought primarily in battlefields but in villages and towns where women and children remain. Further, violence often flows back home.

In Northern Ireland, men in security forces have approved arms because of being potential targets, while paramilitary groups retain illicit arms. In war zones and in conflict societies, women are not just victims, many are active peace-builders. The 1995 Fourth World Conference on Women, in Beijing, was instrumental in defining those areas of concern considered to represent the major obstacles to women's advancement and making recommendations for change.

Since then, the global network of NGOs working on women's rights has expanded. This includes lobbying the UN in the lead up to the 24 October 2000 Security Council session on Women, Peace and Security. The resultant resolution is a global advocacy tool. It is a necessary resolution because women are active in informal peace protests, community dialogue, promoting intercultural tolerance and in practical peace initiatives. However, they are overwhelmingly absent in formal peace processes. They must be included in formal processes in order to establish meaningful gender equality.

Does it really matter if women are present at negotiating tables or in formal peace processes? Yes it does.

- First, women and men are affected by conflict and therefore also are affected by the consequences of peace agreements. These agreements are not merely about ending war, they are also about establishing the conditions for new just societies where plural perspectives are taken into account.
- Second, women's inclusion in all stages of peace processes is essential for inclusive social justice.
- Third, the presence of women in political, policy and legal decision-making contexts often makes a difference to the sorts of issues addressed like education, health, nutrition, childcare and human security needs in places as varied as South Africa, Israel, Palestine, Liberia or Guatemala.

Women universally are prime careers in families and communities and they have a huge interest in community stability, so they play important roles in peace-building in unofficial ways. Some women are peace activists advocating for non-violence, others are mediators, trauma healing councillors, practitioners addressing the root causes of violence, educators or facilitators of capacity-building. Many women assist dialogue between husbands or brothers in warring factions, tribes, clans or ethnic groups. Women often bridge divides across traditional ethnic, religious and cultural divisions, coming together on the shared concerns about practicalities of life.

In Azerbaijan, Colombia, the Democratic Republic of Congo, the Great Lakes Region, the Middle East, Northern Ireland and Somalia, women work collaboratively across ethnic and religious lines to make valuable contributions to peace processes despite little awareness of 1325. Stella Tamang of one of Nepal's largest indigenous groups argues that women at the negotiating table "will introduce practical workable solutions to the conflict". The Mano River Women's Peace Network of women from Liberia, Guinea and Sierra Leone opened pathways of communication between warring factions that led to reopening of borders and restoring of diplomatic relations.

THE UNDERSTANDING OF PEACE-BUILDING BE EXPANDED

Narrow definitions of peace-building sit within the post-conflict reconstruction stage, after peace settlements. This definition has two significant consequences for women.

- First, it overlooks all the hands-on, unofficial work women do to build peace in grassroots groups, communities and families.
- Second, it provides inadequate validation for including women at negotiating tables. Failure to accord acknowledgment for women's active conciliation in all stages of peace processes, consistently results in their exclusion from political decision-making.

Peace-building is a process that needs to flow through the pre-conflict, conflict and post-conflict stages and elaborate this in my forthcoming book, *Peace-building: Women in International Perspectives*. Peace processes consist of both formal and informal activities. Women are prominent in informal peace work. However, despite 1325, they are rare in formal peace processes as defined by the UN to include "early warning, preventive diplomacy, conflict prevention, peacemaking, peace-building and global disarmament". The UN distinguishes between different aspects of these processes.

Peacemaking includes mediation, conciliation, arbitration and negotiation to bring hostile parties to agreement. Peacekeeping involves keeping parties from fighting or harming each other through multinational forces of armed soldiers and police. Peace-building includes constructing the conditions of society to foster peace through development, aid, human rights education, reconciliation and the restoration of community life. In the UN, peace-building typically refers to formal approaches used in post-conflict reconstruction. As Christine Chinkin argues, for many women this concept of 'post-conflict' is a problem.

When active conflict or violence ceases, women still have to deal with traumatized children, family members who were combatants and the inevitable difficulties of meeting everyday needs while dealing with intense traumas. The notion of 'reconstruction' may also seem meaningless for women who never have known full citizenship, social justice or a respect for human dignity and rights. So it is a positive thing that the UN Secretary-General, Kofi Anan is expanding his view and says, 'the participation of women and girls and inclusion of gender perspectives in both formal and informal peace processes are crucial in the establishment of sustainable peace'. Certainly, UNIFEM's emphasis on peaceful, just relationships of equality contrasts with orthodox emphases on structural reconstruction.

Most women's understandings of peace-building are far broader and more holistic than UN or conventional usages of the term. As Sanam Anderlini writes in *Women, Violent Conflict and Peace-building: Global Perspectives*, "the intricate tapestry of what constitutes real peace and security...[includes] social justice, domestic reform, women's rights, co-existence, tolerance, participatory democracy, transparency and non-violent dialogue as necessary ingredients for addressing social differences and building sustainable peace".

HUMAN SECURITY AND WELL-BEING

Part of translating 1325's rhetoric into reality is understanding that there are gendered and cultural views on security. Whilst foreign policy assumes that a military presence tightens security, such militarism threatens security for women who are victims of war-rape or are used sexually by peacekeepers. In their book, Susan McKay and Dyan Mazurana provide examples of how women understand peace-building and security. In South Sudan, for Nuer women, "making peace means figuring out how to meet the material, social and spiritual requirements of life". Similarly, with women in Somalia, "peace is not seen as a matter of discussion, but as a way of living, of security and food for your family, of the future for your children".

In Sierra Leone, building peace means "taking in the children of neighbours, friends or family members who were killed in the war". In Kosovo, "peace work means rebuilding damaged houses as well as friendships with former neighbours who had turned against them during conflict". Lebanese women discover peace-building is building bridges between factions involved in the civil war. All these activities revolve around connections, healing, spiritual wounds, rebuilding relationships and meeting everyday family needs.

Accordingly, when women are present around negotiating tables (Guatemala, South Africa, Northern Ireland, East Timor), they initiate different issues -questions related to human security and well-being -like feeling safe and being inclusive, as well as focusing on the practical needs of food, water, health, education, land rights and economic livelihood. As Johan Galtung puts it, 'human security' initiates a new paradigm where people's needs are central to international security and root causes of insecurity are tackled.

In Guatemala, women's participation in formal negotiations resulted in specific commitments to women on housing, credit and land, attempts to locate children and orphans, penalising sexual harassment and creating the National Women's Forum. In South Africa, women across all parties agreed that each party should have one-third female representation in each negotiating team for the Constitution process. The South African Constitution includes a comprehensive Bill of Rights with gains for women on reproduction, property rights, healthcare, education and culture. In Northern Ireland, the two representatives of the Northern Ireland Women's Coalition lobbied for mixed housing and the early release and reintegration of political prisoners.

There are many positive instances of 1325 helping women to make a difference. In Sri Lanka, in 2002, the Government and the *Liberation Tigers of Tamil Eelam*, supported by Norway, established a subcommittee on gender issues to elaborate gender-sensitive guidelines for the peace process. In Somalia, in 2002, fifty women undertook training in negotiation skills and the provisions of 1325 in order to take part in the peace process. It is overwhelmingly the case that it is women in NGOs and feminist academics who are really utilising the resolution -more than politicians and policy-makers. In Rwanda, even in a context where almost every woman survivor of the genocide has a dramatic story of rape, hunger, fear, flight and loss -women began forming groups to confront common problems.

By 1999, Rwandan women's organization's exceeded 15,000. After 1994, the UNHCR began the Rwanda Women's Initiative, taking a practical approach to assisting income, agriculture, land title, childcare and gender-related violence. When Erin Baines, researcher, asked a Rwandan woman if the Initiative had made a difference in her life, she replied, "you cannot dance if you cannot stand".

Many women's organizations involve both Hutu and Tutsi groups. These groups concentrate on what unites rather than divides, that is, the commonalities women face everywhere such as poverty, violence against women, feeding their children and shelter. *Pro-Femmes*? the umbrella organization of women's groups mobilizes women "to spearhead the promotion of a culture of peace, tolerance and non-violence in grassroots activities". There is the view among survivors that women are better than men at forgiving, reconciling and building peace. Ironically, Rwanda has now surpassed Sweden as the country with the highest proportion of women legislators. From the 2003 elections, women hold 48.8% of the seats in the National Assembly and nine out of 28 ministerial posts.

Funding from the Netherlands trained women in decision-making and political awareness. Such a commitment helps translate rhetoric into reality. But let us return to Northern Ireland, where there are many dedicated women peace activists and hundreds of small women's groups, for a final example. Betty Williams and Mairead Corrigan led large demonstrations of Catholics and Protestants to protest against terrorist violence in 1976 and were awarded the Nobel Prize. Despite being deeply divided politically, activists in Northern Ireland come together over basic issues of childcare, housing, education and job skills, avoiding political differences. Two historic examples of women making a difference include the Northern Ireland Women's Coalition and their place at the negotiating table, and the McCartney sisters' stance against the IRA and the demand that there can be no peace without justice.

'The Northern Ireland Women's Coalition was initiated by women with long histories of engagement in civil, human and workers' rights. The Women's Coalition adopted equality, human rights and inclusion as their principles. They also agreed that participants should acknowledge their political identity differences rather than do what is more typical in Northern Ireland, keep silent or fight about controversial differences. An explicit discussion of differences, divisions, discord and political dissonance is necessary to move beyond intolerance of others' views and sectarian attitudes and practices. In 'transversal politics', you keep your identity intact while openly trying to understand others' identities. In 1996, the Coalition gained enough votes to secure two seats in the multi-party peace negotiations on the future of Northern Ireland that led to the *Belfast Agreement* in April 1998. They put on the agenda issues like victims' rights, reconciliation and the need for a Civic Forum.

Monica McWilliams, the Coalition's leader talks of "women's central role in conflict prevention, peacekeeping and peace-building"; of the dangers of sectarianism, which see "the world exclusively in terms of the interest of your "own" side as against the other side"; and of the importance of "working with, not burying, our differences". The Coalition made a noteworthy difference to electoral politics in Northern Ireland, with forthright and positive women presenting a vision of how politics should be different. Whenever the parties were bogged down, the women brought the debates back to personal issues of bereavement, loss and hopes for children's future.

In a bar fight on 30 January 2005, Robert McCartney was murdered by a known leader of the IRA and several of his associates. McCartney's five sisters -Paula, Catherine, Gemma, Claire and Donna -and his fiancé Bridgeen Hagans are demanding justice. These women "are being seen as a metaphor for where the nation finds itself -still struggling for unity, torn by savage grief yet looking for justice, peace and reconciliation".

Five days after the murder, the women held a candlelight vigil attended by 600 people to protest at the IRA cover-up. Sometimes, women prompt the conscience of the nation. Since 1982, Sicilian women have challenged the iron grip of the mafia; since 1996 the committee of soldiers' mothers in Russia have campaigned against conscription in the war in Chechnya; and more recently in Northern Ireland, the McCartney sisters have taken an important stance.

Paula McCartney says, "Yes, absolutely, this is about women standing up. The men tend to huff and puff and egos come in to play, and it goes round and round, and it always ends in more violence...But we want real justice, not more violence". Peace and violence cannot coexist. Anger is 'a crippling emotion' when tied with revenge. These women say, "we have no fear of the IRA...and we will not be bullied by them". This is worth mentioning because Northern Ireland sectarian conflict has claimed more than 200 lives since the paramilitary organizations called their 1994 ceasefires and only thirty people have been prosecuted for murder. Such women motivate other families who have lost family through paramilitary murders.

Women's global participation in peace and security concerns continues in mediation, conciliation, trauma counsel, healing and memory work, providing health care for survivors of rape and HIV/AIDs sufferers. Women and men continue to build bridges across ethnic, religious and cultural divisions, opposing war and militarism in innovative and creative ways. Despite the significance of Resolution 1325 on Women, Peace and Security, women remain absent or are marginalized from negotiating tables, political decision-making opportunities and senior advisory positions. Inclusion matters. Without plural inclusivity, there is no peace with justice and equality and 1325's call to "all actors involved, when negotiating and implementing peace agreements, to adopt a gender perspective" goes unheeded. The substantive content and implementation of peace agreements require balance between women-specific provisions and gender mainstreaming.

What exactly do I mean by the latter? "Mainstreaming gender equality" means transforming the "mainstream" and focusing on the systems and structures that create disadvantages for women and men. Mainstreaming gender is all about working within institutions to integrate equality concerns into all policies, programs and projects so that issues of gender equality become part of organizations' actions, beliefs, values, priorities, needs and actual decisions. Sometimes, this can result in a token gesture, so an organization makes sure there is a woman on a committee but some men still make sexist jokes or ridicule the woman's contribution. Thus, often it is important to have women-only events to enable women's voices to come through clearly, particularly if there are sensitive issues to discuss like women's discrimination, rape or dowry price.

For example, Astrid Heiberg was a Norwegian representative to a Gender Sub-Committee to the Sri Lankan peace talks of 2003. She tells how women's interaction in negotiations between the Government of Sri Lanka and the women in the *Liberation Tigers of Tamil Eelam* became more open when the Government men left, and she created a "women-only space". In 2000, Sanam Anderlini gave four warnings in a preliminary audit on the international community's response to women, peace and security.

First, while the explicit endorsement of women's groups and civil society participation in peace processes is unprecedented, the absence of actual quotas, benchmarks and timelines is of concern. Second, while the endorsement of the need for peacekeepers and civilian personnel in peace processes is clear, "without the core commitment of governments to provide additional funds, these measures can be ignored or not implemented adequately". Third, with regard to protection of women, "without an effective monitoring and evaluation mechanism and incentives for compliance...it is likely that the necessary changes are not made". Fourth, much more gender mainstreaming needs to be done to translate rhetoric into concrete progress.

Ways to reduce gender disparity need to be built into organizations' policies, programs and projects. The UN Economic and Social Council (ECOSOC) define gender mainstreaming as "a strategy for making the concerns and experiences of women as well as men an integral part of the design, implementation, monitoring and evaluation of policies and programs in all political, economic and societal spheres, so that women and men benefit equally, and inequality is not perpetuated". Five years on, these concerns remain.

During 2001 and 2002, Elisabeth Rehn and Ellen Johnson-Sirleaf travelled to Bosnia and Herzegovina, Cambodia, Colombia, the Democratic Republic of Congo, East Timor, the former Yugoslavia Republic of Macedonia, the Federal Republic of Yugoslavia, Guinea, Israel, Liberia, the occupied Palestinian territories, Rwanda, Sierra Leone and Somalia to present an independent assessment in their *Women, War and Peace*. They found terrible stories, but also women who were surviving trauma and rebuilding communities. Yet, "time and again women described the wonderful documents that had been created and signed -and the failure to implement most of what has been promised".

Lack of will among member states, consistently seeing women's participation as not a priority, institutionalized sexism and patriarchal cultural mores remain major obstacles in translating the grand rhetoric of Resolution 1325 into practical reality. To include women in political decision-making in transitional societies is to take seriously gender justice, gender equality, women's human rights and the rebuilding of relationships in formerly militarized societies.

Peace-building is a process that is important in pre-conflict, conflict and post-conflict stages in both formal and informal settings. Practical peace-building must be truly inclusive of women and men from all branches of life. The 2005 World Summit Document commits states "to fully and effectively implement Security Council Resolution 1325". This commitment must translate into reality.

Proponents of democracy believe that it offers the best hope for justice in any given society. Yet there is very little discussion on how that state of justice can be achieved. Democracy is a concept that gained popularity in the late 19th and the early 20th centuries. As an ideology its rise was closely linked to the rise of the nation-state in Western Europe. In a democracy sovereignty supposedly rests with "the people."

In a nation state it is nationalism that constitute a legitimate definition of who belongs to the category of people. In a pluralistic society such as in India, it often leads to a reinforcement of traditional cleavages based on religion, language, ethnicity caste and gender and transforms them into newer inequalities.

This is because central to the processes of democratic (and in this case post-colonial) nation-state formation is the question of identity. The state machinery seeks to create a homogenized identity of the Nation and it citizenry that accepts the central role of the existing elite. This is done through privileging majoritarian, male and monolithic cultural values that deny the space for difference. As has been pointed by Etienne Balibar (1990) and Nira Yuval-Davis (1991), the denial is legitimized through liberal and social democratic discourses of state formation that camouflages the political will that consciously decides who belong and who does not.

Feminist scholarship and women's struggles alike have drawn attention to the incomplete nature of certain political projects such as democracy. For Carol Paterman (1988) "the social contract presupposed the sexual contract, and civil freedom presupposed patriarchal right." Women were long excluded from the collective "we" of the body politic in Western Europe even after democracy was considered achieved. For example, in France the "Declaration of the Rights of Man and Citizen," negated the rights of women and all those Dam was built were liable to being punished by death if they so much as demanded suffrage, not until the 20th century.

The second wave of feminism in the second half of the 20th century portrayed that even if in the West women acquired civil and political right but social and sexual rights still eluded them that had serious ramifications for democratic processes. In Africa and Asia the project of national independence gave certain political space to women. According to feminist writers such as Jawardena (1986) in the post-colonial developing world for a time feminism and nationalism were compatible and allied, sharing similar objectives. During the period of decolonization, political rights including the right to vote were given to men and women alike. Yet during the process of state formation male-female differences were reinforced. The new states formulated rights and obligations in ways "that strengthened the masculinity of the public sphere and the femininity of the private sphere."

According to Moghadam (2000) in so doing their policies and discourses ironically recall the early Western model of exclusivity and male privilege. The paper will discuss the gendered nature of the Indian state building processes from the time of the Constituent Assembly debates and how in one instance women have been able to subvert such marginalization . Before beginning a discussion on the gendered nature of state formation it is essential to clarify what we mean by gender. Lorber (1994) defines gender as "an institution that establishes patterns of expectations for individuals, orders the social processes of everyday life, is built into major social organizations of society, such as economy, ideology, the family, and politics, and is also an entity in and of itself."

For our purposes gender refers to a structural relationship of inequality between women and men based on perceived sex difference, which is manifested in society, politics, economy, ideology and in culture. Even in the West, modern state formation was a gendered process. The British Nationality and the Status of Aliens Act of 1914 portrayed that rights in nationality could be transferred only through the male like. Women were considered as subjects or aliens primarily vs. Attorney-General in 1922 showed that a female British subject could contract a marriage in good faith during war and lose her British nationality. Thus women were neither full subjects nor foreigners. Even when they were subjects they could lose their nationality through marriage to an alien.

The post-colonial states of South Asia inherited many of its legal practices from Britain. The first Indian Passport Act was formulated in 1920. This Act did not define who an Indian citizen is. But it made it mandatory for any foreigner entering India to carry a passport. In it the male pronounce "he" described the foreigner. In subsequent Acts dealing with immigration and emigration the same practice was continued. The Foreigners Act of 1946 stated that wives of foreigners were also to be considered as foreigners. The Act prohibited Foreigners to change their names while in India. Exception was made if a marriage occurred between the foreigner and a woman ("native" or foreign) who was then permitted to take her husbands name, which presumed that a women's legal status depended on that of her husbands status. Thus women as independent legal identity did not emerge in the colonial period even though women got the right to vote. Even in the Constituent Assembly debates it was presumed by many members that the "masculine, as it is well known, embraces the feminine." This made the passage of the Abducted Person's Recovery Act possible.

The Abducted Persons (Recovery and Restoration) Act, 1949 was an Act provided in pursuance of an agreement with Pakistan for the recovery and restoration of abducted persons. It defined an abducted person as "a male child under the age of sixteen years or a female of whatever age who is, or immediately before the 1st day of March, 1947, was, a Muslim and who, on or after that day and before the 1st day of January, 1949, has become separated from his or her family and is found to be living with or under the control of any other individual or family." There are some outstanding features of this Act.

During partition some 50,000 Muslim women in India and 33,000 non-Muslim women in Pakistan were abducted, abandoned or separated from their families.

The two states of India and Pakistan embarked on a massive Central Recovery Project during which some 30,000 women were recovered by their respective states. Some incidents relating to these abducted women exemplify the politics of gender during partition. Even when the two countries could decide on little else they decided that the abducted women must be restored to their families. Problems arose over the process and progress of recovery. An Abducted Persons bill was brought in the Indian Parliament. The bill gave unlimited power to police officers regarding abducted persons. If a police officer detained any women under this bill they could not be questioned in any court of law. Although numerous amendments were proposed in the House the bill passed unchanged on 19 December 1949.

According to Rameshwari Nehru, adviser to GOI, Ministry of Rehabilitation, many abducted women showed extreme unwillingness to leave their "captors." Ritu Menon and Kamla Bhasin in their recent book on partition observes that women were:

Abducted as Hindus, converted and married as Muslims, recovered as Hindus but required to relinquish their children because they were born of Muslim fathers, and disowned as 'unpure' and ineligible for marriage within their erstwhile family and community, their identities were in a continuous state of construction and reconstruction, making of them … 'permanent refugees'.

These women were forcibly repatriated though refused rehabilitation by their families. How did India and Pakistan achieve such commonality of interest regarding abducted women? Many explanations are given for this forcible repatriation of women. Menon and Bhasin point out how national honour was bound to women's bodies. According to Jan Jindy Pettman repatriation was made a nationalist project because women's bodies became markers of male honour. As usual women's bodies became "part of other people's agendas." Both countries made claims of moral superiority over the other based on their ability to protect/control female bodies. This control was essential for the self-definition of the male identity that was in a state of crisis.

Abducted women were not considered as legal entities with political and constitutional rights. All choices were denied to them and while the state patronized them verbally by portraying their "need" for protection it also infantilized them by giving decision making power to their guardians who were defined by the male pronoun "he". By insisting that the abducted women could not represent themselves and had to be represented, the State marginalized them from the decision making process and made them non-participants.

For the abducted it was their sexuality that threatened their security and the honour of the nation. Thus, their vulnerability was focused on their body. This made all women susceptible to such threats and so had to be protected/controlled. By denying agency to the abducted women the State made it conceivable to deny agency to all women. Even after fifty three years, state politics in South Asia regarding women remain essentially similar to the partition days. The male centrism of Indian project of state formation continued with the Citizenship Act of 1955. As its title suggests the Act dealt with modes of acquiring, renunciation, termination and deprivation of citizenship. Although the Act was meant to give rise to the category of universal citizen in actuality it did not. It continued the gender dichotomy evolved by the colonial state.

The section of citizenship by registration stated that "women who are, or have been, married to citizens of India;" were to given citizenship if they applied for it. No such stipulations were made for men marrying women who were Indian citizens. Thus citizenship by registration was largely transferred through the male line. In the section on the termination of citizenship it was stated that where a male person "ceases to be a citizen of India under sub-section (1), every minor child of that person shall thereupon cease to be a citizen of India." This portrayed once again that citizenship was transferable largely through the male line giving women a second class citizenship.

Although in later Acts women could transfer citizenship rights to their spouses and to their children it did not alter the maleness of Indian State as conceived in the formative years. Adequate testimony to this male centrism of the Indian State is provided by the debates over the Shah Bano case and in present day by State attitude towards the riot in Gujarat. Thus the male character of the state ensured that women would have hardly any space in formal politics. But what about space in the informal sector? To understand the informal space that women acquire within the public sector one can study women's role in conflict resolution in Nagaland. To understand women's role in conflict resolution in Nagaland one has to keep in mind that Nagaland has witnessed protracted conflict over last 52 years.

It has also to be remembered that during state verses community conflict men withdraw from civic life for compulsions of war and self-defense. In such a situation the public sphere retreats into the private and women form the civil societies. They assume roles that are completely new to them and confront and negotiate with the massive power of the state machinery in their everyday lives. Further, as transmitters of cultural value women construct differences that shape the future of the conflict. We will explore some moments of conflict in the life and times of Indian democracy and analyze how women negotiate during these conflicts. This is an analysis of how by their engagements these women transform the traditional definitions of democracy, nationalism and resistance.

In most of Northeast, as well as in Nagaland women are marginalized in institutional politics. The Naga women have one of the worst sex ratios even in Northeast Indian standards but the second best literacy rate. The sex ratio is 890 and the literacy rate is about 55.72%. The sex ratio for women in rural areas in 912 and in urban areas 789. This shows greater out migration of men from villages and the on-going conflict is the main cause for that. Naga women are extremely independent and there are more women cultivators in Nagaland than men. Yet in electoral politics the record of Naga women are hardly any better than the women from the other regions of the Northeast.

Although Nagaland had some extraordinary women parliamentarians such as Rano Shaiza, the present day record is much worse. There are no women in either the Assembly or in the parliament. Electoral politics in the Nagaland is thus completely dominated by men. They dominate the seats of power. Sometimes women are given token representations but very often they become invisible. According to one observer this exclusion of women from electoral politics is a "deliberate exclusion" imposed on them by the men. Thus electoral politics have in no way empowered women in the Nagaland rather it has led to their further marginalization. However, there are other areas in the public sphere where women have made spaces for negotiations.

It is in the politics for peace that they are able to negotiate some spaces of action. The peace movements if not led by women, are overwhelmingly supported by them. Women dominate the peace movements in sheer numbers. Women in the peace movements negotiate with both the army and the insurgents and yet are able to carve out an independent space for their actions. The best known among these organizations for peace is the Naga Mother's Association (NMA). The head office of the NMA is in the largely Angami city of Kohima. It came into existence on February 14, 1984, with a preamble that stated, "Naga mothers of Nagaland shall express the need of conscientizing citizens toward more responsible living and human development through the voluntary organization of the Naga Mother's Association."

Membership of NMA is open to any adult Naga women irrespective of whether she is married or single. Members can join through the women's organizations of their own tribes. The organization encourages human development through education and it efforts to eradicate social evils and economic exploitations and work towards peace and progress. The NMA has rendered valuable service for the cause of peace. It mediated between the Government of Nagaland and the Naga Student's Federation over age limit for jobs and came to an equitable settlement. An achievement of NMA is the formation of the Peace Team in October 1994 to confront the deteriorating political situation. Their theme was "Shed No More Blood."

The NMA spoke against killings not only by the army but also by the militants. In a pamphlet released on 25th May 1995 the representatives of NMA wrote that "the way in which our society is being run whether by the overground government or the underground government, have become simply intolerable." The NMA celebrates the 12th of May each year as the Mother's Day and renew their appeal for peace. Apart from peace initiatives the NMA has worked for social regeneration. In Nagaland there is rampant abuse of alcohol and drug. The NMA provides facilities for de-addiction. They collaborate with the Kripa foundation of Mumbai for rehabilitation of drug doers. The NMA has also started anonymous HIV testing. They are probably the first women's organization in the Northeast to test pregnant women for HIV virus.

The NMA is providing pioneering service for care of patients afflicted with Aids. An important issue that is preoccupying the doctors of NMA is the increase in HIV positive cases among pregnant women. An NMA spokesperson is of the opinion that conflict in Nagaland is a result of chronic underdevelopment. Therefore the NMA believes that without addressing developmental issues there cannot be any peace in Nagaland. NMA's greatest achievement is that most Naga women's organizations are its collaborators. The members of NMA also collaborate with the Naga Women's Union of Manipur. The rallies organized by NMA are always well attended by other Naga women's organizations. The NMA work very closely with the Naga Hohos.

That the NMA has assumed enormous influence in Naga politics is borne out by the fact that they are the only women's group in South Asia who has participated in a cease-fire negotiation. In 1997 they mediated between the GOI and the NSCN (IM) faction and facilitated a cease-fire. The NMA however is not the only women's group. There are a number of others of which an important organization is the Watsu Mongdung. And extraordinary case catapulted the Watsu Mongdung to fame. The incident took place on 27th December 1994 in Mokokchung town. Ten members of the Assam Rifles entered the town and carried on indiscriminate rape and arson. Innumerable women were raped. The Naga Human Rights Commission entrusted Watsu Mongdung to investigate and identify the victims. The Watsu Mongdung formed a special committee and investigated the matter. They identified eight victims and reconstructed the incident after a thorough discussion with them.

None of the other social organization wanted to take this up. So members of the Watsu Mongdung decided to litigate on behalf of the rape victims. The case is still pending. Although the Watsu Mongdung is largely an Ao organization they have participated in protest marches organized by the Lothas and such other tribes. However, they are one of the few women's organizations that do not collaborate with the NMA. This may be because of traditional Ao and Angami antagonism. The Watsu Mongdung carries out relief work during calamities, man-made or otherwise. They have led protests against any kind of oppression and violence. Once during a combing operation in Mokokchung when the army wanted to separate the men and women, they refused to be separated since they feared that the army would kill the men. Ultimately the army had to interrogate both men and women together and then released most of them.

The Watsu Mongdung is not the only group that provides such services. There are other women's groups such as the Tangkhul Shanao Long (TSL) which operate both in Nagaland and Manipur. The TSL worked in Ukhrul district. It has its branches in all the Tangkhul Naga villages. In July 1997 after an ambush by the NSCN-IM the Assam Rifles went on a rampage in Ukhrul town beating up the men including schoolteachers. People were so traumatized that life came to a standstill in Ukhrul town. The TSL not only spoke to the army and convinced them to release over forty civilians but also tried to instill confidence among the people of the town and its adjoining villages. They helped the people of the area to return to normal life by requesting the shopkeepers to open their shops. They appealed to the stranded people to go back home which brought back some semblance of normalcy in the town.

In recent years groups such as the NMA, the Watsu Mongdung or the TSL have gained recognition as serious actors in the peace process. Their organized campaigns and rallies have facilitated the cease-fire. They continue working with other Naga organizations to reduce the violence and brutalization of the Naga society. They actively participate in discussions on peace and human rights. Through their negotiations for peace they have created a niche for themselves in the public sphere.

There are a number of Naga women activists in Manipur whose activities fall within this genre of peace movement. The Naga Women's Union in Manipur has fifteen constituent units and one of the more exceptional ones is Moyon Sanuw Ruwrkheh (MSR). The Moyon tribe inhabits the Chandel district that is in the southeastern part of Manipur. The Moyon women's organization included a number of political demands in their annual resolutions. They called for equal right of women to inherit property. They also began an agitation for women to be in decision making bodies. These resolutions were brought up for discussions in the Moyon Naga Council and the President of the MSR was given the right to vote. She was the first woman to vote in the elections of the council.

In 1997 for the first time a Moyon woman became the speaker of the Assembly of the Naga Moyon Council. No other Naga tribe in Manipur has given their women the right to vote in their Legislative Councils. The Moyon women are extraordinary in another way as well. These women tried to initiate dialogue with Kuki women living in proximity.

Initially they had some success but later the Kuki women activists told them that their men are unwilling to let such a dialogue continue. Notwithstanding the pressures from the men the Kuki women and the representatives of the MSR organized a formal dialogue between the women activists of the two groups. But on the day of the dialogue they were informed through an emissary that it will not take place as the Kukis were unwilling to continue it.

The Moyon women are of the opinion that although the Kuki women were willing to dialogue on peace their men felt threatened by such a dialogue. Thus, they stopped their women from attending such dialogues. Even after this set back the MSR have continued their activities towards peace. They established networks with other Naga groups and are trying to organize a women's dialogue between the Isaac -Muvah and the Khaplang factions of the NSCN.

They crossed international borders to speak to the leaders of the Khaplang faction. In the process the Border Security Force arrested them. But as a result of interventions by the Chief Ministers of Nagaland and Manipur all charges were dropped. Apart from these senzation al endeavours the representatives of MSR organize peace campaigns through awareness raising programmes, seminars and workshops on peace and harmonious co-existence in different localities. They collaborate with other human rights organizations on fact-finding investigations.

Apart from peace activities the Naga Women's Union in Manipur also undertakes developmental activities. They campaign for women candidates in Lok Sabha elections. They have begun campaigning for the inclusion of women in Naga village councils. None of the Naga village councils include women as office bearers. This is a source of great disappointment among the Naga women. Hence campaign on this issue is a priority for the Naga Women's Union. They also work towards income generation programmes for the women. Their other priority area is to work towards equal wages for women. There is a disparity in wages between male and female workers in Naga society which the Union seeks to correct. However, their greatest achievement has been over property rights.

Traditionally Naga women do not inherit immovable parental property such as land. But due to the campaigning of these women the Naga tribes in Manipur are slowly trying to correct this discrimination against women. This is possible because the Naga Hohos (tribal council) view this issue favourably and they have also included it in their agenda. The numerous Naga women's peace groups successfully maintained their independent stand. They have convinced all the parties in the politics of peace that they are not to be dictated by any specific faction. Most of these women retain their belief in their Cause. But their actions show that they are on the side of peace. They want to achieve their goals through political actions and not through brutalization of society. Women's peace groups in Nagaland have achieved enormous success. They have become an important and necessary component of the Naga Hohos. Yet even the state machinery is not averse to using them for purposes of peace.

There are a number of reasons for the success achieved by the Naga women. The Naga women have been able to situate their political maneuverings within their traditional roles. Peace to them is not just a political phenomenon it is also economic and social. They believe that without development there cannot be peace and here they differ from the majoritarian result in equity and they equate it with progress. The Naga women also successfully mix social work with their political actions. Whenever they face political opposition they shift their focus and work on issues of health, de-addiction and rights of women. Their involvement in developmental activities has increased their effectiveness and their acceptance in Naga society.

The experiences of women's peace activism in Nagaland portray that if women are successful in defining peace making as a woman's job then they are not severely challenged. The experiences of Nagaland show that through peacemaking women are able to negotiate spaces in the public sphere. This recognition then helps them in their other negotiations such as the reworking of property rights. Women's negotiations for peace have the potential to change the situation of women even in traditional societies. It also leads to a democratization of society in as much as democracy can be equated with social justice. Therefore women not only redefine peace but their own situation is also redefined by the politics of peace.

DEMOCRACY AND CITIZENSHIP -THE CASE OF SRI LANKA

Sri Lanka's protracted ethno-political and armed conflict now spans a period of nearly thirty years. This ongoing conflict is fundamentally rooted in the failure of post independence nation building to accommodate the interests and needs of the country's multi ethnic society within a framework of pluralist democracy. Instead democracy as experienced by post colonial Sri Lanka has re-affirmed majority rule and entrenched ethnic, language and religious marginalization. It has also strengthened existing social inequalities, including those of class and gender. Women's activism, in Sri Lanka, to bring about a sustainable and just peace based on a politically negotiated solution to its ethnic conflict, has therefore to be understood within this context of vested interest and political advantage wielded by the Sinhala majoritarian and patriarchal state.

In the context of the conflict, women's activism for a political solution was first articulated via their agitations against the Prevention of Terrorism Act, which came into effect in Sri Lanka in 1979. Anti terrorism legislation in the country was thus a reality long before September 11th and the resulting spate of similar legislation by a number of countries. Women joined or took the lead in forming human rights organizations in the 1970s and early 1980s evolving into some of the strongest human rights defenders in the country. These early organizations included the Civil Rights Movement, the Movement for Inter Racial Justice and Equality and the

Movement for the Defence of Democratic Rights. By 1982, feminists and progressive women's organizations had come together as the Women's Action Committee to advocate for women's rights, human rights protection and a negotiated settlement to the ethnic conflict.

In 1984, a broader coalition of women formed Women for Peace which called on all political parties as well as the political representation of the Tamil militant groups fighting for self determination in the north east of the country, to meet at an All Party Conference. This coalition was also the first to highlight war related internal displacement as a situation which gives rise to the violation of a range of socio-economic and political rights with specific gender based repercussions. By 1984, Tamil women in the Northern Province, where the armed conflict between the state and Tamil militants was intensifying, had banded into a Mothers Front to protest against arbitrary arrests and disappearances of young persons.

In 1989, a similar Mothers Front was formed in the south of the country demanding information on the disappeared, filing *habeaous corpus* petitions, fighting against illegal detentions, involuntary disappearances, arbitrary arrests and extra judicial executions. Both Fronts operated under conditions of severe threat and gross human rights violations by both state and non state entities. In a situation where traditional forms of struggle were either ineffective or not possible due to political violence and terror, women employed the cultural and gendered construct of motherhood in response to increased militarization. Motherhood was used as protection against reprisals, an expression of anger and outrage as well as a moral duty and obligation to safeguard life.

The years of war also transformed the gendered roles of non-combatant women. Often marginalized and rarely acknowledge these women used a multitude of other strategies to survive the many ravages of war. Commonly perceived merely as victims, untold numbers of Tamil, Muslims and Sinhala women affected by the conflict were forced to defy or overcome traditional norms and barriers to ensure the survival of their families and communities. They assumed de-facto and de-jure responsibility for the emotional as well as economic survival of their families; dealt with multiple displacements; engaged with political and military institutions on behalf of detained, tortured, raped, disappeared or executed loved ones; led movements demanding the protection of human rights; negotiated mutual co-existence with hostile neighbours, and campaigned for an end to the fighting.

By the 1990s women's rights work was linked to the discussion around the contours of a political solution to the ethnic conflict that ranged from constitutional reform to political decision making and citizenship, with particular reference to gender concerns and women. Following a number of failed efforts at peace making by the state during this period, women's political activism determinedly transformed to deal with the tenuous 'peace process' and sustain the 'ceasefire' of 2002. Building on past experiences, the women's movement used a number of strategies to influence the peace process. Women were the first to rally publicly in support of the ceszation of hostilities between the government and the LTTE and the positive atmosphere created in which it was hoped peace negotiations could commence.

At the same time women also made a constructive critique of the CFA and called for its strengthening. They reminded both sides that transparency and inclusiveness should be important features of agreements made during process seeking to establish peace. Women emphasized that new agreements must be committed to democracy and pluralism, respect the rights of women and all minority groups and enshrine the principles of equality. Women reiterated that the burden of peacemaking must be shared by all those affected by the conflict, including minority communities and women. They also called for the inclusion of women and gender concerns in the formal peace process that was unfolding. Petitions to the state and the LTTE were followed by memorandums and representations. However although the Prime Minister promised to consider a more inclusive and gender sensitive framework and include a mechanism to engage women in the peace process this was not reflected at the peace talks.

As the plenary talks progressed and gender concerns continued to be marginalized from the formal process, women decided to carry out a fact-finding mission in the conflict-affected districts bringing feminists/women activists from the international peace movement to join local women. This report was used strategically to lobby the international donor community, the UN and bilateral governments. Ten months after the ceasefire agreement, the government and the LTTE agreed to establish a women's committee to 'explore the effective inclusion of gender concerns in the peace process'. The Committee subsequently known as the Sub Committee on Gender Issues (SGI), which was mandated to report directly to the plenary sessions of the peace talks and work closely with other Sub-Committees to the peace process was facilitated by a Norwegian woman minister and comprised ten nominees, five each from the government and the LTTE.

It sought to identify issues of concern to women and bring those into the agenda of the peace process. This mechanism is possibly the first of its kind established within a formal peace process at a pre-substantive stage of negotiations. It is also the first effort by the Sri Lankan government and the LTTE to recognize the involvement of women in peace building and peace making. By its second meeting the SGI was able to agree on terms of reference that focused broadly on: sustaining the peace process; resettlement; personal security and safety; infrastructure and services; livelihood and employment; political representation and decision making and reconciliation. However, when the LTTE withdrew from the formal peace process by mid 2003 all the joint sub committees were also effectively made redundant. Though many attempts were made by women's groups, bilaterals and others to keep the Gender Sub Committee going, the LTTE was reluctant to resume partial engagement.

It is also doubtful if the new government, which is now pursuing a more militaristic strategy to deal with the conflict, will revive the SGI if negotiations resume. The SGI was without doubt an important first step in the process of including gender issues in the formal negotiation process. Whatever its future fate this initial ground work together with the precedent setting agreement at the peace talks that gender concerns must be effectively included in the peace process will be both a standard and a strong foundation for future negotiations and the women's movement to build on. As positive as the mechanism was, the SGI can be subjected to a fair degree of criticism.

The manner in which it was set up, its composition, its links to the formal peace process, its autonomy or the limits to its autonomy, its links with gender concerns on the ground, its links to the broader women's movement, its accessibility, its communication strategies, the perception of its role by the peace constituency, policy makers, implementers and the media, must be interrogated critically. The need for such a mechanism or mechanisms that may be created in the future, to maintain some independence from the official process and negotiating parties is crucial. This is only possible if constant interaction and a free flow of information between such a mechanism and women directly affected by the conflict and those working on gender and conflict related issues and concerns can be established and maintained. Such concerns must also be incorporated into terms of reference, policy formulation and implementation processes and must also be open to constant evaluation and monitoring.

A further concern was that the SGI could be perceived as a supplementary mechanism that was expendable which ignored the fact that if women are to be represented in the peace process they must be directly present at the negotiation table. Analogous with this criticism however is that nominal representation of women at the negotiation table will not in itself resolve the gendered nature of the talks and the peace process and that gender concerns should be included through an inclusive and interactive mechanism that is an intrinsic component at the talks. This is the only guarantee to women's political security and the only route to enabling economic and social security for women in the interim and post agreement period. The success any such mechanism will be a vital factor in ensuring this political security and achieving a sustainable peace.

The fact the SGI had no definite link to the other Sub Committees in the peace process, such as that dealing with immediate humanitarian and relief needs (SIHRN), and had no mechanism to access independent funding was also reflective of its marginalization from fundamental decision making processes that addressed economic concerns. It is therefore imperative that any mechanism dealing with gender concerns must also be linked to all other mechanisms dealing with political, economic, social and cultural issues in the course of peace processes. The interdependency of such concerns has to be recognized and a holistic approach to dealing with the range of securities in all these spheres must be developed.

Though the SGI was affiliated to the formal peace process as an advisory body there was no clear direction of how this affiliation could be operationalized. The terms of reference of the SGI, drafted independently by the Committee itself, and therefore an extremely positive first step, had to be formally agreed upon at the plenary. Since the plenary talks stalled before the SGI terms of reference could be placed before it, the SGI was left in a state of limbo unable to access any financial or material resources and unable to meet officially. The unanticipated postponement of the peace talks was followed by a LTTE decision to unilaterally pull out of all other subcommittees to the plenary. Consequently, there was no opportunity for the SGI to negotiate its continuity, independent of the stops and starts to the peace process. For both the LTTE and the Government, gender issues were subsidiary to the main agenda of political power sharing.

The agenda of the peace process was framed around issues of power, territory and resource-sharing so that the consideration of gender issues was possible only while consistent with them. While bringing a keen understanding of gender concerns to their work, the LTTE women in particular gave primacy to the politics of the Tamil liberation struggle. The Government delegation too was constrained by the government's political agenda. There was thus no real democratic and independent inclusion of women in the peace process. As last week's discussions at the Feminist Dialogues proposed, we as women need to develop a deep and profound critique of democracy that will enable its transformation and radicalization.

Feminists noted that "The radicalization of democracy calls for the re-construction of the notion of citizenship as well. Taking into consideration the various exclusions and marginalization that are an integral part of democracy as we know it, we must re-cast the identity of the citizen within a political mould". They also noted that among the challenges posed for activists "within the hegemonic democratic frameworks now in place is that of overcoming the systems of exclusion of women from the public/political space, incorporating the recognition of the urgent processes of democracy in the private".

In the process of radicalizing democracy, women's movements and feminist movements therefore proposed "to take the struggle into a variety of terrains: Among these are struggles against material and symbolic exclusions; struggles for redistributive justice and the justice of recognition; struggles for local, global and inter-societal justice and peace; struggles for recognition of body politics; struggles for the recognition and dialogue between diversities". As the Feminist dialogues noted "Some of us have been retrieving and radicalizing the most progressive aspects of liberal democracy -liberty, equality, self-determination, autonomy - and combining these with socialist conceptions of the common good.

2

Fascism Today

Historically, control over our bodies and sexualities has been central to feminist struggles; it has been an area of intense analysis and political struggle. Revealing the suffering and violence inflicted on women's bodies, varied forms of repression and sexual exploitation constitute the feminist legacy for a democratic conception of social transformation that is at simultaneously more radical and more human. This is what brings fundamentalist reactions all around the world. They are premised on crucial and specific interpretation of the body. This interpretation also involves a re-construction of the body, giving rise to a particular kind of body politics. Indeed the body has been central to fundamentalism, just as much as it is central to most political processes.

A FRAMEWORK FOR DISCUSSION

The framework in which this reflection is presented tries to take into account the new scenarios in which our lives and liberation struggles occur.

- Expanding hegemonic control of neo-liberalism, militarism, fundamentalisms;
- The impact of a globalized network based capitalism on gender relations (expanding from binaries);
- Resistance to these hegemonies, specifically the George W Bush symbol of global patriarchy, the Vatican, the political Islam of Osama Bin Laden, the Catholicism of

Latin America and eastern Europe, the Hindu fundamentalism in south Asia.

We are living through the change of an era. Old paradigms are becoming redundant. Accompanying this is the slow process of building new paradigms from new realities and meanings of liberation; and from the new subjective and symbolic changes. On the one hand, is coordinated intervention of three forces: neo-liberalism, militarism and fundamentalisms that induce new exclusions and put human survival itself at risk. These are new risks and new forms of organization that strengthen expansion and hegemonic control. On the other hand, coordinated efforts and collective impacts have been deepened and expanded. New actors have appeared, thus modifying paradigms and enriching a global-local perspective of liberation.

With the transition from industrial capitalism to a globalized network based capitalism, the paradigm of gender has changed. These changes, which have excluded women in many ways, have also generated broader room for manoeuvre: women have politicized the domestic sphere. Gender has taken on a more complex dimension. The binary opposites of man/woman no longer predominate our thinking, other "sexual identities" have been incorporated into the ontology of gender. This gives new meaning to what it is to be a man or a woman. It is in this context, of resistance to these new paradigms and liberating changes, that fundamentalisms with diverse faces and masks have risen and expanded; religious, political, economic, cultural fundamentalisms that defend the sole and unchanging way of thinking as a norm for society.

The fundamentalisms take advantage of wars, of racism, of poverty and, in all cases, those who lose the most rights are women. George Bush and his cohorts are in the forefront in terms of pushing the neo-liberal agenda throughout the world. Militarism is an effective way of fulfilling this aim. Coupled with that is the imposition of a model of the traditional patriarchal family. Christianity and its control of women's bodies is as fundamentalist as the political Islam of Bin Laden, the Vatican which in Latin America converts the sins of Catholicism into a crime for the whole society or Hindu cultural nationalism that blatantly uses fascist methods to contain dissent and dismantle all democratic mechanisms.

FEMINIST RESISTANCE AND BODY POLITICS

The historical challenge for feminists has been to incorporate new forms of relationships between people–with their bodies and sexualities- creating new social subjectivities and favouring ways of living together in the "world as a whole" as lived bodies with social, cultural and political expression. This form of body politics for feminists is an essential dimension of the new paradigms. This implies politicizing the private sphere and providing evidence for the close relationship between sexuality and democracy, because recovering other dimensions for democratic change (personal/ interpersonal relations, democratization of the private sphere and daily life) and strengthening the meanings and contents of democracy.

Disputing the meanings and content of this hegemonic globalization requires politicization and active visibility of feminist agendas–as part of the radical democratic agenda, from the visibility and demand for recognition of the contribution itself. This is a profoundly counter-cultural, because all forms of hegemonic power generates resistances and alternatives that confront the existing power. That is why culture is also an area of transformation par excellence: violation of rights in name of tradition, fundamentalisms in name of cultural purity or religious submission, or the western as the hegemonic cultural ideal, are all rooted in the cultural arena. However, it is also the dimension that sustains counter-cultural changes in the subjective and symbolic horizons of society.

A counter-cultural dimension that feeds counter power emerging from new meanings orients itself to the coordinated efforts of personal change with the processes of social transformation, feeding alternative subjectivities that put "impertinent ways of knowing" for the traditional discourse, at the centre of the agenda, highlighting all the dimensions that the hegemonic power obscures or marginalizes. The body is an "impertinent way of knowing". It broadens the terms of reference for transformation and is one of the contributions of feminism in its construction of counter powers to confront the hegemonic culture and economy that has made the body a war zone, especially as booty in the case of women and other expressions of gender such as transvestites (both women and men).

Some examples of such violations are: women raped in armed conflicts; denial of sexual and reproductive rights through the biomedical dimension; racism that discriminates because of skin colour; impacts of a hegemonic model that removes capacities from the bodies of the new generations. Each one of these dimensions has given rise to strong movements of resistance and expansion of rights. The body has been converted into a field of citizenship. From this stems the importance of linking the political dimension of the body with democracy.

Sexual freedom in this context is an aspiration, an attitude of searching and construction the social, political and economic conditions that broaden the margins of exercise and election among multiple options/orientations. It is an area for autonomous liberation and liberation in relationships, modifying the conditions of inequality among people and the pre-conceived ideas about the nature of a love relationship. In this way the conditions of choice and autonomous decision of individuals are broadened and individuals recover the conditions to be able to decide about their lives and circumstances.

DISCUSSION POINTS

- How are women in different regions responding to these profound paradigmatic and ideological changes?
- How do women's movements in your region perceive and analyze body politics?

- What are the impertinent ways of knowing? That feminisms are putting at stage?
- How is sexuality linked to democracy? How are women's bodies being acted upon? How do women exercise agency or mobilize and strategize to deal with body politics in your region?

RESISTANCES, REPRODUCTIVE RIGHTS AND HEALTH

The women's reproductive capacity constitutes an area of control and an area of freedom. Women's reproductive capacity has been the historical mechanism for subjugating women in the economic, political, social, cultural and sexual spheres. Recovering the autonomous and liberating decision requires confronting the sexual division of labour that strengthens appropriating reproductive capacity to women, as well as registering the reproductive rights of men and the shared responsibility of both. Reproduction is a right and a pleasure when it is freely decided.

It is a source of pain, stigma and intolerance when this freedom it is constrained by religious, moral influences, economic limitations. It is necessary to liberate reproductive rights from the framework of reproductive health, which is sustained by the traditional role of women, leaving aside other sexual diversities like reproduction among lesbian women.

Additionally, it is necessary to overcome the legal conditioning that denies women the right to the decision of abortion. In recent decades there have been unprecedented advances that have created new reproductive technologies and new stimulants for good sexual functioning. It is an ambivalent victory because although on the one hand it has a high liberating content, on the other it can be dehumanized by profit and mercantilism. It is a problem of access and an ethical problem of orientation in its use (for example the use of reproductive technologies for improvement of the human race or for sex selection of the foetus).

For this reason, it is fundamental to reject the commercialization of the conditions of production/reproduction of life, as well as the democratization of scientific technologies, recovering their liberating content since these technologies extend the universe of the citizens rights (for example the right of lesbians to reproduction or the right to the reconstruction of the body itself). It is also urgent to control them and alert the population about the threat of their dehumanizing potential and morally reprehensible profit motive in the use of such technology. It is necessary to nourish a liberating public ethic that replaces the existing public morality defined by hegemonic groups of power.

Discussion Points:

- How is reproduction a right and freedom?
- What are the strategies employed in different regions with regard to abortion?
- What are your responses to new reproductive technologies? What are the ambivalences and fears around this?
- What are the inter-linkages between body politics and democracy bodies as sites of contestation and resistance? How does it manifest itself in your region?

RADICAL DEMOCRACY AND SEXUALITY

There is growing recognition and celebration of the diversity of expression of the multiplicity of genders. This has led to a redefinition of masculinities, feminities, transgender options. It debunks the viewpoint that pigeonholes gender or reproduce stereotypes. The different forms of gender (masculine, feminine, transvestites, androgyny, intersex) are expressions culturally available for everybody and are culturally open to permanent redefinition. Core to these discussions are the theorizing around sex work and the politics of desire as debated in queer theory that challenges mainstream morality around the selling of sex and marketing of desire. From this arises the importance of the construction of a liberating public ethic that substitutes the existing public morality.

This public ethic would incorporate human rights and would be built from a plurality of visions. Thus it would recover democratic meaning as pertaining to all citizens instead of individualized stances that lend themselves to the possibility of being converted into a single vision that excludes all those who do not fall within the ambit of this framework. To deepen democracy it is necessary to break with the liberal perspective of freedom, recovering it as a process that transcends the individualism and competition inherent in the logic of the market. By linking sexuality and democracy, a new perspective of radicalization opens up in the construction of a more just and equal society. Today's global industry of pleasure is build on the sexualized body creating in the process desire, in many manifestations, as a product to be developed, sold and consumed.

Through diverse channels the market launches ever more voracious strategies of capture and redefinitions of the meanings of sexual liberty. It turns sexual freedom into a profit-making enterprise and ends up objectifying relationships. When sexuality is not separated from reproduction, pleasure as autonomous dimension is denied. Sexual pleasure is the most stigmatized and subject to the stringent prohibitions. This is especially true for women, young people and those with different sexual orientations. Historically, pleasure has been hijacked by religion and puritanism. Monopolized by the specific vision of masculine sexuality, it is repressive and obscurantist for women and all people whose bodies escape the hegemonic heterosexual norm.

The search for pleasure is a fundamental expression of individual autonomy and the quest for autonomy in relationships. Pleasure is not only a sexual love game but is also present in other spheres of life such as maternity. When it is freely chosen maternity can be an invaluable source of pleasure. Pleasure can be genital, corporal, sensorial, emotional, individual or shared. It is conditioned by existing democracies, which need to be expanded. For this reason, in order to search for adequate conditions, the affirmation of a lay state and a secular culture is fundamental in addition to a democratic education as public policy.

Discussion Points:

- How do women's movements accommodate the issue of varied sexualities?
- Do you think democracy and pleasure can be linked? Do you think this is liberating potential in terms of women's movements and their political strategies?
- What are the different regimes that oversee your regions (for example, democracy, military states, monarchies, quasi-military state, theocratic state, or even statelessness)? What are the kinds of influences they wield over the religious, cultural, legal, social and economic spheres? How do these affect women's sexual and reproductive rights?
- What are the possible strategies for a liberating framework vis-à-vis the body, sexual pleasure, sexuality and democracy? How can we link up with women's movements that are focused on other areas like hygiene, food, work, water, the right to rest and pleasure?

Owpsee brings you the essay by Nada Ler Sofroniæ, originally published in "Zenièke sveske" magazine. Nada Ler Sofroniæ holds Ph.D. in social psychology. She is university professor, feminist theorist, one of the founders and most important figure in Bosnia and Herzegovina women movement. She is executive director of NGO research centre "Women and Society" from Sarajevo. She has published a great number of articles, essays and books. Together with Staša Zajoviæ, she edited *Fundamentalism Today -Democratic and Feminist Responses,* collection of essays by Marieme Helie Lucas.

"The postmodern condition gave us nothing to die for and nothing to live for, but it seems to have given us a great deal we are willing to kill for-" Tina Beattie, leading British feminist theologian.

Back in 1996, Eagleton talked of fascism as a (possible) future for contemporary world to which the leftist, postmodern philosophy and political theory have no answer. Today, ten years later, his words seem to me more tangible and truer than ever. The process of fascization of the world today, pressed forward by the religious fundamentalisms in a seemingly paradoxical alliance with capitalist market fundamentalism, social theory and the left are caught unprepared and confused, averting their eyes from the increasingly successful attempts to create a retrograde and totalitarian world order.

This text focuses on the women and the contradictory and ambivalent approach of the "progressive world" and social theory to the consequences that the process produced for women as its primary and most vulnerable targets. Assisted by religious fundamentalisms, (ab)use of the teachings of the Bible, the Qur'an, the Torah, the Vedas, the Pali Buddhist canons, contemporary fascism, while misleading the spiritual movements aimed to restore the God's laws for women, family and society, successfully covers its eminently political ambitions and nature.

They are seconded successfully by the global market fundamentalism that has made the status of women, globally, worse than ever in history: it increased discrimination at the workplace, in education, and in legal status; it seriously threatens and undermines women's social and reproductive rights; pushes them to the margins of public and political life; revises and re-traditionalizes gender and family roles and opens the door to unprecedented trade in women from the impoverished post-socialist and post-colonial world. For the first time in the new era we see authentic slavery relations, white-slave trade, and trade with women as a commodity for labour and sexual exploitations. The militarized global scene and the wars make the women most vulnerable targets of sexual violence and murder. From Rwanda, Myanmar, through Bosnia and the Congo, and so on.

At the same time, religious fundamentalisms are increasingly stronger in many countries, especially in the so-called third world, and they manifest themselves primarily as movements that aim towards control of female sexuality, female body, relations in the family, control of women's movement, and the way they dress. Unlike the more subtle instruments for marginalization of women from the public life and decision-making processes applied by the "enlightened world", they openly impose the ideal of prohibition of women's participation in public affairs. Furthermore, some have engaged in constant campaign to use the dress code to make women invisible in public, on both symbolic and real levels, and completely deny them their individual identity.

The religious fundamentalists influence social norms, impose their views of everyday life, introduce legislation, especially in the domain of the family life, regressing the status of women to slavery. Compared to fascism, which put the absolute emphasis on the community, giving it supremacy over the individual, these movements make additional step backwards from the sociological and historical point of view. They not only secure absolute supremacy to the community, they revive on of its most retrograde forms -the "slavery-community".

Why do we find it justified to view the waves of religious fundamentalisms today as eminent tools for fascization of societies? Specifically, what do the authentic fascism and these movements have in common? Fascism and religious fundamentalism are both anti-liberal and anti-democratic totalitarian mass movements. The fascist worldview, just like the fundamentalist one, as opposed to the liberal individualism and cosmopolitism, promote creation of an exclusive community as the sole condition and form of functioning society. The community is understood as either a unified, organic state (Italian version of fascism) or as nation/state whose unity is guaranteed by blood and soil (German fascism), just as contemporary religious fundamentalisms promote religious unity in a single orthodox religion as the basis of statehood.

Both fascism and religious fundamentalisms put the community above the individual (especially the female individuals), and retains the right to control the privacy of the members of the community, on the behalf of the community. It is also justified, in the name of the holy community and its ideals, to subject certain social groups-especially those labelled as "alien", dangerous and hostile -to its will, strict control and, ultimately, violence until they are destroyed. In fascism and fundamentalism, unity and uniformity of the community is the condition for spiritual, social, political and economy renaissance, return to the original values of the supreme authorities, manifested in the united will of the community.

The will of the community is expressed and guaranteed by the leader, whose will is the source of community laws. Anti-liberalism, anti-democracy and authoritarianism are the constitutional elements of the fascist worldview, just as they are for religious fundamentalisms. Fascism and religious fundamentalism promote violent suppression of diversity that could disrupt the creation of non-mediated unity of the community. Fascism and religious fundamentalisms hold the position that the unity of the community should be created through purity of blood of its members and/or primacy of the only true faith.

Through the promotion of nationalism, racism, religious exclusivity and sexism, fascists denounce the members of minority nations/groups as the main culprits for any crisis of established order, and see the freedom of the woman to control her own body as subversive for the needs of the community. The same is done by religious fundamentalisms, which express even more open and drastic extreme misogyny and utter contempt for women. Fascism promotes violent termination of the worldviews and associated practices it disapproves of, as well as all cultural, religious and political differences whose very existence, in its view, question the very foundations of unity.

Terror as organized, systemic, brutal and unlimited violence is seen as legitimate instruments in the struggle to reach uniformity in the community. Both previous characteristics are equally valid for religious fundamentalisms. Fascist and religious fundamentalist movements create their own armed, paramilitary organizations (for example, squadre d'azione in Italy, Sturmabteilung in Germany, GIA in Algeria) that use terror to exercise power, cruelty and punish the dissidents.

Fascist order, just as religious fundamentalisms, suppress all elements of liberal order of the state (rule of law, parliamentary system of governance, independent judiciary, federalism, multiparty system, autonomous public, etc.) and create autarchy of the fascist political party/movement, i.e. fundamentalist movement. The declared unity of the community is secured, in addition to the terror that often progresses into genocide and with religious fundamentalisms, as we shall see later, into femicide through monopoly of levelled propaganda, and subordination of pedagogical and educational institutions from the earliest childhood to adulthood.

Populist manifestations frequent the calendar to stimulate the enthusiasm of the masses and their permanent mobilization. Fascism was a lethal threat to the civil society, marginalized social groups and minorities. It was especially strict in the control of sexuality, family, women, population and demographic policies. Brutal terror against sexual minorities is a well-known fascist and totalitarian practice. The same is applied by religious fundamentalisms, which are especially zealous in the promotion of absolute apartheid for women (separate schools, baths, medical institutions, etc.).

Contemporary religious fundamentalisms are characteristic for their strong penetration of state policies: they aim to control the media, influence national policies and international institutions, undermining the universal norms and institutions of human rights. All their efforts are directed towards de-secularization of societies and make religion the focus, the central point of state and national affairs. The growing influence and domination of religion in public life dramatically undermine the available space for plurality and increase the possibility of misunderstanding and discord. That may be the most important factor that makes the political movements of totalitarian, fascisoid and fascist nature.

The demands for retrograde reforms in family law in Islamic countries and the rise of Christian Evangelical movements in the U.S. demonstrate the impact of such movements on women rights, while incidents in the European Parliament in 2005, with the appalling anti-abortion exhibition in the Parliament Hall in Strasbourg, used pictorial horror to show that such tendencies are not restricted to the distant and "exotic" third world or puritan America, but are alive and well in the very centre of most important democratic institutions in Europe.

Therefore, a very serious conflict between essential democratic, libertarian on one hand and backward, extremely right-wing and conservative values is simmering in the very heart of Europe. What is interesting is that the conflict was initiated, above all, by the associated post-communist countries of Central and Eastern Europe, which have experienced a revival of the strong influence of the Catholic Church. They use their right-wing representatives in the European Parliament to pave the way for religious conservativism and fundamentalist values that have engaged in furious attacks on women rights amidst European democratic institutions.

POST-SOCIALIST WORLD, DE-SECULARIZATION, WOMEN

There is no true strong response to the right-wing, clericalist tendencies and the radical de-secularization in the "new democracies" of the post-socialist world, where women face growing erosion of vested social, economic, reproductive rights, and the right to control their own bodies. The so-called left-wing opposition, the feeble social-democratic forces, are not focused on women rights (or, for that matter, minority, labour or rights of any of the marginalized social groups), especially in countries ruled by the clero-nationalist right. A good portion of the "leftist opposition", in those places where there is one, is itself imbued with populist policies and its views on women and family are very close to the official positions.

Nation, family as a pillar of society and woman as mother are the left's favourite subjects of apology, both because of authentic conviction and the need to tender to the assumed or real conservative mentality of the majority of the electorate. There is no tradition of independent progressive women movements and feminism in those countries. Moreover, sometimes even the women who declared themselves feminists when it was in, tend to close their eyes to what is going on in the name of "religious freedoms" and "the right of women to choose for themselves", even if it meant they "chose" slavery and polygamy, for example.

Women nongovernmental organizations in BiH didn't react strongly, with a single voice, to the introduction of religious education for three-year old children in kindergartens in Sarajevo, a move that has every chance of going through, being supported by the Government, not to mention the fact that they never reacted with united position on the increasingly frequent instances of polygamy, promoted by the highest religious authorities in the country. In the current global situation, the retrograde values seem to have greater chance to win in the conflict with the democratic ones. That is, by the way, the unfortunate possibility of a fascisoid future after the end-of-the-history in the post-socialist world that Eagleton wrote about.

The latest emergence of right-wing political forces in the traditionally democratic West, like Italy and the UK, and the counter-productive bickering between the two democratic candidates for the 2008 elections in the U.S. that gives serious chances to the conservative Republican option, will certainly deteriorate the overall situation for women both in "new democracies" and in the so-called third world. Regarding global trends of restriction of women rights, it seems that it gives a chance to the infamous anti-women Gag Rule to gain in strength.

Women, cultural relativism or the crime of non-intervention in the name of "the right to difference". How do the "enlightened world" in general, the countries of developed Western democracy, the international community and international press, the left, finally, how do social theory and science react to the totalitarian political projects that are centred on the attack on women and women rights?

In spite of the difference in historic age and global contexts, the situation, in my mind, carries an irresistible resemblance to the ostrich-like behaviour of democratic and civic actors who hid their heads in the sand faced with the surge of fascism and Nazism in the 1930s. The world back then watched almost silently how the monster grew and destroyed everything that stood in its way. The majority of the intellectual elite failed to stand up to it, and a significant portion of that elite even provided the theoretical legitimacy to totalitarian and nazi regimes. There was, in particular, mass understanding of the manner they treated (in the current postmodernist theoretical discourse) the very popular concept of "difference". This is in particular true of the understanding for the treatment reserved to ethnic diversity which, as we know all to well, culminated in pogroms, persecution and mass extermination of "different" minorities.

There is no adequate response by the so-called democratic world, the left, the social and political theory to the far-right, fundamentalist movements that, hidden behind the mask of religious and spiritual movements in the so-called third world, post-colonial and post-communist societies, attempt to realize their totalitarian political projects. The democratic world is mostly indifferent to the old and new forms of violence and repression against women somewhere in the "exotic" countries and "different cultures", or, faced with the drama that the women go through, hides behind "politically correct" rationalizations, using the ultimate proof of the political correctness -the respect for the "right to difference".

The leftist, progressive circles, fearing they may be accused of racism, have adopted the approach to avoid or reduce to the minimum the criticism of the concept of female roles practiced by fundamentalist theocracies of the "third", post-colonial world. The left's resistance to the violations of women rights under surging fundamentalisms is lukewarm and pale, almost inexistent, in fact. The left has been entangled in lesser points of cultural relativism and often opposes reports on violations of women rights in the developing countries of the third world and the rights of women living under Islamic law, declaring them racist and tendentious. As M.H. Lucas noted, the left usually is not opposed to fundamentalists ascending to power if they kicked out the western imperialist forces, regardless of the horrible effects that fundamentalism in power would have on women.

There is a good illustration of the type of exotic "differences" in question in the book that reports on the horrors women face under fundamentalist attacks in Algeria. *Describing the situation in* Algeria that ultimately grew into a civil war, M.H-Lucas shows how both women and men were targeted because of their political convictions opposed to the positions of the barbaric theocratic regime, while women were under attack for the simple reason of being women. She describes how women workers were attacked while going to work in the factories by men who stoned them and beat them up with iron bars. At the same time, attacks on women who lived alone with their children started. Fundamentalists started terrorizing divorced women and widows and burned their houses down. In the town of Ouargla, writes M.H. Lucas, a house of a woman who lived alone with her seven children was burned, and the youngest child was killed being unable to run and save itself. There were a number of cases of exorcism registered during that period. Women were forcibly taken into a mosque that was held by fundamentalists, or their male relatives would lock them up at home and call for fundamentalist mullah to kill the devil in them... meaning torturing them until they admitted they were possessed by the Devil. Lists of individual "traitors" that were to be killed were published, with categories of citizens that were targeted: Intellectuals, artists, journalists and all media professionals, foreigners (by default the enemy of fundamentalist policies) and above all and in any way possible -women. Women were set as one of the main targets among civilian population.

There is an impressive description of the notorious pogrom of women in Hasi Mesud (the town in Sahara is the location of the oldest oil well in the country) in Algeria, on the night between Friday, July 13 and Saturday, July 14, 2001, after the evening service held by the Islamist *imam* Amar Taleb in the local mosque. The book describes the crime which, as M.Helie-Lucas says, was not committed by organized armed fundamentalist groups on the behalf of a fascist party, but a lynch at the hands of common people inspired by that very same fascist ideology.

"... a mob of 300 men fell on the working women... mostly cleaning ladies, couple of secretaries and cooks, all employed by foreign oil companies. These women were widowed or divorced..... migrant workers pushed by poverty, using their meagre salaries to feed whole extended families... children, parents, siblings, relatives... Witnesses say the imam accused them of "immoral" behaviour and called the men in the mosque to a "jihad against evil" and to expel the harlots from the area, explaining they lived alone, i.e. without a "wali", a male guardian in the Maliki tradition, therefore equal to prostitutes.

During the process of "purging of the area", they killed, tortured, stabbed, mutilated and raped women... They broke into their houses, robbed them and torched some of them to the ground. Security forces intervened at three in the morning. The pogrom continued on July 14 and 15 in Hasi Mesuda area known as "Area 136", and on July 16 in "Area 200"... then in Tebesa, the town in the south of the country, where not only houses of single women, but also women owned businesses, like hair-dresser salons were attacked.

The authorities decided, "for the sake of security of women themselves" to lock 95 of the attacked women, as well as some "...that could be attacked" into a youth hostel guarded by the security forces... They are held there, without enough food and medicine... more and more women... gather in front of the hostel, begging the armed guards to let them in -all in vain, because the hostel is filled to the maximum... Independent journalists reports that the imam and, depending to their sources, between nine and 40 identified attackers -some of them the landlords that rented substandard flats to the working women at high prices -were arrested and may be charged and tried in the court..."

The fiercely misogynous character of religious fundamentalism is especially moving in the following description:

...The way in which women and girls are killed in Algeria today... illustrates how much fundamentalists hate women. The bodies of women and girls are often mutilated before or after death. It happens quite often that their breasts and genitals are mutilated. Usually, fundamentalists slit their throats and decapitate them, and then parade through the streets or leave the heads in public places as a warning... it is all done publicly, to terrorize the population...

We face today the incredulous hypocrisy of liberal, democratic "human rights oriented" forces, which either remain silent, justify, or consciously tolerate and even approve of totalitarian, hermetic projects in post-colonial societies that focus on absolute control and apartheid for women, ban on their appearance in public, polygamy, violence and even genital mutilation. In the post-socialist world engulfed in a wave of clericalism and neo-conservatism, there is no serious criticism of the treatment those societies reserve for women, and even women who claim they were feminists are inclined opportunistically to "not see" the danger of penetration of fundamentalisms into those societies, all in the name of respect for "religious freedoms and freedom of choice for women".

The non-interference and toleration of misogynous practices in the distant "exotic" world is, quite perversely, theoretically justified with the otherwise legitimated, progressive proposition of "right to difference" and "maintaining distance from cultural imperialism". Instead of using all its power to prevent massacres of women in those parts of the world, the so-called progressive public and intelligence of the democratic West doesn't seek and, usually, doesn't publicize the authentic testimonies of what is going on there, but continues, head in sand, to promote "better understanding and recognition of cultural practices different from ours!"

The "postmodern-liberal" jugglers of theory in the post-socialist world have declared, whenever critical view on threatening waves of fundamentalism and fascization of society was expected from intellectual and academic communities, quite firmly their devotion to respect for cultural differences, directing us all cynically that we should view the world of exploitation of women in "its specific cultural context". It is so touching, so consistent, so "postmodernly contextualising"! Structural violence against women and girls is euphemistically dubbed "cultural practices" that are, as it is, somewhat different from the democratic standards we hold so dear, but we have no right to judge them or, god forbid, interfere.

There they are over there... (but there they are over here, it seems!) The same lenient approach is reserved even for practices that are in direct collision with our positive legislation. For instance, the polygamy that has become quite common practice in some parts of our country is increasingly treated as the matter of faith and customs and official institutions don't get involved -the public prosecutor remains silent in spite of the fact that polygamy is legally prohibited and punishable by law.

CULTURAL RELATIVISM AS A SPECIAL FORM OF RACISM AND FASCISM

The theoretical and practical perversion of cultural relativism results, actually, from the fact that, often, it is not just pure opportunism, but an essentially racist and sexist approach that uses for rationalization the very theoretical concepts introduced into social theory and human rights standards for the very purpose of resisting racism, sexism and misogyny. Namely, the concepts of "right to difference" and "right to choice" originate in the liberation practices and re-vindication of "Others", different, marginalized, oppressed, "invisible" social groups subjected to violence, to which the neo-feminism of the "second wave" gave its invaluable contribution. The essence of such revindications is to prevent any use of differences as basis for discrimination and violence.

Now, the situation has been reversed and discriminating and violent treatment of women is tolerated in the name of "the right to difference"! So, it become customary to contextualize, in the very "post-modern" and "elegant" fashion, the understanding of darkest gender policies and regimes, the dramatic violence and massacre of women and grave violations of women human rights in misogynous communities. The rationale was that such cultural practices were the norm in those communities. The "human rights fighters", the "democrats", social theory and institutions charged with distribution of justice in democratic world implicitly instruct us from their lofty heights that the culture of gender segregation, apartheid and violence should be understood and accepted, even tolerated.

Sometimes even the judicial practice in the democratic societies of the West adapt and rule in cases concerning members of "exotic" cultures in accordance with principle of cultural relativism. One example is the oft quoted court decision widely reported by German press, and even the media in Bosnia and Herzegovina. Namely, a female judge of the Frankfurt on the Mein court dismissed the request by a German citizen, a Muslim woman of Moroccan descent, who filed for divorce on the ground of prolonged physical abuse in the family. The judge explained that her ruling took into account the religious affiliation of the married couple which "comes from Moroccan cultural background" in which it is not unusually for the man to exercise his right, by the Qur'an to educate his wife with beatings, if necessary. Ronald Pofalla, the Secretary General of the Demo-Christian Union protested the decision that the Qur'an should overrule the German Constitution. The decision was criticized by the left, too. Green party's Hans-Christian Ströbele reminded that German judge is to follow German Law, warning that grave cases of abuse are punishable in Germany for a good reason. The Central Council of Muslims in Germany also reacted negatively to the decision. Nurhan Soykan, the Council spokeswoman, explained at the time that violence and abuse, regardless of the gender, are sufficient grounds for divorce in Islam, too. Mina Ahadi(8), Iranian woman the lives and works in Germany, watching at the justification of the ruling in disbelief, declared "cultural relativism dangerous and even racist", since every person, regardless of cultural background, is entitled to universal human rights. She warned that German judicial system sometimes, for reasons of "sensitivity to cultural differences", relativises the crime, so that so called "honour killings" committed by Muslims are treated more leniently than other homicide cases in Germany.

It often happens that true racism and sexism uses liberal mask of cultural terminology instead of open calls for racial and gender segregation. While democratic, liberal and "human rights oriented" forces mask their inaction with cultural relativism, right-wing forces use it as a source of a brilliant argument: Cultural relativism implies that human rights do depend, in fact, on nationality, religion, culture and tradition (which is by default patriarchal and misogynous) so that, in the end, the level of won human rights by necessity has to depend on all identities listed above, and in particular of one's gender.

CONCEPT OF UNIVERSAL HUMAN RIGHTS AND CULTURAL RELATIVISM

Alas, the "understanding", the justification for discrimination and violence against women in other cultures through "contextualization " has turned into a source of legitimacy for anti-discrimination culture and democratic, libertarian wide scope. So, we have the additional hypocritical explanation: Out of respect for the right of difference, the described anti-women practices of cultures alien to us should not be measured with the scales of Western/democratic concept of human rights! That view has many implications, but this imposes itself as the crucial one: The concept of universal human rights, being of Western provenance itself, is potentially incompatible with another world that is entitled to its own practices, established by "folklore" and its own culture. It matters not if they are repressive and even brutal to women.

If follows that the West should refrain from universalization and practice to impose its own democratic achievements in the area of women rights to the rest of the world. It creates an illusion that the powerful West grants that world a democratic right to choose which of its achievements and practices shall be adopted and which will be left out. At the same time, the most powerful global powers offer very tangible proof, on daily basis, that they want to export their democratic and human rights standards to the rest of the world and will do it by force, if necessary. Naturally, they do it mostly when it suits there direct economic and political interests.

Namely, we could hardly say that the globalizing instrument of Western capitalism to profit from natural resources and cheap labour in post-colonial and transition countries of "new democracies" offer them any possibility to choose. Quite to the contrary, those instruments are applied exactly regardless of specific local contexts, the authentic interests and production methods of those communities. Especially the extremely important role women play in that production is disregarded. Even if we agreed that the concept of human rights was exclusive achievement of Western democracy, and I hold some serious reserves on that regard, it has to, by virtue of its universality, apply to the whole of humanity. All women in the world should be entitled to their women rights in spite of and, in fact, because of the resistance of misogynous societies, cultures and traditions they live in, not in line with them.

GENDER RELATIONS AS "CULTURAL PHENOMENON"

In my mind, the key problem of cultural relativism, regarding women rights, is that it reduces gender relations and patriarchal practices to mere "cultural phenomena". Gender relations are, above all, structurally conditions social relations of power. In addition to their social component, these relations have a very important political connotation. Just as fascisoid, fascist, fundamentalist and theocratic regimes are not cultural phenomena and spiritual movements, but represent totalitarian socio-political projects in which the woman are just one, albeit most numerous and vulnerable, of the targets. Even if we viewed patriarchal relations exclusively in their cultural dimension, gender relations are not set in stone, a historical, unchangeable and lasting categories.

RIGHT OF CHOICE

The instrumentalization of the fundament of human rights, the right of choice, seems to me even more perverse than the abuses of the "right to difference". The common phrase that fundamentalist rules for women, whether we find them good or bad, are acceptable if women themselves (perhaps even joyfully) chose to accept them, giving in to the role of devout believers, subjects, servants, children-bearers, invisible persons, mothers that sacrifice their sons for the benefit of the Nation, Faith, the Leader, with pleasure and pride. The freedom of choice, therefore, should be respected no matter how foreign we found the choice in question to be.

Well, isn't the prostitution in the market of female flesh in fact a matter of choice of the involved women, and shouldn't we legalize it for that reason alone? The abuse of the principle of the right of choice turns it, in some almost Orwellian perverse way, into justification for oppression and non-freedom. There, all contextualization stops. Namely, the "right of choice" in economic, social, psychological, cultural, ideological realms, where possibility to choose is extremely limited, reduced and controlled by huge ideological, financial and, usually, militarized and clericalized power, is nothing more than a hypocritical farce. Moreover, that power is, as a rule, facilitated by the State which, through its institutional mechanisms, denies the principle of equal opportunities and choice for all, especially for women.

To be able to choose in the first place, a public and private socio-cultural space is required, devoid of visible or invisible, direct or indirect repressive social control. From the women rights view-point, structurally non-egalitarian and antagonized, non-secular societies, by default patriarchal and misogynous, are not, to put it simply, spaces that offer equal opportunities to all. Especially not to women. For that reason, it doesn't suffice to determine that it was a case of personal choice if, say, a woman lives a life not worthy of a human being because she says herself she chose that life.

The place in which the women today have to chose whether they will accept it or resist it, is the world ruled by the militarized capital, the world in which most powerful economic and technological actors provoke and manage wars, world in which the very global "promoters of democracy" themselves promote reactionary politics and reduction of women rights and often, when it suits their economic, military or political interests, enter pacts and alliances with the darkest fundamentalist regimes that maim, rape and massacre women. That is a dangerous ground for resistance and not easy at all.

To be able to truly choose, women should possess equal quantities of social power as men, together with institutions of system based on the same principles. It is difficult to see women voluntarily trade their own power for life in slavery. Still, inside the predominantly repressive and misogynous context that exists, more or less, all over the planet, the only real choice presented to women is whether they will adapt and accept it or renounce it and resist. That is the only true field of choice for women today. Globalization was imposed on the world with a promise of peace and prosperity. Instead we are faced with war and economic crisis. Not only has prosperity proved elusive, the minimal economic securities of people and countries are fast disappearing.

Hunger deaths have started to occur in countries such as Argentina where hunger was never a problem, and starvation has returned to countries like India which had driven away famine like the one of 1942 which killed 2 million people under colonial, and provided food security through public policy shaped by the democratic process of an independent and sovereign country. Even the rich economies of U.S., Europe and Japan are facing a decline. Globalization has clearly failed to improve the well being of citizens or countries. It has helped some corporations increase their profits and markets, but many corporations like AOL/Time Warner and Enron whose non-sustainable growth was based on deregulation accompanying globalization have themselves either gone bankrupt or lost their value.

Following the globalization path is proving to be a recipe for non-sustainability for the rich and impoverishment and destitution for the poor. Peace was the other promise of globalization but terrorism and war is what we have inherited. Peace was to be a result of increased global prosperity through globalization. Increased poverty is the unfolding reality. And economic insecurity and exclusion is creating conditions for the rise of terrorism and fundamentalism. Economic and political exclusion, and the erosion of national economic sovereignty is making many young men turn to terrorism and violence as a way of achieving their goals.

The erosion of economic nationalism and the growth of economic security is also providing fertile ground for the rise of right wing fundamentalist politics, with parties using the reality of economic insecurity to fan the flames of cultural insecurity, and filling the vacuum left by the collapse of economic nationalism and economic sovereignty with the pseudo nationalist agenda of "cultural nationalism". At the global level, the rhetoric of "clash of civilizations", and the war against Islam performs the same function as the exclusivist political agendas of cultural nationalism and fundamentalist ideology at the national level.

THE CONVERGENCE OF FUNDAMENTALISM

Two forms of fundamentalism seem to be converging and becoming mutually reinforcing and mutually supportive. The first is the market fundamentalism of globalization itself. This fundamentalism redefines life as commodity, society as economy, and the market as the means and end of the human enterprise. The market is being made the organizing principle for the provisioning of food, water, health, education and other basic needs, it is being made the organizing principle for governance, it is being made the measure of our humanity.

Our being human is no longer predicated on the fundamental human rights enshrined in all constitutions and in the U.N. declaration of human rights. It is now conditional on our ability to "buy" our needs on the global marketplace in which the conditions of life-food, water, health, knowledge have become the ultimate commodities controlled by a handful of corporations.

In the market fundamentalism of globalization, everything is a commodity, everything is for sale. Nothing is sacred, there are no fundamental rights of citizens and no fundamental duties of governments.

The market fundamentalism of globalization and the economic exclusion inherent to it is giving rise to, and being reinforced and supported by politics of exclusion emerging in the form of political parties based on "religious fundamentalism" / xenophobia /ethnic cleansing and reinforcement of patriarchies and castism. The culture of commodification has increased violence against women, whether it is in the form of rising domestic violence, increasing cases of rape, an epidemic of female foeticide, and increased trafficking in women.

Globalization as a patriarchal project has reinforced patriarchal exclusions. Atrocities against dalits have also seen an increase as a result of globalization, with higher castes enjoying new power with their integration into the global market place and also wanting to usurp the resources of the poor and marginalized, especially dalits and tribals, for commercial exploitation. Land reform laws which made the land rights of dalits inalienable have been undone. An attempt is under way to undo the constitutional protection of tribal land rights under Schedule V of the Constitution.

Women, dalits, tribals, minorities are special victims of the social and economic impact of globalization. New movements of solidarity such as the Indian People's Campaign against W.T.O. are forging new alliances between diverse movements. However, people's movements are being overtaken by the emerging politics of exclusion. Economic insecurity makes citizens vulnerable to politics based on exclusion. For those in power, or seeking power, a politics of exclusion is becoming political a necessity. It becomes necessary for filling the vacuum created by the demise of economic sovereignty and the welfare state and substituting a politics based on economic rights with politics identity.

It becomes necessary for deflecting public attention away from the negative impact of globalization and explaining the lack of jobs and livelihoods, and the lack of basic needs satisfaction which result from economic globalization in terms of competition for scarce jobs and resources from "minorities" and "immigrants". Fundamentalism and xenophobia emerge as handmaidens of corporate globalization, dividing, diverting and distracting people, and thus providing insularity and immunity to the globalization project.

In India, every vote since 1991 has been a vote against globalization and trade liberalization which is creating 10 million new unemployed people every year, is pauperizing the peasantry and disenfranchising the marginalized. This changed in 2002 with the Gujarat elections which followed the massacre of 2000 Muslims and the violent engineering of the electoral agenda away from basic needs to a majority-minority conflict and contest. The arithmetic guaranteed victory to the party which had created a divide between the majority and minority communities and sown mutual fear and hatred through rapes and killings. This violent and exclusivist agenda is now being developed for all forthcoming elections.

And while the killings were underway, and national concern was focussed on fighting communalism and fundamentalism, the globalization agenda was put on fast forward. GMOs were given clearance, Patent laws were changed to allow patents on life, a new water policy was introduced based on water privatization, and new policies were introduced to dismantle farmers livelihood security and people's food security. The 2003 budget has further pushed the globalization agenda, using the diversion of communal and religious divide to dissipate democratic opposition.

In the U.S. and U.K., the war against Iraq has become a convenient diversion from issues of globalization and the rise in unemployment and economic insecurity. A politics of hate is becoming the indirect support for the failed and failing project of globalization. We need a new politics of solidarity and peace which simultaneously addresses violent and exclusion inherent to globalization, the violence of terrorism and fundamentalism and the violence of war. The different forms of violence and different forms of fundamentalism have common roots, and need a common response. Globalization is intolerant of economic decentralization, economic democracy and economic diversity.

Terrorism and fundamentalism are intolerant of cultural diversity. And the war machine is intolerant of the "other" and of peaceful resolution of conflict. The response to globalization is the protection and defense of our diverse economies at local and national levels. The response to fundamentalism is celebrating our cultural diversities. The response to war is the recognition that the "other" is not a threat but the very precondition of our being. Imagine how different the world would be if it was based on a philosophy of mutual interdependence instead of the current dominant philosophy which is based on "If I have to be, you must be exterminated" or "Your existence is a threat to my existence".

In the world based on interdependence rather than domination, exclusion, extermination, Monsanto would not push a TRIPS agreement that treats the farmers whose seeds Monsanto has patented at "thieves". Monsanto, Syngenta, Ricetec and other Biopirates would recognize that their breeding is based on prior breeding by farmers. If Biotech corporations could see that humanity depends on biodiversity, and food security needs pollinators and diverse plant species, they would not deploy genetically engineering Bt crops which kill bees and butterflies, they would not create herbicide resistant plants and wipe out plant diversity.

If President Bush could see the Tigris and Euphrates and the Mesopotamian civilization as ancestors and recognize our common roots in a common evolution, he would not be rushing in to wipe out the historical roots with unmanned bombs and weapons of mass destruction. If those who control capital could see that their wealth embodies nature's creativity and people's labour, they would not be creating rules of trade that destroy nature and the livelihoods. The fundamentalism of the market and the fundamentalism of ideologies of hate and intolerance are rooted in fear-fear of the other, fear of the capacity and creativity of the other, fear of the sovereignty of the other.

We are witnessing the worst expressions of organized violence of humanity against humanity because we are witnessing the wiping out of philosophies of inclusion, compassion and solidarity. This is the highest cost of globalization-it is destroying our very capacity to be human. Rediscovering our humanity is the highest imperative to resist and reverse this inhuman project. The debate on globalization is not about the market or the economy. It is about remembering our common humanity. And the danger of forgetting the meaning of being human.

It is the argument of free market fundamentalists that "deregulated free markets are the only solution to erase social inequality". Certain saviors of underprivileged people also fall for this propaganda due to their ignorance and difficulty in making sense out of data available from USA. Remember, the social inequality in USA is mild compared to the kind of inequality we are facing in India. The only argument put forward by the saviors of underprivileged in India is that 45 years of socialism didn't erase it so let us try deregulated free markets. They tend to compare the unorganized sector in India, where underprivileged people get some living by doing commerce, to a deregulated market system. Such a comparison is illogical and shows the clear ignorance about the effect these deregulated market systems will have on underprivileged people. A fast food chain will run over road side *dhabas* and send them out of business.

A reliance kinda retail outlet will send many mom and pop stores (where underprivileged sections of our society have some presence) running to save their underwear. Equating the unorganized sector to a completely deregulated free market system is too simplistic and it is a case of plain ignorance. On top of it, if the saviors of underprivileged, who support a deregulated free market system, also expect the government to support underprivileged through policies like reservations, it is a case of plain hypocrisy. A capitalistic system, without the mandatory humanism component inside it, will wipe out socially underprivileged people. If the arguments of free market fundamentalists are true, why did underprivileged people fail to come up during the British rule.

It was, of course, a capitalistic society in play. There was no socialism and the underprivileged people had a good chance to come up with the free market forces in play there. It is time for these saviors of underprivileged people to do a hard thinking. Socialism failed to uplift the underprivileged sections in the first 45 years after independence, when India was a socialist country. It is time for us to change from the socialist setup towards a more proactive market economy. However, if we live in a fools paradise and imagine that a totally deregulated market system will solve the social ills in the country, then we have to take responsibility for hitting the final nail in the coffins of the socially underprivileged people.

Even though the socialist era didn't lift the underprivileged people out of their problems, it didn't have a negative impact either. However, a deregulated market system will have a negative impact on them. Let us take the data from USA, a country where the social inequality is not all too bad compared to India, and see how things have shaped up. I am relying on this study by the Brookings Institution about the income inequality between blacks and white during the period of excessive deregulation (from the Nixon period onwards).

While incomes have grown for both black and white families, white families still have considerably lesser income than the black families. Some of the differences in economic outcomes reflect the persistent effect of income differences from the early

1970s, passed down from parents to children. The analysis also shows that white children have better economic outcomes than black children. Black children born into the bottom fifth of the economic distribution have a hard time escaping upwards, and a harder time than poor white children. Many middle income black parents have seen their children's income fall behind their own and higher number of black children have fallen from the middle to the lower end of the economic distribution.

What can we infer from the data and the conclusion? The most obvious inference is that deregulated free market system has not helped to bridge the social inequality. If you dig a bit deeper, you can even find that it has increased the gap between whites and blacks. Also, a deregulated free market systems will never bridge the inequality gap. We have seen this with this data in USA and we have also seen it during the British rule in India. First, let us shut down the ridiculous propaganda of free market fundamentalists that a deregulated free market system is the cure for all social evils. Those saviors of underprivileged, who think that such deregulated systems will help their cause, should come out of their delusions and take a hard look at the data. It is time for them to be realistic and make a decision based on hard data. Should India go back to the socialist economy? No way.

We needed it after the independence and the system has outlived its utility long back. India should embrace the free market system but, unlike America, India should ask hard questions. India should take a hard look at the data and understand that a highly deregulated system is not suitable for our country. Socialism doesn't work in the current scenario and deregulated market system will also not work. The best case is to have a "free market" system that has humanism built into it. A market economy that offers a level playing field on which both the privileged sections and underprivileged sections compete on an equal footing. To ensure this, we need strong regulations to keep the players in control. A strong regulatory body which ensures that we don't have bullies in the playing field. A compassionate government which ensures such a level playing field.

This can only be achieved if we ignore the crap propaganda of free market fundamentalists and the delusions fostered by certain saviors of underprivileged. We need to ask hard questions. We need to look deeply on the existing data. We need to learn from the history (the market system under British rule). If Indians fall into the trap of the free market fundamentalists, like the Americans, no one can save the socially underprivileged people. We can as well write an obituary for them right now. It is time for Indians to actually think.

Women's empowerment and gender equality are no longer theoretical notions with hard-to-grasp meanings. They are terms bandied about by development agencies, not just implying different things to different people as was the analysis a few years back, but also more or less unburdened of their reference to 'power', and transformed into what Andrea Cornwall, in her essay - Pathways of women's empowerment - refers to as "today's softer, more conciliatory, calls ..... that have none of the rough edges of older demands for justice and equality." It may seem a bit exaggerated, but the onus now is on those actors who actually push for sustained institutional and structural change focusing on micro-macro connections about issues like poverty, marginalization, discrimination and violence to clarify that their conception of gender justice and women's empowerment is "NOT" the formulaic variety, but more embedded in women's realities and the need for more fundamental change in the ways we imagine and implement development policies and programmes.

Indeed access to productive resources such as land, property and credit are indispensable to the journeys of empowerment, and formal, legal-policy mechanisms to guarantee women their claims to such means of economic independence are vital. However, empowerment is essentially about being able to see how to negotiate one's condition in a process of sustained change - that builds capabilities for well-being and autonomy - even as it allows societies real choices for determining their paths to progress. This freedom to shape the "parameters of the possible", as Cornwall observes succinctly, is severely constrained for a majority of the world's women, who owing to neo-liberal macro-economic frameworks have suffered debilitating impacts on their productive and reproductive roles and rights.

Land itself is being commercialized and taken away from indigenous peoples and small farmers by states colluding with transnational corporations, and disenfranchised communities from around the world have had no recourse, not even in global governance systems, because of huge democratic deficits characterising existing global systems. The larger structural rubric of development today has also led to a rapid and rampant consumerist discourse, with deep consequences for women's autonomy. Research shows how in parts of India there is an increase in dowry because of increased mobility of IT professionals with disturbing consequences for those underprivileged and seemingly unconcerned with the global IT industry. Legal-policy measures do have their limits and therefore, gender equality presupposes changes to society's basic visions and conceptions of progress.

In respect of the lessons from micro-credit, the writing is on the wall and yet, the business instinct of micro-finance squelches development wisdom about poverty, gender and credit. Let us not forget, as Walden Bello says, that "many of the same institutions that pushed and are continuing to push failed macro programs (sometimes under new labels like "Poverty Reduction Strategy Papers"), like the World Bank, are often the same institutions pushing microcredit programs." The narrative of micro-credit seems to correspond to the tale of the Emperor's New Clothes. Everyone sees the truth and yet we go on. It is true that access to credit is significant to women's survival; it is a means by which the poor tide over contingencies, particularly in health.

And yet, as has been observed by policy experts, the odds are stacked against the self-employed in the global marketplace and the strong clout of transnational corporations places the poor, especially poor women, at a particularly unfair advantage in the global marketplace. More recently, as the formal banking sector becomes more and more happy with the "prospects" of micro-finance, there seems to be an anomaly between women's empowerment goals and the fundamental rationale of the micro-credit approach. A few years ago, *Nirantar*, a leading NGO in India working on women's right to education conducted a research that shows how women who are part of micro-credit forums are denied the right to educational opportunities, and how increasingly, the government is presenting the mere creation of micro-credit forums as the primary continuing education strategy as well as the women's empowerment strategy in the country.

Development strategies have a responsibility to expand capabilities, not take them away. A report of the Planning Commission in India that scopes the micro-credit market concludes that "Banks could be encouraged to undertake such lending and could be incentivised to do this through being allowed to charge commercial rates of the order of 18-20% on such loans." With such high interest rates, and with the instrumentalization of women's SHGs for business interests, the micro-credit approach may simply lend legitimacy and greater financial clout to an exploitative form of organized money-lending.

There are models of credit that are women-centred. Organizations like SEWA in Ahmedabad India, which is a trade union of women, locate their low-interest lending strategies as one of a multi-pronged approach that addresses rights of women in the informal sector, their capacity and training requirements, and health care, also providing critical institutional mediation for women producers to global markets, actively negotiating their interests. SEWA locates access to credit as one important dimension of women's rights as workers, especially to secure livelihoods.

In a discussion on productive assets, the discussion on access to ICTs seems a bit misplaced. Not because ICTs cannot be productive assets, but because access to ICTs is a more fundamental capability, that cannot be seen merely as translating into monetary or economic gains. Rather, an enterprise based approach to ICTs can backfire, as is increasingly the evidence from programs that see women as franchisees of ICT services.

In state after state in India, many government promoted schemes, where young unemployed youth were enticed to set up telecentres with bank loans, have run into huge debts because they were promised profits from e-governance and e-commerce ventures, which simply did not materialize. A similar story of the phone-women of Bangladesh indicates that their income has petered down with greatly increased mobile telephony penetration in the country.

A progressive framework of access to ICTs that addresses questions of women's empowerment needs to see access to ICTs as a 'capability right'. Marginalized women can, through the appropriation of ICTs, gain legitimacy for their concerns; demand accountability from public institutions and explore new platforms for building solidarities and for learning and knowledge sharing. The ICT diffusion paradigm is however deeply entrenched in market fundamentalism and in an undermining of the public policy role of governments to nurture and sustain local and community media and networks that are based on equity and social justice considerations.

A public goods approach is vital for women's groups to access ICTs, and leverage the propensities of the emerging information and communication ecology for furthering their struggles, whether around the right to information, right to livelihoods, the need for educational content in local languages or running community radio initiatives. Public financing instruments are critical to realize the capability rights of women through ICT access.

The simple truth about access to resources is that unless we are able to put the politics back into the framework of access - dealing with structural issues of injustice, we are bound to be left with quick-fix solutions, bereft of ethical and ideological values, in the common pursuit of what may, unfortunately have become empowerment's bane -efficiency, at all costs. Often these costs are simply too high for most women.

3

Women and Politics

The law to reserve one-third of the total numb r of seats for women was implemented at the *panchayat* and *zilla parishad* level in all the states of India without any opposition from any political quarter whatsoever. Ramakrishna Hegde's government in Karnataka started this process in 1983 before the central legislation mandating representation for women was passed. It provided for 25 percent reservation for women at village *panchayat* levels. This was before any powerful women's lobby emerged in Karnataka to press for this move and before there was any popular groundswell of opinion in favour of women's reservation.

In the mid 1980s, the *Shetkari Sangathana* of Maharashtra, led by Sharad Joshi, pioneered the move to field all-women panels for *panchayat* elections in that state and subsequently focused on getting women elected to *zilla parishads* in as many constituencies as possible, with men of the *Sangathana* playing a supportive role. However, the Bill introduced in the Parliament in September 1996 to reserve one-third of the seats in Parliament and state legislatures has evoked a good deal of resistance and opposition.

This despite the fact that all our major national parties - the Congress, the BJP, the Janata Dal, and even the two Communist parties have committed themselves to reserving 33 percent of the seats in legislatures for women by including this promise in their respective election manifestos. The

Common Minimum Programme (CMP) agreed upon by the various parties constituting the present UF government starts its section entitled "Social Justice" with the declaration that "one-third of the elected membership in Parliament and state legislatures will be reserved for women. Legislation, including an amendment to the Constitution, if necessary, will be introduced to reserve one-third of all posts in government for women.... All laws will be reviewed to remove provisions which discriminate against women." Though they dare not openly backtrack from their promise, it is evident that they did not expect to be called to account so soon and so earnestly. News reports indicate that the greatest opposition to this bill is coming from the United Front MPs. Some of them have openly declared their intention to even defy the party whip (if one is issued) and vote against the bill.

Compare the present day controversy over the issue of women's representation in legislatures to the atmosphere that prevailed in the 1920s. In response to the Indian agitation for representative government, the British government set up a committee headed by Montague and Chelmsford in 1919 to work out a proposal for constitutional reforms aiming at the inclusion of some Indians in government.

Many groups presented their case for representation before the committee. Among the many delegations that met this committee, Sarojini Naidu and Margaret Cousins led a small delegation of women to demand that women be granted the same rights of representation in legislatures as men.

The British government predictably thought this demand was quite preposterous because women in most Western countries had still not been given the right to vote, despite a protracted struggle. The Southborough Committee stated that "the extension of the vote to women would be premature in a society which continued to enforce *purdah* and prohibitions against female education." However, instead of taking on themselves the onus of rejecting the demand outright, the British government simply skirted the issue by leaving it up to each of the individual provincial legislatures that they had just set up in India to grant or to refuse the franchise to women.

Their assumption was that since Indians were so "backward", they would never accept the idea of equal political rights for women. But despite the fact that at this time there was no mass-based women's suffrage movement in India, each of the Indian provincial legislatures voted to make it possible within a short span of time for women to be represented at par with men without much fuss. The testimony of Margaret Cousins, an Irish feminist who played a major role in women's organizations in India as well as in Britain, brings out the contrast between the Western and Indian response to women's political rights very clearly.

"Perhaps only women like myself who had suffered from the cruelties, the injustices of men politicians, the man-controlled press, the man in the street, in England and Ireland while we waged our militant campaign for eight years there after all peaceful and constitutional means had been tried for fifty previous years, could fully appreciate the wisdom, nobility and the suffrage. When a meeting of representative women's organizations in 1930 drafted a memorandum demanding immediate acceptance of adult franchise without gender discrimination, it was turned down by the British government.

The same demand received a totally different response from the Indian leaders. The very next year, in 1931, the Karachi session of the Indian National Congress took the historic decision committing itself to the political equality of women, regardless of their status and qualifications. This proposal met with virtually no opposition. Laws claiming to protect women's rights have seldom evoked the same amount of hostility or opposition in India that they provoke in many other countries of the world and get to be easily endorsed by the entire political spectrum. In fact, in India there is very little difference between parties of the right or left on women's issues.

For instance, the BJP's current manifesto sounds even more progressive than the left parties on women's issues. It took women in Europe a century-long struggle to win the right to vote. By contrast, the right to vote and other legal rights came without a fuss or fight in India. The right to abortion, right to equal employment and educational opportunities, equal remuneration for equal work, protection against domestic violence - all came to be passed as laws in India without any hostility or resistance. However, since our government neither has the political will nor the appropriate machinery to implement any of its laws (not just those relating to women but even traffic laws) little of our progressive legislation makes an impact on citizens' lives.

PEOPLE'S RESPONSE

Our country has had a well-entrenched tradition whereby a party, politician or public figure bad-mouthing women in public or opposing moves for women's empowerment are strongly disapproved of and usually rejected. Among our male politicians, only Bal Thackeray of the Shiv Sena had the stupidity to make some brazenly anti-women statements some years ago. In the assembly elections that followed, his party suffered a major setback in Maharashtra, which was attributed to his indiscreet anti-women remarks, among other things. Because of this, very few politicians dare attack women from public platforms except when they are in direct electoral competition with a woman.

This is not just due to the pressure on our politicians to be "politically correct" on women's issues. Indira Gandhi as the first woman Prime Minister of India was rarely attacked on account of her gender. If anything, she was able to use her gender to her advantage projecting herself as Mother India and Durga incarnate rolled into one. There was no fuss made over her assuming the highest political office in the land. By contrast, many of the supposed advanced democracies of the West are still not ready for women in such high offices.

The first woman Prime Minister of France was constantly derided and attacked for being a woman till she simply resigned from the job. There is indeed a widespread social opinion in favour of women's active political participation. The recent countrywide post-election opinion survey conducted by the Centre for the Study of Developing Societies for India Today provides the most encouraging and definitive endorsement that there is no real divide between men and women in India on this issue. 75 percent of men and 79 percent of women favour active participation of women in politics and 75 percent of men and an equal number of women favour reservations for women in legislatures.

Barring one Sikh couple, everyone I interviewed expressed strong feelings in favour of reservations for women. This included men and women from supposedly conservative Muslim families, illiterate working-class Hindus and Muslims, and representatives of the *Balmiki* and *Jatav* (sweeper) communities, apart from the middle and upper classes. Men and women alike said that the inclusion of women was equal participation.

In these societies women have begun to seriously alter the very nature of politics and have made enduring and substantial gains for themselves in every field. In India, the problem is more serious because while in many other countries women are inching forward bit by bit, in India the participation of women in politics is actually declining. There were many more outstanding women leaders and workers in the Congress Party at all levels during the freedom movement than are present today in all the parties put together.

PUZZLING CONTRADICTIONS

One of the most puzzling features of low political representation of women in our legislative bodies is that it seems to have no direct correlation with literacy and other seemingly logical indicators. A comparison between the states of Kerala and Rajasthan, whose literacy rates are at opposite ends of the spectrum, demonstrates this clearly. In Kerala, the overall literacy rate is reportedly 90 percent with 86 percent female literacy. By contrast, in Rajasthan, female literacy is a mere 20 percent and only 12 percent of the females are literate in rural areas. Kerala has a matrilineal tradition in which women have a much larger measure of autonomy and freedom of movement.

Kerala's women also tend to marry at a much later age compared to women in other states. Most women in Rajasthan live far more restricted lives in aggressively patriarchal communities, many of whom still practice *purdah* very early or even child marriages. However, all these cultural and educational advantages women have in Kerala have not translated into higher political participation. The percentage of women in the Kerala legislative assembly rose from less than one percent in 1967 to six percent in 1991. In Rajasthan, the representation of women was four percent in 1967 and reached eight percent in 1985-90. Since then it has been going down.

Similarly, the state of Manipur, which has a tradition of women playing a dominant role in family and community, again due to a matrilineal heritage, never elected a single woman legislator up to 1990 - when it elected its first. A similar low level of women's representation is true for Nagaland and other North-eastern states, which are known for a less repressive culture for women. By contrast, UP, Bihar, and Madhya Pradesh, which are known for their low education levels and repressive cultural norms for women, have not only sent a relatively larger proportion of women to the Lok Sabha but have also elected relatively more women MLAs.

POST-INDEPENDENCE POLITICS

In independent India, politics has proved to be very inhospitable for women. One important reason is the pervasive gender discrimination which results in making even veteran women politicians feel bypassed and ignored. For new entrants, discrimination makes it very difficult for them to establish a foothold without patronage from powerful men in the party. However, it is important to recognise that the sidelining of women in our polity goes beyond gender discrimination. It is part of a larger process in which most honest, decent people have become politically marginalized as our politics and government have become the hotbed of crooks, thugs and even outright criminals. Very few honest men or women have survived in electoral politics and kept their honesty intact.

Today the political scene has come to be dominated by anti-social elements because we have reduced our democracy to the sole ritual of the electorate casting its vote whenever called upon to do so. After they vote, the people have virtually no role in the functioning of civic and other institutions. After Independence, the brown sahibs led by Nehru, who inherited power from the *gora sahibs*, allowed the colonial bureaucracy to strengthen its stranglehold over our civic, administrative, and political institutions from the village to the national level.

Even today, a young collector in his 20s rules supreme like a colonial master over the district he governs. He can dismiss *panchayat*s and *zilla parishads* at will and people have to appear before *sarkari babus* as hapless supplicants for every little thing. In such an atmosphere, local leaders, including elected representatives, tend to establish a nexus with bureaucrats so that both can join in unrestrained loot and plunder of public resources. No effective monitoring mechanisms exist to restrain our *netas* and *babus* or call them to account when they systematically abuse their authority.

Politics has become the quickest and shortest route to getting rich without doing any work other than brokerage. If the rules of the game remain as corrupt as they are now, only those women politicians who are good at emulating the worst of male politicians in the art of power-grabbing and plundering will be able to survive. Career graphs of Indira Gandhi, Jayalalitha, Mayawati, Rithambara, Sheila Kaul, and a host of other prominent women in power politics is a testimony that women become as vicious, corrupt, and authoritarian as the worst of men when they occupy positions of power which demand little or no accountability.

Such specimens of the female gender serve neither the cause of women nor that of society. They are as harmful for our democracy as are the Bal Thackerays, Chandraswamis,

H.K.L. Bhagats and Advanis. The presence of this type of woman is neither worth fighting for nor celebrating. This is not to suggest that I am in favour of leaving the political arena to the male crooks who dominate our Parliament and state legislatures today.

Far from it, I would like to see women enter politics with a vision for restoring the health of our dysfunctional political system, to make our politics truly representative and overhaul our institutions of governance - the local corporations, police stations, courts, and various government offices - in such a way that they become actually accountable to ordinary citizens in their everyday functioning.

EXTRA LOAD OF MORALITY

Many argue that to expect women to carry an extra load of morality is to make unreasonable demands of them which only strengthen the stereotype of women as self-sacrificing creatures who can be easily sidelined. While it is legitimate for women to demand a share of the pie, it is equally important to ensure the pie is worth eating and that there is enough there for everyone to share. Women's entry into politics will not change anything for the better if the overall character of politics does not improve.

If women join politics in greater numbers through the present scheme of reservation this change alone is not going to create a new political culture by itself. While the inadequate representation of women in governance is a serious flaw of our democracy which needs correction, to stop at merely that would be suicidal as it will only lead to making a sizable space for women in the world of organized corruption and crime.

As things stand today, even those women who have made a mark in electoral politics find it hard to sustain their involvement unless they too become money making racketeers. For the honest, the heavy investment of time and money that is required proves too burdensome to be sustained for more than a short time. A good example from among the many accounts I have heard of the special hurdles women face in politics, is that of Sarojatai Kashikar, who was a member of the Maharashtra assembly between 1991 and 1995.

Sarojatai was initially drawn into politics through her husband's close association with the *Shetkari Sangathana*. Before her exposure to the *Sangathan,* she was an ordinary housewife whose only connection with political life for years was cooking and serving her husband's colleagues in the movement. Though she was well-educated, she had no interest in or knowledge of the political world. However, as the *Sangathana* leader Sharad Joshi insisted that women must participate actively in the movement, she slowly came to be one of the leading cadres of the *Sangathana.*

In 1991, the *Sangathana* fielded her as a candidate for the Maharashtra state assembly elections as part of their campaign to get as many women elected as possible.

Though new to electoral politics, she won by a convincing margin and within a short span of time came to be one of the most respected legislators in the state assembly. She took her work seriously, studied the required documents, kept in good contact with her constituency and was respected even by district officials for her honesty and integrity. However, her job as a MLA required that long periods had to be spent away from home attending assembly sessions in Bombay. Since she did not feel safe living alone in the MLA's hostel in Bombay, a young brother-in-law was deputed to accompany and stay with her in Bombay.

She told me that even for a middle-aged married woman like herself, to be seen chatting and freely socialising with male political colleagues was likely to be misunderstood and become cause for character assassination. To avoid this, her brother-in-law remained by her side to act as a protective shield. In addition, in Sarojatai's case she could also count on her four other male colleagues from the *Sangathana* who also became MLAs at the same time as her. Having been trained in the political culture of the *Sangathana,* her colleagues were not only exceptionally honest and decent but also used to dealing with women as colleagues.

These men acted as buffers, yet provided her the necessary communication channel with the world of politicians without her having to directly hobnob with all kinds of unsavory characters. Since they were all close and trusted friends of her husband, interaction with them provided much less scope for misunderstanding. Yet she did find herself handicapped in many respects and had to watch her every step. Hence the dependence on her young and relatively inexperienced brother-in-law.

Sarojatai's accomplishments would have been nearly impossible without her supportive husband and even more supportive sister in-law who cheerfully took over the entire load of her domestic responsibility as well as caring for her two growing sons. Fortunately, her two sons were already responsible teenagers and were cooperative, but they missed her during her long absences from home. If her kids had been small, political work would have been even more stressful. Apart from the substantial sum of money that had to be spent on her election campaign, her husband had to spend a lot of additional money to support her politics because, unlike most other MLAs, she did not make any "extra" money.

The amount of money and resources officially provided to each MLA for their salary and political work simply does not cover the actual expenses of nursing a constituency. Due to all this, Sarojatai simply refused to stand for the recent parliamentary election though she continues to be active in *Sangathana* work. They say behind every great man there is usually a great woman. However, behind each politically effective woman, not just a cooperative husband is required, but an extremely supportive and resourceful extended family and in addition a strong movement-based organization ready to encourage women into public life.

THE INHIBITING FACTORS

A key component of politics is the art of building alliances. In a culture where even formal interaction with men unconnected to one's own family is frowned upon, women are severely handicapped in politics because they cannot cultivate close association with men without jeopardising their position in the family. A woman operating on her own strength in a party filled with corrupt politicians who think nothing of slandering their own women colleagues would find the going very tough, even if she can somehow mobilize other compensatory resources by her own special efforts.

Not too long ago, Uma Bharti of the BJP was driven to a suicide attempt because of the slander campaign unleashed by her own colleagues who saw her independent mass popularity as a threat to their power. They used her supposed personal closeness to one of the BJP's respected male leaders to spread all kinds of vicious rumours about her, both within the party and in the media. The fact that politics is dominated by the most unsavoury kind of men makes most women themselves reluctant to break taboos regarding free intermixing with men.

A woman risks her reputation by even being seen with many of them, whereas a man does not have to prove his credentials by such fierce avoidance. Thus women are handicapped from getting crucial information which men pick up easily from casual gossip with all kinds of people. So much of our politics is carried out in late night sessions, often over booze, where deals are made and strategies planned. Most women politicians, including the corrupt ones, don't dare to be seen participating in such sessions. The breakdown of institutional politics in favour of gangster politics has made things much tougher for women, especially given the strict regime of restrictions that most women are made to live under.

Even though most men in India favour women's political participation, this does not easily translate into relaxing restrictions on the women in their own families. Behavioral change at the family level will require consistent hard work to change cultural norms and reduce women's domestic responsibilities. Even in educated middle class neighbourhoods of Delhi, *mohalla* associations are usually run by men. While a few families are willing to relax some restrictions on women and are supportive of their activism, the workload of women and the nature of their domestic responsibilities makes it extremely hard for them to spare the kind of time required for making even a small difference in politics.

When I was studying the functioning of an all-women *panchayat* in a Maharashtra village, one of the leading members described the difficulties of keeping women active and involved, except intermittently: "For every little thing, we have to go and petition the district level officials - whether you want a road repaired or a bus service extended to your village, a water tank built or a phone connection sanctioned - each of these tasks require numerous trips to district headquarters with each trip involving loss of one full work day for a woman. Often meeting officials won't get the work done. You have to organise protests, sit on *dharnas* and what not.

Women simply can't spare that kind of time even if their husbands are not objecting to their participation. There should be no requirement that a person become a full-time politician and make it a profession (as well as a means of livelihood) if we want meaningful participation by large numbers of women in this country's political life on a consistent, long-term basis, rather than fitful, sporadic involvement in *morchas* and *dharnas*, as happens at present. The more centralized and authoritarian a polity, the lower the involvement of women will be in it.

ADDITIONAL DISADVANTAGES

By keeping more than three-quarters of India's women illiterate and providing shamelessly poor quality education to the few who manage to reach *sarkari* schools, the government plays a crucial role in discouraging and obstructing women's participation in public affairs.

Even for participation at the *panchayat* level, it is no longer possible for an illiterate person to function effectively because the *sarkari panchayat*s have been integrated into the vast bureaucratic network, with its reams of forms to fill out and its dust-covered volumes of rules and procedures.

Moreover, the rules are rendered in such opaque Hindi or regional languages that even the literate members of *panchayats* find it difficult to make any sense of them. Wherever the *panchayat* members are incapable of or diffident about handling rules and accounts, the government-appointed *gram sevak* simply takes control of the *panchayats*. Most women, especially those who are uneducated, feel helpless and lost when they are required to deal with the impenetrable maze of the bureaucratic world which defines the parameters of the *panchayat*'s role.

What appears to be a woman *panchayat* member's incapacity is actually proof of our system's ridiculous procedures and insensitivity to people's requirements. What goes by the name of politics in our country is an overly time consuming and debased activity. Even for those who are honest and sincere in their work, the nature of our political institutions makes it very difficult to make a real difference. Nothing comes to our citizens without *sifarish* and influence because the government encroaches on too many aspects of our lives in negative ways.

Our MPs and MLAs are constantly mobbed by favour-seekers and petition-mongers. They waste a good part of their time doing out favours to their supporters and people who seek their intervention in getting a water or electricity connection, a telephone or gas cylinder sanctioned, jobs or school admission, out-of-turn railway reservations from the MP quota, and generally mediating with various *sarkari* offices for "getting work done" (*kaam karwana*) since our *babus* don't believe in doing anything unless kicked from above or bribed from below.

This includes intervening in cases of harassment by the police, corporation or other government agencies. In addition, an MP or an MLA is expected to lobby to get funds sanctioned for repair of roads or to get *sarkari* approval for the opening of an engineering or medical college. Even to get a primary health centre opened or a public sector enterprise started in their constituency requires lobbying. In other words, all those things that ought to happen in the normal course of events require constant string-pulling in India.

The kind of politicians who can thrive in such an atmosphere are not likely to have the time or the skills required of a legislator such as initiating meaningful changes in government policy and making appropriate laws to translate that policy into action. This cultivation of a network of favour-seekers is essentially the only political activity commonly recognized as "political work" and "constituency building". Within this system how can a legislator do any meaningful work in her/ his constituency?

No matter how hard an MLA may try, she/he is not likely to succeed in getting a primary health centre or primary school of that constituency to function properly. However, very little effort is required for an MLA to become a part of the corruption network and make money by keeping the malfunctioning system intact. The constant pressure from favour-seekers means that an MP/MLA has no time for a normal family life. Women find this part of politics especially hard to cope with. That is why most of our women legislators tend to be from political families which are conditioned to withstand such a stressful life-style. No ordinary person can put up with so much strain and stay sane.

STAYING POWER OF WOMEN

The staying power of women in politics is also limited due to the fact that while they may get support and even get to be treated as heroines if they win an election, very few women are allowed to remain politically active once they lose an election. According to Sharad Joshi, whose *Shetkari Sangathana* worked hard to bring large number of women into the electoral arena, it is extremely difficult to keep women politically active after they have lost an election because a woman who continues to devote time to politics even after the electoral setback gets to be looked down on as a hopeless addict, like a wayward man hooked on drugs or liquor. Therefore, unlike men, women cannot take defeat in their stride and tend to fade out soon thereafter. Considering all this, it is perhaps not a coincidence that the few women who have developed an independent political base and are able to compete with men in electoral politics are mostly single or widowed - as for example, Uma Bharti of the BJP, Mamta Banerjee of the Congress Party, and Maneka Gandhi of the Janata Dal. These women are able to give their undivided attention to politics because there is no man to hold them back and, therefore, they are not easily cowed down by scandal or character assassination.

These three women have had to wage relentless battles within their respective parties for due recognition because their popularity, mass appeal and their organizational skills which are resented by their male colleagues. Yet these women have mostly emerged triumphant because they are celebrities to their supporters. While Indian society may not be very kind to ordinary women, it loves to celebrate women who appear and prove themselves to be stronger than men.

In Maneka Gandhi's case, the aura around the Gandhi family name has played an important role in adding to her charisma, while both Uma Bharti and Mamta Banerjee come from very ordinary families and were not groomed by any powerful patriarchs. Women who show extraordinary resilience, courage and the capacity to withstand character assassination get to be treated with special awe and reverence in our country. Despite all the muck-raking regarding Uma Bharti's alleged affairs, her opponents in the party have not been able to eclipse her. She is a popular cult figure among the BJP followers, far more influential in electoral campaigns of the party than even Rajmata Scindia with all her royal antecedents.

However, none of these women have the clout their popularity should have earned them within their respective parties. At the same time, it is ironic that none of these three women make a special point of mobilizing other women. They would see that as a downgrading of their status if they were projected primarily as leaders of women. The more successful among women politicians do not like to be seen as representing women's interests. It is unfortunate that by and large only those who find it hard to maintain a secure foothold for themselves in elective politics tend to gravitate towards women's issues.

POLITICS FOR ORDINARY WOMEN

Our democracy will become more meaningful when ordinary women can take part in political deliberations without having to make heroic sacrifices and prove themselves stronger than men over and over again. In the existing circumstances, even talented women cannot stay in politics on their own steam, especially if they are married and have families. Women need the following conducive conditions in order to participate effectively in the public realm: a supportive family, preferably one with a political backgrounds someone from within the extended family willing to take over a large part of the family responsibility, especially the care of her kids. a good amount of surplus money in the family.

Not only in India, but even in the West, very few women can count on all these factors combining together in their favour. The nuclear family and the high divorce rate in the West make it that much harder for women to give much time to sustained political activity, especially since most Western women are simultaneously engaged in employment outside the house. If a woman's day revolves around dropping off and picking up kids from crèches after an eight or ten hour job outside the house, there is not much energy or time left for political work, except sporadic participation in campaigns and demonstrations.

If the nature and demands of politics are such that a woman has to choose between her children and politics, most women are likely to avoid politics. Therefore, it is crucially important for women to have more leisure for them to want to participate in politics. They tend to prefer political work that doesn't take them too far away from home on a regular basis. Thus women can be effective only in decentralized polities where decisions affecting people's lives can be taken locally.

If we look around the world, we find that women have secured a strong political foothold only in those societies where institutions function according to well-defined democratic norms, where the crime, violence, and overall corruption levels are low, where decision-making is not concentrated in the hands of a few, and where citizens actively participate in local governance without needing to become full-time politicians. It is no coincidence that the representation of women is highest in the parliaments of the Scandinavian countries.

By contrast, in the more macho and aggressive political climate of the USA, women's representation in the Senate is barely nine percent. This is despite the long history of the militant women's movement in the United States. Apart from the above mentioned factors, family life in the Scandinavian countries has changed dramatically due to changes from above and below, allowing women relatively greater leisure and freedom.

According to 1994 statistics, 66 percent of Swedish women in the age group 25- 29 were never married or remained single. In the 40-49 age group this figure drops to 16 percent - still high by Indian standards, where marriage is nearly universal. This doesn't count the people who are divorced and separated, but only those who remain single. In Sweden, according to 1994 data, the average number of children a woman has in her entire lifetime is 1.9, and according to 1992-93 figures, 28 percent of Swedish couples were cohabiting without children.

In 1990- 91, Swedish women spent an average of 17 hours per week on household work excluding childcare, with men contributing six hours. In 1990-91, women had 33 hours per week for leisure activities with men having only a slight advantage with 35 hours of leisure per week. The state provides high-quality childcare through municipal institutions and in 1993, 58 percent of kids aged one to six attended state-supported daycare centres. The state also provides "cash benefits" up to 450 days after a baby is born for both fathers and mothers of young children.

There are many other special benefits provided for children who have special needs. The functional and streamlined democracies typical of Scandinavia have opened up a substantial amount of time for both women and men who are interested in political work or any other work outside the domestic sphere. However, the support system that is enjoyed by people living in Scandinavian countries is only possible because these countries have: very high income levels not a very dramatic gap between the rich and the poor small and culturally homogeneous populations well-developed traditions of the state playing a social welfare role a substantial number of women living independently very high education levels for both men and women and high participation of women in the income earning labour force.

For instance, in 1994, only five percent of women were unemployed in Sweden while the figure for unemployed men was a little higher at seven percent a situation in which families are spending less and less time on housework and care of children. Interaction with "other family members", such as elderly parents, let alone other relatives, is at a minimum. It is no wonder that having freed themselves from the domestic sphere, Scandinavian women lead the women of the world in political participation. However, this has been achieved at the very heavy cost which most of us in India may not be willing to pay.

Care of others outside the family takes up about 30 minutes a week for both women and men in Sweden. By contrast, Swedish women spend 32.6 and men spend 35.2 hours a week on leisure activities. All of this paints a picture of an increasing atomization of human life and rapid erosion of family ties. If one compares the time involvement of Swedish parents with their children or relatives to the amount of importance given to family life in India, including time with children, old parents, relatives, neighbours, and friends, it becomes obvious why most people in India, not just women, are averse to sustained political work.

However, the gains Scandinavian women have made in the public realm are indeed substantial. In this respect, Japan provides an interesting contrast where politics at the top is highly male-dominated but at the bottom is becoming rather woman-centric. In Japan, a majority of women do not work outside the house, while men are expected to work extremely hard to support their families. Employers control not only men's long working hours, but also their leisure time when they are expected to socialise with male colleagues going in groups to bars or geisha houses.

Consequently, men have hardly any time for family life. They come home too late, too tired, and leave too early to be able to take an active interest in family or neighbourhood affairs. Consequently, the whole domestic terrain and neighbourhood is left to women who have lots of free time on their hands once their husbands and kids leave the house. In addition, men are expected to hand over their earnings to women - family finances are controlled and managed mostly by women.

The male-centric traditional culture of Japan does expect women to remain servile to men and nurture them obediently. But since men are home so little, the time women spend serving and pleasing men is very small. During such time they tend to wear a Kabuki-mask-like expression and do the required rituals, only to shed that mask of servility as soon as men leave home. Unlike women in India, they socialise with other women freely, especially in their neighbourhoods and they do not live under a regime of restrictions over their movements and interactions with the outside world, provided they are not spending too much time with other men or having extramarital affairs.

Consequently, women as a group have the time and the resources to take an active interest in local neighbourhood affairs - including civic matters. The politics at this level is heavily female-centred. The famous socialist party woman leader, Takako Doi, came into prominence by quietly building a vast political base by mobilising such female networks and energy into the political mainstream. Thus, women in Japan have carved out a special space for themselves in politics at the base level without the confrontational militancy of the Western feminists. In this case, the fact that most Japanese women are relatively leisured housewives proved to be a positive asset.

It would have been much harder had they been running from high-pressured jobs, to household shopping, to crèches, and to the kitchens, as most Western women do. All this only goes to underscore the fact that the problem is far more complex than simply that Indian women are lagging behind due to discrimination. We have to make politics worthy of women, tune it sensitively to their requirements or else even with reserved seats, only those who become like *saree*-wearing men will be able to survive in politics.

Among many other reasons, the latest Assembly elections were interesting was for the number of women stakeholders. There was Sonia Gandhi in Rai Bareili using the tried and tested renunciation weapon; Mamta Bannerjee in West Bengal trying to storm the Left bastion; and the one and only Amma in Tamil Nadu fighting a rearguard battle to save her fiefdom from Karunanadhi. The results are out and all but Sonia have fallen by the way side. No surprises there, really. Now, broadly speaking, women in Indian politics can be divided into two groups:

1. 1.The *Pallu* group(with the families ties): Sonia Gandhi, Vasundhara Raje Scindhia, Amma, Rabri Devi
2. Hysterical group: Mamta, Mayawati, Sushma Swaraj, Uma Bharti

Generally, the *Pallu* group commands much more "respect" and has a much better chance of being in power. The Hysterical women on the other hand are cynically used as rabble rousers at best or at worst provide entertainment to the rest of the country. Remember Sushma Swaraj's threat to shave off her head if Sonia became the PM? Mamta or Sushma are genetically incapable of making a coherent argument without resorting to hysteria. Unfortunately, unless you belong to the

Pallu group and have family lineage or better still family sacrifices to hang on to, its very difficult for women to break into the Indian political scene. So what they do, they try to outdo the men in being "men." The entrenched political class plays along till it suits them but when it comes to giving real power, they draw the line.

Conversely, some like Mamta Banerjee are never able to outgrow their rebel image and have become more or less a relic in the changed political situation. The most interesting thing is that the *Pallu* group is no pushover. In fact, they demand and command supreme political power and in their intolerance for dissent behave worse than any despot-remember Emergency? But the real source of their power is the *Pallu*–they keep the pretense of being the *bahu*/daughter/ mother, emotionally blackmail voters, and exploit their womanhood to the hilt. Almost all of Sonia Gandhi's political renunciations shenanigans have been built on the platform of being the wronged Indian *bahu*.

It is an indicator of the inherent hypocrisy in Indian society where we are all ready to prostate before a *bahu*, hail her as the next *Devi* as long as she remembers the *Pallu* on her head! There is an urgent need for women of substance in Indian politics-Women who don't come from a politically well-connected family nor mistake lung power and hysteria as an argument. Till then, we can't really call Indian politics inclusive. And neither can we hope for India to truly develop. Women's experience with and in formal politics - meaning in political parties, elections, and legislatures and local councils - would seem to bear testimony to this prophetic woman's words. In more recent waves of feminist activism, we have focused on women's access to power and decision-making authority in formal political institutions as critical to achieving gender equality in the long term.

Political empowerment of women became a clarion call by the mid-seventies, based on several assumptions about how this would change things for all women: that lasting gender equality could be achieved only through political change (enabling policies, legislation, enforcement and protection of rights); that women in politics would advance the cause of gender equality and women's rights; that unless women themselves were represented in local, national and global political bodies, the momentum for such change could not be sustained; that a critical mass of women in political institutions would also initiate broader social justice and peace - by fostering non-violent conflict resolution, sustainable and socially just development, access to and protection of the full body of human rights, and placing people above profits; and most of all, that this critical mass of women in political institutions would transform the very nature of power and the practice of politics through more transparent, accountable and consultative political behaviour - in other words, that women would play politics differently and practise power accountably.

It's certainly true that thousands of courageous women who entered politics have attempted to do all this and more - undoubtedly, women have made a significant impact on politics and political institutions at multiple levels.

But we must also confront the fact that increased representation of women in elected bodies has not transformed these institutions or engendered policies in the way we hoped - not even in those handful of countries where women elected representatives have reached more than a critical mass. Women have not been able to advance this notion of democracy as wholeness, as something that enables every voice, perspective, and priority, to become part of the 'collective will'.

Indeed, AWID's recent study of women's movements worldwide indicates that the women who have been experimenting with and participating in this very essence of democracy, are women in social movements - their own and others. As Parker Follett foresaw, it is women in organized movements - or "group organizations" as she termed it - who advance democratic process in ways that women in formal political institutions are unable to do because of the very male, hierarchical, and centralized cultures of these institutions. They do so by confronting the structures and relations of power in private and public spheres, challenging the ideologies that justify or rationalize these relations, and by accessing and redistributing resources. They create struggles that redefine notions of development, sustainability, and peace.

Most of all, they struggle with, and through, the complexity and heartache of constructing 'wholes' that hear and include the minorities within their own movements - this is much harder than the majoritarianism that marks most democratic political regimes. To illustrate these characteristics from the AWID case studies, the Indigenous Women's movement of Mexico has challenged the patriarchy within their own culture, while at the same time developing an intricate new construct of the relationship between themselves and the natural environment. The Domestic Workers movement of the United States, the Mothers movement of East Europe, and the *Dalit* Women's movement in Northern India have all struggled to build the most democratic forms of internal governance even as they claim their rights from formal political structures around them.

The One in Nine Campaign in South Africa and the GROOTS Kenya network challenge both the patriarchal violence against women that deprives poor women of their physical integrity or their inheritance rights as AIDS widows, and challenge the failure of their so-called democratic states to address their needs. These are only a small handful of the women's movements around the world that demonstrate that given the consciousness and opportunity to organize and build collective power, women are in a constant process of claiming true citizenship. They are not just champions of democracy but its true architects.

Women in Singapore traditionally played a small role in the politics of Singapore and Singapore's public life. Nonetheless in recent years, there is an increasing women representation in public life as more women have started running for political office. Notable female politicians include the highest ranked female politician in the history of Singapore; former Acting Minister Seet Ai Mee, Minister of State Yu-Fu Yee Shoon, and Amy Khor Lean Suan, a district mayor. Several women also became Nominated Members of Parliament, representing a range of societal interests such as women groups and conservation groups.

Unlike their Western counterparts, universal suffrage was granted and thus the women in Singapore did not have to fight for enfranchisement. The first women representatives in the Legislative Councils were those reflecting the English-educated and middle-class interests. Chinese-educated women leaders came into prominence as the proportion of women voters expanded from 8% to 50% in the 1955 Rendel Constitution elections. However, some of these Chinese-educated leaders like Linda Chen Mock Hock were linked with communism and thus were subsequently clamped down by the fiercely anti-communist Lim Yew Hock administration.

As the People's Action Party rose to power in 1959, as many as four female PAP candidates were voted into the self-governing Assembly. They included Women League's founders Chan Choy Siong and Ho Puay Choo. The PAP-Barisan Sosialis schism caused two women members to defect to the Barisan Sosialis. The two and from 1968, one remaining PAP woman members were considered moderate and relatively passive compared to the radicals, perhaps leaving a legacy of a weakened and subsequently, lack of female representation in politics for more than a decade.

ABSENCE OF FEMALE REPRESENTATION

With the retirement of Chan Choy Siong in 1970, there were no female representation in parliament from 1970 to 1984-a total of 14 years. Nonetheless, there were sporadic failed electoral bids by female opposition candidates. In 1984, the dominant PAP fielded 3 women candidates whom all entered parliament successfully. They were Dr. Dixie Tan, Dr. Aline Wong and current Minister of State, Mrs. Yu-Foo Yu Shoon.

Another woman, Dr. Seet Ai Mee joined the trio in 1988 and she subsequently was promoted to Acting Minister for Community Development- the highest political post ever held by a woman. However, Seet lost her seat to Singapore Democratic Party's Ling How Doong in the 1991 General Election by a razor-thin margin. The ruling PAP Women's Wing was formed in 1989. In 1992, Dr Kanwaljit Soin became the first female Nominated Member of Parliament and she played a major role in raising important social issues, such as violence against women, in the parliament. Other notable NMPs include Ms Claire Chiang and Ms. Braema Mathiaparanam.

CURRENT WOMEN PARLIAMENTARIANS

Since the 1990s, the number of women participating in politics progressively increases, but women remain significantly underrepresented in government and parliament. There are currently 17 elected women parliamentarians out of a total of 84 elected members. All female members are from the ruling PAP. There are two ministers of states and one district mayor. There are 5 females of a total of 9 Nominated Members of Parliament, while there is only 1 first-ever female NCMP. While Christianity has traditionally taught the equality of souls for God, the Church has been a patriarchal institution based on an anthropology in which man is the 'head' and woman subordinate.

Augustine of Hippo helpfully explained: 'Woman does not possess the image of God herself, but only when taken together with the male who is her head'. The theology has clearly influenced Gordon Brown's 'Presbyterian conscience'. The most significant shot fired across his bow by Caroline Flint -the fickle and capricious erstwhile Europe Minister -was that he treats women in the Cabinet as 'little more than female window dressing'.

The Prime Minister does not, she avers, view women as equals, preferring instead structures which secure and perpetuate male dominion. To her frustration, he has not grasped the emancipatory ideas of the Enlightenment. Feminist politics is a murky as feminist theology, but they are united by their fundamental antithesis to patriarchy. In his *Dogmatics*, Barth observed: 'Different ages, peoples and cultures have had very different ideas of what is concretely appropriate, salutary and necessary in man and woman.'

While the liberal tradition has been concerned with an equality of liberties and opportunities, Marxist feminism has been more radical in its identification and elimination of the prevalent androcentric fallacy -that men and women do not only differ physiologically, but also in their experience, perception and appropriation of reality; and that this difference has been masked because the normative representation of humanity in Western culture has been the experiences, values and conceptual constructs of males. Ms Flint has simply discovered the consequence of Gordon Brown's failure to find femininity in God. Gordon Brown's God is a father, husband, king, clan leader and warrior.

Caroline Flint's is a pregnant woman, mother, midwife, mistress. Gordon Brown's testosterone-charged, self-asserting and self-aggrandising 'inner circle' has no need of the goddess and no use for the 'feminine experience'. And so Caroline Flint feels that she exists on the periphery of misogyny, enduring an intolerable oppression. In the worldview of the Prime Minister, men possess all dignity, virtue, and power, while women, as a mere derivative of man, are inferior, defective, passive, somehow less than fully human. Therefore the female contribution to Cabinet can be largely ignored. But Ms Flint's error of judgement (and it is a considerable one) is that her emotional outburst, pettiness and inconsistency (not to mention posing for this sort of photograph) will simply be taken as corroboration that she was never qualified to be any more than 'window dressing' in the first place: her feminist quest to join the male-dominated 'inner circle' was the superficial pursuit of gender, not of merit.

By resigning from the Cabinet, she can no longer be a critical voice within it, but is reduced to being just another feminist revolt against it. Hers is now the 'advocacy stance' adopted by all liberation theologies which favour the oppressed. Her desire was to join the male-dominated 'inner circle' in order to realise the full equality of male and female: by removing herself from it she has just set back by years the struggle for the political liberation of women. She has simply proved herself to be the incarnation of all that Gordon Brown intuitively felt but, with his commitment to Marxist principles of equality, could never actually state.

Ms Flint ought to reflect on the fact that it was the women who did not desert Jesus but were united with him in his crucifixion and death; they were first to witness the resurrection; and they were the first to receive the apostolic commission to go and tell others. But those women were not obsessed with a trivial political feminist quest: they kept their eyes fixed on the super-objective, and they had the balls to persevere.

4

Women of Today

Their Issues and Challenge

For over two years Africa and the world has seen and witnessed the rise and fall of Liberia. Starting from the 1800s with the arrival of free slaves to the shores of West Africa, leading to the declaration and independence of Liberia in July 26, 1847. Since that time, Liberia has served as a beacon of hope for Africa, until 1980 when this "proclaimed" peaceful country experienced its first calamity of a bloody *coup de tait*. The country thereafter degenerated into anarchy and chaos, with rampant corruption, human rights abuses and bad governance as its hall mark.

1990 civil war was the final result of one hundred and forty years of rule of successive governments. It is estimated that over 250.000 Liberians and other nationals died in this crisis; including raping of women/girls, sporadic killing, execution of civilians and destruction of millions of dollars of property, infrastructure and a complete break down of the rule of Law. Liberia became a "no mans" land with its people fleeing and seeking refugee in various African, European countries including America; thousands languishing in refugee camps. The once beloved nation, one that African countries strived to emulate had become a sad story.

Just as everything must come to an end, so it was that the civil crisis came to an end in 2003.The ushering in of another interim government with the support of regional and international organizatons, countries lead the process of the general elections of Liberia. The election of 2005 saw again the transformation of Liberia, setting once more a record in African history as the first African country to elect a woman as their President H.E Ellen Johnson -Salieaf. Liberia is once again on the rise, showing to Africa and the world at large that indeed women are capable of leading their nations.

African women as well as Liberian women are now singing the song "this is our time" while African men are now realizing that times have changed and that women also can be Heads of state. Fingers are pointing to, heads are turning towards, and eyes are focused on Liberian not in pity but in admiration- setting the pace once more for true democracy in the African continent.

DEFINING A NEW ERA FOR LIBERIAN WOMEN

Liberian women have felt the tied of woes over the years, paid the price of successes, failures in blood, tears, sacrifice even unto death. Their sufferings are untold, their numerous contributions, yet not recorded. Today, Liberian women are more conscious of their rights to political, social and economic inclusion and their significant contributions. It is in recognition of these rights that their issues are identified in order to correct the wrongs and rebuild Liberia for sustainable and lasting peace. There are many issues that women are faced with in Liberia that were never considered National issues, but norms of the society and community.

This orientation is a major cause of women marginalization, discrimination, exclusion and human rights abuse. Some of the prevalent issues that are of grave concern are; Gender Based Violence (GBV) rape, domestic violence, Sexual exploitation, Harmful Cultural practices, particularly FGM, the lack of marketable vocational and technical skills, illiteracy and access to Justice. Before the civil war, women/girls were seen as sex objects, to provide sex for the pleasure of men be it by coercion, force, exploitation, mutual agreement or violence. Sexual abuse was never a topic to be discussed in private or public.

The Liberian government and society perpetuated a culture of violence against women that saw the escalation of rampant sexual abuse against women and girls during the war. Even though the guns are silent, women and girls continue to suffer sexual violence. The lack of political will to implement laws to protect women/girls and the acceptance of harmful cultural practices,(FGM, beatings, killings, arranged child manages, incest, rape, dowry or bride price) are major contributing factors to the high rate of illiteracy, violence and vulnerability of women in Liberia. For this and many other reasons, WOLPNET- Women of Liberia Peace Network, a non political, governmental organization, has joined the vanguard to promote women's rights and to advocate for the adherence to and implementation of national conventions such as the AU Protocol to support, protect and enhance women social economic, civil, liberty and political development.

With the collaboration and financial support from regional and international organizations, WOLPNET is engaging communities, public and policy makers through its program/ projects to sensitize and highlight these issues affecting women Advocating for change in policy, ending violence against women, elimination of harmful cultural practices (Female Genital Mutilation), right to dignity, life, and integrity. Through its media program, Women Agenda, WOLPNET is spreading the message of positive change; a change that is transforming and defining politics in Liberia; a change that must also be realized in the lives of women by the elimination of vices that impede women progress, calling for full implementation of; Article 2 elimination of discrimination against women, Article ¾ rights to dignity, life integrity and security of the person Article 8, Access to justice and equal protection before the law by the AU Protocol on Human and peoples rights on the right of women in Africa.

To my sisters and women, I urge you to say no to male supremacy, superiority, political domination, exclusion, discrimination and Violence against Women (VAW). Stand for peace, justice, equality and unity. The road is rocky and very rough right now, but my sisters, it has been for a long time before now. Like Liberian women, you have been excluded, abused, misused, disgraced, discriminated against and persecuted. Nevertheless, stand firm. Liberian women can do it you can do the same. Do not go down but stand up fighting for women's right; your bodies may be broken but do not allow your spirit and minds to be broken. Remember, many are called but few are chosen to lead the cause for justice and equality.

A small-scale farming is a farm holding established on a land area of not less than 5 hectares. In Nigeria, most of the small-scale farming enterprises are owned by men. This does not imply that Nigerian women agriculturists are not desirous of expanding their businesses due to so many challenges which border on gender issues, economic or socio-cultural barriers as well as government unfavourable policies. This chapter, a purely descriptive research, employs secondary data to expound on the issues and challenges confronting the development of the Nigerian women to full blown agro-entrepreneurs for national economic advancement. The rest of the discussion in this chapter is organized along the following issues:

- Women's potentials in entrepreneurial skills.
- Why women entrepreneurship development?
- Policy Framework for Women Entrepreneurship Development.
- Challenges faced by women agro-entrepreneurs.
- Strategies for development of women agro-entrepreneurs.

WOMEN'S POTENTIALS IN ENTREPRENEURIAL SKILLS

Women in general are naturally endowed with some exceptional abilities, which if properly harnessed for entrepreneurship purpose, could result in positive and enviable results. Women by nature:

- Have creative abilities
- Are blessed with ability to persist and pursue their desires

- Are good and patient nurtures of children, and this tenacity is usually transferred into business
- Are good innovators
- Have ability to develop passion for what they believe in

Waton (undated) cited in Okara (2005) identified the basic requirements of an entrepreneur to include: hard work, teamwork, commitment, appreciation, listening, high expectations, setting achievable goals. Women, by nature and exposure to family relationships, possess most of these qualities that are essential and can be enhanced for entrepreneurial success. Many researchers have shown that poverty is a malady that incapacitates its victim economically and indirectly subject him/her to a state of destitution, voicelessness, powerlessness and even violence.

Unfortunately, the most affected sex by the above incapacitation are women and children. Statistics show that women are poorer than men. The UNDP (1995) estimated that, about 60% of the world-poors, are women. Women are poorer because they are more vulnerable economically. The findings of Thane (1978), Showalter (1987) and Lewis and Piachered (1987) cited in Magaji (2004) showed that women have been the poor sex throughout the 20th Century and have formed a substantial majority of the poor since poverty was first recognized. On why women are the poorest sex, the physical strength of women and various challenges limit them to specific soft duties making it difficult to be enterprising.

Entrepreneurship development therefore is a crucial tool for women's economic empowerment. The benefits derivable from empowering the women folk are far reaching, starting with family advancement and eventually touching on the national and global economic advancement. According to the Nigerian Minister of Women Affairs and Social Development, Hajiya H. S. Bungudu, the latest Nigerian census revealed that women constitute 49.9% of the nation's population; the underrepresentation of women (2%) in the nation's development processes in finance, business and investment fronts renders 40% of the population inadequately positioned to contribute to the economic growth of the country. It is the nation that blends the strengths of women and men that will lead the world in development in the field of agriculture and other sectors.

Entrepreneurship or investing is not an exclusive reserve of any gender. Both women and men generate the same result provided they follow the principles of investment. Kiyosaki (1993) proves with statistical data in United States, that women are better investors than men. A year 2000 National Association of Investors Corporation (NAIC) study found that women-only clubs achieved average annual returns of 32% since 1951 versus 23% for men-only investment clubs. The verdict is; women know how to handle money and can be greater entrepreneurs than men if the various obstacles to development is removed or minimized.

POLICY FRAMEWORK FOR WOMEN ENTREPRENEURSHIP DEVELOPMENT

There are neither policies nor strategies for entrepreneurship development that is specifically tailored to women. The Nigerian government's policy of promoting entrepreneurship dated back to the early 1970s. The hope of promoting small scale enterprises to stimulate entrepreneurship was documented in the 2nd National Development Plan (1970-74). This policy continued in the 3rd (1975-80) and the 4th National Development Plan through various strategies of technical, financial and management of the small scale industries. The Federal Government's concern for the menacing problem of mass unemployment in the mid-1980s spurred the setting up of the National Directorate of Employment (NDE) in 1986 and the Work For Yourself Programme (WFYP) in 1987. Both were essentially joint programmes of training and financial support to entrepreneurs.

The NDE operations included three core programmes (i) Youth Employment and Vocational Skills Development Program (YEVSDP) (ii) agricultural programs (iii) the small scale industries and graduate employment scheme. The NDE, though starved of fund for some time, has achieved a lot in promoting employment, create wealth and alleviating women poverty. The Better Life for Rural Women Programme (BLRWP) initiative of a first lady of the Federal Republic of Nigeria, Maryam Babangida, was an entrepreneurship development programme specifically for promoting education, health and economic development of women.

It made unprecedented contribution to women through the cooperative organizations. The spirit of BLRWP is still operating today through the subsequent first ladies. A number of Non-Governmental Organizations (NGOs) also came up to promote entrepreneurship development. Prominent amongst them was the Country Women Association of Nigeria (COWAN) which contributed immensely towards women entrepreneurship development through organization of many cooperatives and micro-credit schemes and in partnership with the United Nations.

THE ROLE OF WOMEN IN AGRICULTURE

A significant amount of work has been carried out in developing countries on the potential of women in boosting food production. Boserup (1970) described Black Africa as the region of female farming par excellence. FAO (1982) estimated that the rural women contribute two-third of all the time that is put into traditional agriculture in Africa. Accat (1983) also pointed out that 80% of African women are engaged in agriculture. Patel and Antonio (1973) reported that 95% of the Yoruba women of the Southwestern Nigeria are engaged in farm works, growing yams, maize, tobacco and cassava, poultry and fish farming. They also participate in bush clearing, land preparation and weeding. In addition to their role in production, they are actively engaged in harvesting, processing and marketing of farm produce.

The participation of Igbo men in nonfarm activities and waged employment has resulted in an increased workload for women in food crop production as well as a breakdown of the gender division of labor in agriculture. Igbo women now undertake some of the conventional male agricultural tasks in addition to those in the female domain. The predominance of women in the small-scale fisheries post-harvest activities: micro-fish retailing, fish processing, fish distribution and marketing, make women the major players in the socio-economic development of the West African countries.

Despite women's extensive and varied participation in agriculture, they continue to have less access to credit and modern agriculture inputs. Consequently, their farm works is labor-intensive, yields meager economic returns and operate mostly at subsistence level. International Labour Organization (ILO 2003) quoted in Akpera and Sunday (2008) reported that Nigerian and African women entrepreneurs in general are in the micro enterprise sector and almost invisible in the small and medium enterprise categories.

THE CHALLENGES OF NIGERIAN WOMEN AGRO-ENTREPRENEURS

Some of the many obstacles that hinder women enterprise development, agribusiness growth and improved income earnings include;

1. Finance

The greatest challenge for Nigerian women in agribusiness is lack of finance. Women in agribusiness need substantial finance both for start-up and expansion. Finance could be in form of equity or from external sources. Equity from informal sources includes personal savings, friends and relatives, traditional (*esusu*), professional and age-group associations as well as formal co-operative societies.

External finance is majorly from banks (specialized, development, commercial, etc), government agencies, Non-Governmental Organizations (NGOs), international donors, etc. Entrepreneurs are expected to provide, in some cases, 25% of fund applied for and/or produce collaterals before accessing these external finances. It has been difficult for women to raise equity for own business because most women interested or engaged in farming earn low income. Many of the commercial or development banks are reluctant to grant agricultural loans due generally to the high agricultural risk factor or because they do not have competent assessors as in the case of fish farming. The high interest rate charged as well as the demand for collateral of landed property or other assets also compound the issue.

Currently, the Microfinance banks (MFB) are the government's latest major organ of policy for entrepreneurship finance in Nigeria. In an ongoing research conducted recently, it was discovered that male to female application and approval by MFB are in the ratio 65% to 35%. This discrepancy was linked to women entrepreneurs approaching banks on an individual basis and lack of soundly written business plan and/or feasibility studies.

2. Manpower and Education

The whole business be- it agricultural or any other, revolves around the entrepreneur (visionary) as she combines all other human, financial and material resources to create an enterprise of value. The chief executive of the business outfit must be knowledgeable to effectively mobilize resources to advantage. Agribusiness at small or medium scale is highly professional, technologically driven and require some level of education. Education not only provides basic knowledge and skills to improve health and livelihood, but it empowers women to take their rightful place in society and the development process.

Entrepreneurial education seems to be the major key policy to promote entrepreneurship development for women in Nigeria. Entrepreneurship education should be inculcated into school curriculum at all levels. Research indicates that Small and Medium Enterprise Industrial Empowerment Scheme (SMEIES) operators ranked the reasons for failure of entrepreneurs' application for loans and came up with reasons that range from bad feasibility studies, poor management skills, lack of proper accounting, poor character checks and attitudes among others. All these are challenges that can be remedied by entrepreneurship education. Even as the 93 approved Nigerian universities have adopted entrepreneurial studies, funds and the dearth of teachers to train the students has remained an obstacle.

A number of current training centers/programs are urban-based, for example, the Industrial Development Centers established in the 1960s are urban-based. Small Medium Entrepreneurial Development Agency of Nigeria (SMEDAN) aimed at facilitating credit, technology markets, capacity building, training and technical support for SMEs and provide adequate linkage with women bodies is urban-based and starved of funds. Agribusiness is rural-based and better educated farmers are more likely to adopt new technologies and have access to credit and extension services.

3. Technology

Many women, due to lack of exposure and financial limitations, still make use of old technology in farming, processing and preservation thus leading to drudgery and low output.

4. Cultural Restrictions/Weak Land Rights

The Nigerian culture cannot be described as being gender friendly. For example, the "Kule" policy in the North where married women are forbidden from going out of the house in daylight for business is an initiative/development-killer policy that should be discouraged in this 21st Century. In Sub-Saharan Africa, including Nigeria, where women have prime responsibility for food production, they are generally limited to user rights to land and subject to the consent of a male relative. Culture and social practices discriminate against women to be enterprise successors/inheritors or own independent assets which could easily serve as collaterals. Such unequal land rights are reflected in the smaller land sizes of women farmers thus limiting them economically.

5. Lack of Equipment and Appropriate Technology

Despite women's extensive and varied participation in agriculture, they continue to have less access to modern agriculture inputs. Consequently, women agro-entrepreneurs work under very difficult and laborious conditions, using crude traditional technology. Technology is closely related to finance and education. Nigerian women entrepreneurs, especially in agriculture, work under very difficult and laborious conditions, using crude traditional technology. There is urgent need for provision of modern, cost effective and affordable technologies for the use of women. Moreover, some new technology has often been inappropriate to women's needs. There is a need to define some priority actions to promote the role of women in the economy because it has been showed that women are productive and efficient when they have access to the right technologies and opportunities.

6. Erroneous Ideas about Women and Credit

There are certain myths about women in respect to credit which have made them to remain poor and limited their entrepreneurial prospects. One of such myths is that poor women make poor credit risks. This is being proved wrong as Olutunla (2008) reported that Nigerian women have been found to be more faithful in terms of loan repayment to Banks than men.

7. Entrepreneurial Attitude

According to Akpa (2007), an average entrepreneur is rugged and aggressive. These are common attributes of men while most women are of the gentle and kind disposition. Men tend to focus on getting the job done while women tend to focus on being more inclusive and relational. If a woman entrepreneur is to succeed, she must adopt some level of ruggedness and aggressiveness. Success is not gender-friendly.

8. Research and Extension Services

For a long time, agronomic researchers do not pay attention to the role of women in the farming system. Research into the activities of women in agriculture is gaining attention only recently. A survey in Ogun State, Nigeria and Osun State, Nigeria revealed that Extension Agents visited between 7-10% of women farmers every week compared to 70% of the male farmers who received weekly visits. An FAO (1989) study found government investment on agriculture represented less than half the sector's contribution to national income, therefore, it is reasonable to guess that women's access to extension services and training especially in the area of fish farming, processing, packaging, distribution and marketing are unlikely to improve when the overall funding and availability of services is declining.

9. Misplaced Focus

Many agricultural projects and programs are not suited to the special circumstances of women or may not reach women at all, thus truncating the intended effort to increase food production.

10. Market and Marketing

Due to lack of good roads in Nigeria, electricity, poor access to information and poor networking, many farm produce perish thus discouraging women farmers.

STRATEGIES FOR WOMEN AGRO-ENTREPRENEURSHIP DEVELOPMENT

The complementary policy issues in entrepreneurship education should include increasing women enrolment in schools at all levels especially in the field of agriculture to reduce gender inequality. Budgetary allocation should be made to accommodate more continuing and vocational education. More seminars/workshops should be sponsored and extended to rural areas to increase women's capacity to start and grow their agribusiness, prepare sound business plan/feasibility studies and increase their technical and managerial capacity in agribusiness. Modern processing plants/storage facilities should be installed for women groups on government/private joint partnership basis so that women can process and store their farm produce with ease.

The enabling environment in terms of gender-friendly policies, good roads, pipe-borne water and electricity should be provided by the various arms of government. Cooperatives and women groups should be more formally instituted and encouraged among women to position them strategically to access fund and other inputs with ease. The Government should mandate the commercial Banks to produce more gender-friendly loan packages (low interest rates and more relaxed duration of repayment).

Women should be exposed to the latest agro-technology from time to time to remove drudgery in farming, processing and preservation techniques. Nigerian women should be encouraged to network more, both at the national and international levels for more exposure, to access fund and export information. Agro-extension institutions should be boosted and more women extension agents be trained to reduce women to extension workers ratio and for wider coverage of women agriculturists.

Nigeria's vision of becoming one of the top twenty leading economies of the world by the year 2020, otherwise known simply as vision 20:20 appears compelling enough to energize its over 150 million people (nearly half of which are women) to make the vision a reality. To accomplish this laudable goal, there is urgent need to pay attention to the development of agro-women entrepreneurs so that they can take their place in family advancement and national economic development. The government and development/change agencies must not only be prepared to recognize the economic role of the women but must also extend to them the same recognition and facilities as the men are enjoying.

CHALLENGES FACING MUSLIM WOMEN

The Islamic Resource Foundation (IRFSA), in an endeavour to carry out its mandate of 'helping those who help others', has planned three events that will involve Muslim women who are active in a wide range of community organizations or just act as individuals assisting the needy in their areas. The goal of these programs is to do an 'on the ground' assessment of the needs of our community and define women's role in finding solutions to these common concerns.

The first workshop was attended by 75 women from approximately 27 organizations and institutions.

The full day program used a focus group approach that allows all the participants the opportunity to express their ideas and opinions. All participants were separated into various groups in order to expose each individual to as many new group members as possible. A pre-selected group leader was given the task to facilitate a discussion involving all group members about their organizations and the concerns that face their communities. Main points were recorded on flip chart papers and then reported back to the main body by a member selected by the group. This report (feedback) was posted for all participants to browse and then summarised for the following workshop. An abridged form of these discussions accompanies this report; it will be the task of the second workshop to priorities and begin to find practical solutions to the most pressing concerns.

After lunch and midday prayer the participants were addressed by Sh Ebrahim Gabriels, Dr. Abdulllah Hakim Quick and Sh. Khalid Al Mushawah. These informative talks shed light on the historical rights of women in Islam and the role that the modern Muslim can play in her community. The talks were followed by some challenging questions from the sisters that covered issues such as leadership roles for Muslim women; the need for Muslim men's education around the rights of Muslim women and their own specific responsibility in the family and community. In the concluding session, verbal feedback and creative suggestions for future sessions such as inviting only women speakers, focusing on solutions and skills to begin to address our common problems wrapped up a fruitful event. Suggestions for similar regional events where delegates could plan around common challenges and share solutions were also forwarded to IRFSA.

Most participants felt that there was a comfortable atmosphere which allowed full participation and they appreciated the opportunity to network with many other organizations. Delegates mentioned other issues such as the venue being difficult to access, the need for punctuality and better outreach to ensure an even wider participation. As a minority in the United States, Muslims face many challenges. First and foremost is ignorance about Islam. This ignorance leads to stereotyping, fear, and distrust. The acts of a few Muslim extremists are attributed to all Muslims. Muslim American citizens' loyalty to the United States is questioned.

We are dehumanized and thus easy prey for prejudice. For instance, last April, the federal building in Oklahoma City was bombed. It is probably the most devastating terrorist act to occur on U.S. soil. A few hundred people were killed, several hundred were injured. It was particularly brutal because there was a day care center on one of the bottom floors of this building. As soon as the report of the bombing came out, the first suspects were Muslims. As soon as the building was bombed, news reports said: "Arab looking people were seen leaving the area." Basically, for the next twenty-four hours, we faced harassment, we were threatened, and our lives were very much put in danger.

Muslim schools had to be closed, and individual Muslims were detained and harassed, even physically assaulted. It wasn't until the next day, when it turned out to be a fringe minority white group of people who had done it, could we sort of breathe a sigh of relief that our lives were not in danger, and finally we were able to mourn the victims of that bombing. Another danger resulting from American ignorance about Islam is the omnibus anti-terrorism legislation that President Clinton has proposed, which unfairly targets Muslims as widespread purveyors of terrorism. Despite several generations in this country - Muslims have quite a history in the U.S.-we are still perceived as foreigners; we are still perceived as people out to destroy the United States, and when we attempt to define ourselves, our voices are silenced.

When mainstream Muslims are given the rare opportunity to explain Islam, we are told that we, as moderate Muslims, are the minority, and that most Muslims are actually violent extremists. This image of Muslims as violent extremists is perpetuated by the media which chooses to report primarily negative images of Islam and Muslims. This image is further intensified by the profound ignorance of the average American about Muslims and Islam. This ignorance, unfortunately starts at a very early age-in schools, the textbooks are biased, and have a lot of erroneous information. And, as all minorities must do, American Muslims must struggle to ensure that our civil liberties are not trampled upon. Our accomplishments in being counted as part of the American pluralism, while maintaining our identity as Muslims, are often rebuffed and misunderstood.

We are told, by some Muslims and non-Muslims, that we must choose between being Muslims and being Americans. Among Muslims-who range from every culture on earth, as we've seen in this conference-American culture is unfairly perceived as inherently anti-Islamic, and little attempt is made to understand and accept Muslims of the American culture alongside Muslims of Arab, Asian, African, or any other ethnicity. Among non-Muslims, because the U.S. was founded on the basis of the separation of church and state, the presence of any religious group in the political arena is viewed with suspicion. As Muslims, we carry that burden, but we also carry the additional burden of ignorance about Islam. Our continuing striving to define ourselves as American Muslims is in fact a very challenging *jihad*.

MUSLIM WOMEN IN AMERICA

As women in the United States, we often face gender-based discrimination. While this discrimination may not be as overt as in other parts of the world, or may take different forms, it does exist in America nevertheless. Women often cannot achieve their highest potential in career or education and the media continually depicts women as sex objects and nothing more. American women's salaries are still, dollar-for-dollar, less than the corresponding salaries for their male counterparts. Women who do work to earn a living still have primary responsibility for taking care of the home and family with little domestic support from their husbands. Women in positions of influence in the United States are few and far between. Recently we have had setbacks in affirmative action, and that will only make our struggles for equality more important.

American Muslim women face many unique additional hurdles. We are discriminated against by both non-Muslims and Muslims in America. For instance, a woman who wears *hijab*, which is the traditional head-covering, is often taunted at work and on the street, and the careers of a lot of these women are actually jeopardized-they are discriminated against at work and they are not given jobs. And, women who wear *hijab* in the United States are obvious targets-they are obviously Muslims, and because of this they bear the brunt of the ignorance about Islam; they face sexual harassment, and often their actual physical safety is jeopardized. Muslims come from different backgrounds.

In America, we have immigrant Muslims, who face a whole host of problems such as xenophobia. In the U.S. in recent times, there has been a growing hostility toward immigrants, and they are often erroneously blamed for all of the socio-economic problems that we face in the U.S., and are harassed because of that. And we have a large African-American Muslim population, and they face additional hurdles, because being part of a racial minority in the United States, they have had to deal with the problems of racism, discrimination, segregation and the vestiges of slavery. To that, add religious discrimination and gender discrimination, and these are some of the challenges that are generally faced. But in addition, Muslim women often face discrimination from their own Muslim community. Discrimination by Muslims primarily results from ignorance about Islam and the importation of cultural attitudes that demean women.

Islam is often interpreted in ways that are sexist and not true to the true teachings of equality in the Quran and the model provided by Prophet Muhammad, may God's peace and blessings be upon him. Quran and hadith (the teachings of Prophet Muhammad) are taken out of context and used to justify certain behavior. Because Muslims are a minority in the

United States attempting to portray a positive image of Islam, the true image of the teachings of Islam, Muslims in America are often reluctant to address the problems faced by Muslim women for fear that the enemies of Islam will use this information against us.

But the ironic part is, that everyone knows the problems we face, and everyone knows that we are the only people not addressing them. And unfortunately the media is quick to inform us and others of the more serious forms of abuse or discrimination that Muslim women encounter. And what we hope to achieve in this presentation is to recognize some of the problems that we as American Muslim women face, and give voice to our sisters who have suffered wrongly in the name of Islam. Asifa later will explore opportunities that we as Americans have to attempt to address these issues.

CASE STUDIES

Some of the most serious problems that we American Muslim women face include: domestic violence, abuse of divorce and child custody laws, abuse of the polygamy system, and isolation and exclusion from various aspects of Muslim life. We are going to provide a few anecdotal cases simply to illustrate the depth of the problems. We have given the women in the stories names to make it more personable, but their identities have been changed and their confidentiality is protected. The stories are shared simply to illustrate and give life to the specific suffering of American Muslim women today.

These are true stories, these are real women who have suffered. These stories were compiled by speaking with Muslim community leaders, social workers, psychologists, lawyers, doctors, mostly in southern California, but throughout the United States. We also obtained information from a thing called Sistersnet, which is an E-mail network of Muslim women throughout the United States and other countries. But unfortunately, there is no database, there is no accurate information that exists as to the frequency of any of these abuses that occur. Further research of these issues is desperately needed so that we can adequately address these problems. And, while these cases may not be experienced by a majority of American Muslim women, they are nevertheless serious issues that must be addressed. Now, the story of Mariam is as follows.

MARIAM

Mariam got married to a man named Ali. They were married for several years. Throughout this marriage, Ali abused Mariam. His abuse was verbal and physical. Mariam was often beaten by her husband. When Mariam did attempt to speak with her local Muslim community leader, she was made to feel that the abuse was her fault: if she was a better wife, Ali would not have to beat her. She was also told not to discuss her marital problems with other people, and that it was important for her to stay married at all costs to preserve the family. And, Ali would quote the Quran and hadith to justify his abuse. And so Mariam being told by her local Muslim leader that the abuse was justified, she had Quran and hadith quoted in her face to justify it, she thought it was justified. She was abused for years.

And finally, she couldn't stand it any more. She feared for her life, she left. She left her home, she left her husband, and sought refuge in a local (non-Muslim) battered women's shelter, and there she received the assistance that she needed to put her life back together. Ali was convicted in U.S. court for spousal battery. When Mariam, appeared at Muslim functions, she was shunned; the Muslim community wanted nothing to do with her. She was viewed as a woman who had left her husband for no reason. Ali, on the other hand, when he went to Muslim functions, was viewed as the victim of a broken marriage, as a victim of the U.S. criminal justice system. He was greeted by the Muslim community with open arms. Mariam found no support from the Muslim community.

She continued to go to non-Muslim agencies for support, and she finally stopped attending Muslim functions. Mariam's story, unfortunately, is not an uncommon one in the United

States. Victims of domestic violence have little support from the Muslim community, and the support they do receive, while well-intentioned, is often unorganized and ineffectual. The lives of domestic violence victims are often in danger, and their only recourse is to turn to non-Muslim organizations who are prepared to deal with this issue-which is also a pressing issue in the larger American society as well. So we face issues of domestic violence. The story of Khadija and Fatima shows the abuse of the polygamy system in Islam.

KHADIJA AND FATIMA

Khadija married Omar under the laws of the United States and the state in which he lived, and under Islamic law. Omar later took a second wife, Fatima. But, Omar and Fatima could not get married under U.S. law because he was already married to Khadija, and polygamy is illegal in the United States. So, Omar married Fatima under a-supposed-Islamic tradition which includes simply a marriage proposal and an acceptance of that proposal in front of witnesses. Fatima, the second wife, who was a convert to Islam, learned Islam mostly from Omar and he convinced her that they did not need to be married under U.S. law-Islam would sufficiently protect her rights. And while this is true in the theoretical sense, in the United States, we have no framework to enforce that.

Omar had children through both of his wives-his first wife Khadija and his second wife Fatima. Both marriages failed. Khadija and Omar-the first marriage-divorced. Omar refused to pay any support to Khadija or their children through that marriage. But Khadija could take Omar to U.S. court and get child support and alimony. Now, Omar was obligated under Islamic law to do these things, but he refused, and as a religious minority in the U.S., not living in an Islamic state, Khadija had no recourse other than the laws of the U.S.

But, thankfully, Khadija was married to Omar under U.S. law and could take him to court. Fatima, on the other hand-when Fatima and Omar divorced-couldn't do that, because she was not legally married in the eyes of the U.S. courts. So, Omar shirked his responsibilities under Islamic law-didn't give her anything, didn't give their children anything, even though he had assured her, before the marriage, that he would. And Fatima couldn't do anything under U.S. laws because they weren't legally married. Fatima was able to get no financial support from Omar because there was no legal institution compelling Omar to comply with Islamic law. And next is the story of Iman. While the situation is not as physically or financially serious, it still is extremely emotionally harmful, and it's very common.

IMAN

Iman is a university student. She is very active in her student government on campus. She has formed coalitions with other student groups and they do relief work for Bosnia, Palestine, Chechnya, and other causes. She is on the student senate at her university, after being elected to it. She wants to organize similar relief efforts in her mosque, in her local Muslim community and in other mosques in the area so that she can reach the larger Muslim population. She wants to post flyers and information on the walls in her mosque. But she can't get to the men's section. She can only distribute the information to women, many of whom don't come to this mosque, because the facilities are less than adequate or desirable.

Iman does not have a brother, father, or husband to access the men's side for her when she needs to get information to the Muslims. On occasion, she has approached men to ask them to help her. Many of them ignore her and leave, but on occasion, she has had men help her to post flyers and such information on the walls. But, it's difficult, because the next time she goes, she can't find the same man, and she has to go through the same thing again and again, and she gets really frustrated. She can't make any announcements at the mosque about the work that she's doing. She wants to make an announcement after the Friday prayer, but she is told she can't because she is a woman.

She is getting fed up and she wants to make a change. Elections at this mosque come up, and she wants to run for the board because it's a great way to get involved and to make changes. But she is told she cannot run for the board because she is a woman. But she is told she can join the women's committee and organize Eid carnivals for the children and prepare *iftar* (breakfast) during Ramadan. Iman, of course, is extremely frustrated. She is an activist. She has work that she is doing. So she stops going to the mosque because she knows that she can do more through the non-Muslim human rights groups at her university.

As shown by Iman's story, Muslim American women are regularly excluded from leadership positions in our mosques and in our Islamic centers. They are allowed to participate only in certain areas-preparing lunches, organizing Eid festivities, and events of that sort. Women are absent from educational or spiritual roles, unless they are teaching other women or children. Women with Islamic knowledge and expertise are not allowed to explain the Quran to the congregation nor give lessons in Shariah. Gender segregation is imposed in most American mosques and results in unfair and unequal access to space and facilities. Women are often put in areas with poor sound systems, or none at all, or noisy makeshift childcare areas. They are stuck in back rooms next to the bathrooms, and wherever they are put-even if it's a great facility-they still can't interact with the speaker and ask questions and have their voices heard.

American Muslim women are not just excluded from leadership positions in our communities, but also even excluded from mosques completely. This exclusion can be overt where we are told "you cannot go to the mosque, this is a men's mosque," or it can be subtle, where the facilities provided are so inadequate and the treatment we receive is so horrendous that no reasonable woman is going to go back. All of this exclusion has no basis in the teachings of Islam. It results from culture and tradition. And Muslim women also deal with other problems, many of which are culturally or ethnically based and not unique to Islam. There has been so much cultural baggage that has come to the U.S. with the various waves of Muslims.

And some of these other problems are not unique to Muslims, such as: the general devaluation of women-we are just seen as "not as good" as men, a preference for sons over daughters, women as a source of honor-and therefore shame-in the family, so we carry this horrendous burden of family honor, early marriage which often results in early pregnancy and usually an end to a woman's educational opportunities, double standards which often result in unequal access to education-higher education especially, because women are not allowed to leave their homes or to travel very far to go to universities.

These abuses that I have mentioned are simply a few of those suffered by Muslim women in America. The abuses vary in degree and form. Again, we raise these issues not because we hate Islam, not because we hate Muslims, but because we-as Muslims-need to deal with the problems. It is not enough to say that Islam is a great religion. We need to prove it with our actions. It is increasingly common to see Muslims in the United States-women and men-leave Islam in growing numbers because of the treatment of women. They see Muslims as offering no solutions to these problems and they see Muslims denying that these problems exist, and after awhile it simply becomes unbearable. As Muslims it is our duty to fight against every form of oppression, whatever form it takes, by whatever means we can, and we cannot fight oppression if we do not acknowledge that it exists.

WOMEN'S POLITICAL PARTICIPATION

Women constitute slightly more than half of the world population. Their contribution to the social and economic development of societies is also more than half as compared to that of men by virtue of their dual roles in the productive and reproductive spheres. Yet their participation in formal political structures and processes, where decisions regarding the use of societal resources generated by both men and women are made, remains insignificant. Presently, women's representation in legislatures around the world is 15 percent.

Despite the pronounced commitment of the international community to gender equality and to the bridging the gender gap in the formal political arena, reinforced by the Convention on Elimination of All Forms of Discrimination Against Women (CEDAW) and the Beijing Platform of Action, there are only twelve countries where women hold 33% or more seats in the parliaments (UNDP Report, 2005). This chapter attempts to investigate the conceptual and material bases of women's historic exclusion from the formal arena of politics; analyze strategies adopted around the world to promote women's political participation/representation; identify internal and external conditions and factors that facilitate or hinder the creation of an enabling environment for women's political empowerment; and finally draw policy recommendations for the national and international actors.

The development context of women's political participation at the community and national levels will be reviewed for nuanced understanding of the nature of women's participation and their share in development processes and outcomes. With an increasing recognition among international community of women's historic exclusion from structures of power, a global commitment has been made to redress gender imbalance in politics. Women's enhanced participation in governance structures is viewed as the key to redress gender inequalities in societies. The global debate on the promotion of women's political participation/representation has been surrounded by intrinsic and instrumentalist argument.

The former argues for equal participation of women in politics from the human rights perspective. Women constitute half of the world population and therefore, it is only fair that they should have equal participation and representation in world democracies. Instrumentalist argument pushed for women's greater participation on the essentialist ground that men and women are different. Women have different vision and concepts of politics owning to their sex and their gender roles as mothers. Therefore, it is assumed that women in politics will bring a special caring focus and female values to politics.

There is an extensive research literature produced in support of the varied rationale or theoretical approaches to women's inclusion in politics. However, without debating the merit and demerit of various approaches, this chapter is grounded in the broad agreement that proponents of varied approaches have arrived at - women must be included in politics. The challenge facing all advocates of gender equality in politics today is the wide gap between shared values reflected in the national and international policies and practices.

Before identifying the key strategies for the promotion of women's political participation and the vital elements in the enabling environment for women's political empowerment, we need to strive for a deeper understanding of the structural imperatives of a society in which women's political participation is instituted. Women's historic exclusion from political structures and processes is the result of multiple structural, functional and personal factors that vary in different social contexts across countries. However, beyond these specificities of national and local contexts, there is a generic issue in women's political participation that relates to the wider context of national and international politics, liberal democracy and development.

It is, therefore, imperative to critically review these constructs and decode the gendered nature of Democracy as well as Development, which poses limitations on women's effective political participation. The elements of enabling environment for women's participation in politics and development cannot be discussed and identified without putting the current development and political paradigms under scrutiny. Development today as Rounaq Jahan (1999) maintains has brought tremendous benefits to people all around the world who have gained in terms of education, health and income. But at the same time development leaves behind 2.5 billion people who live on less than $2 dollars a day.

There are glaring disparities among and within countries. Forty percent of world population accounts for 5% of global income while 10% richest account for 54 percent (UNDP, 2005). Presently, the mainstream development paradigms based on capitalist relations of production thrive on opportunities created by gender relations for power and profit. There is an intrinsic link between women's domestic labor with capital accumulation. Leacock further elaborate the same point as "...the inequalities between men and women could not be understood in isolation from polarizing tendencies of the capitalist mode of production which places the 'peripheral' countries of the Third World in a relationship of dependency with the metropolitan centers of the First World. Within an egalitarian world order, so called development could not release women from oppressive social, economic and political institutions; it merely defines 'new conditions of constraints'".

It is imperative for gender equality advocates to focus on the gendered nature of development and challenge the capitalist paradigm of international development that creates and recreates gender disparities, while at the same time working towards creating an enabling environment for women's participation in development. Women's mere participation in mainstream development cannot automatically lead to their advancement and gender equality unless the contradiction in the development claim for equality and justice and the practice is eliminated.

The level and nature of participation is equally important to determine whether women are able to share development gains. Another contextual issue in women's political participation relates to the nature of politics in general and the liberal democracy in particular. Democracy has historically served men better than women. As a political system from the ancient Greece to the modern times of the 21st century, it has built on the public-private dichotomy and excluded women from citizenship.

Women have been kept outside the public domain of politics as most of the political thinkers and philosophers such as Plato, Aristotle, Rousseau, John Lock, Thomas Hobbes and Hegel considered women fit only for domestic roles in the private sphere and maintained that there was no place for women in politics because of their suitability in caring roles as mothers and wives. The public- private divide remains as the foundation of the various forms of world democracies. This is one of the reasons that the normative political theory considered private sphere as non-political and did not make any effort to explore the political nature of the private life.

The ancient and modern democracies failed to recognize women as citizens. Therefore, they sidelined them and their concerns in its theory and practice. It was only the liberal political philosophy of the 19th century that promoted the idea of 'free and rational' individual which was used by suffragists to demand for the right for vote. However, as Rai maintains the conceptual basis of liberal theory is inherently gendered in ways, which perpetuates patterns of patriarchy and ignores gender subordination in both polity and society. Feminist theorists also challenged the notion of abstract individual in liberal theory and argued it is not a gender-neutral category.

This is why despite women had the right to vote they were not able to impact public policy and could not bring private sphere in the preview of the public. Even western democracies left them dislocated on many fronts. When women enter politics within this patriarchal context of modern democracies, they are unable to play a role to radically change the sexual politics rather they largely play political roles on male's terms. The fundamental assumption in liberal democracies needs to be changed in order to create genuine political space for women within.

FACTORS HINDERING WOMEN'S POLITICAL PARTICIPATION

Women's participation and access to formal political power structures vary across countries. There is a steady upward trend in women's political participation and representation in developed countries particularly in Nordic countries. Out of twelve countries where women representation in parliament is more than 33%, nine of them are ranked in the high human development category. However, the improvements in medium and low human development countries are not significant. The structural and functional constraints faced by women are shaped by social and political relations in a society.

The common pattern of women's political exclusion stem from (a) social and political discourses (b) political structures and institutions (c) the socio-cultural and functional constraints that put limits on women's individual and collective agency.

Ideological Factors

Patriarchy as a system of male domination shapes women's relationship in politics. It transforms male and females into men and women and construct the hierarchy of gender relations where men are privileged. Andrienne Rich defines patriarchy as: "A familial-social, ideological, political system in which men by force, direct pressure or through ritual, tradition, law, and language, customs etiquette, education, and the division of labor, determine what part women shall or shall not play in which the female is everywhere subsumed under the male."

The gender role ideology is used as an ideological tool by patriarchy to place women within the private arena of home as mothers and wives and men in the public sphere. This is one of the vital factors that shape the level of women's political participation globally. However, this ideological divide is not reflective of the reality. The boundaries between public and private are often blurred in the daily lives of women.

Nonetheless, domestic domain continues to be perceived in the North as well as in the South as the legitimate space for women while public space is associated with men. Women have to negotiate their entry into and claim on public space according to the discursive and material opportunities available in a given culture and society. Although the gender role ideology is not static rather remained in a flux while intersecting with economic, social and political systems of a particular society, women continue to be defined as private across countries which resulted in their exclusion from politics.

Political Factors

The nature of politics is an important factor for the inclusion or exclusion of women in politics. Vicky Randall defines politics as an "articulation, or working out of relationships within an already given power structure", which is in contrast with the traditional view of politics that defines it as an activity, a conscious, deliberate participation in the process by which resources are allocated among citizens. This conception of politics restricts political activity only in public arena and the private sphere of family life is rendered as apolitical.

This public-private dichotomy in traditional definition of politics is used to exclude women from public political sphere and even when women are brought into politics they are entered as mothers and wives. Male domination of politics, political parties and culture of formal political structures is another factor that hinders women's political participation. Often male dominated political parties have a male perspective on issues of national importance that disillusions women as their perspective is often ignored and not reflected in the politics of their parties. Also women are usually not elected at the position of power within party structures because of gender biases of male leadership.

Meetings of councils or parliamentary sessions are held in odd timings conflicting with women's domestic responsibilities. The larger democratic framework and level of democratization also impact women's political participation. Secular democracies in Europe and also in some of the developing countries have created relatively more space for women's participation in politics as compared to countries where religious orthodoxy has been shaping politics and democracy.

Socio-Cultural Factors

The subordinate status of women vis-à-vis men is a universal phenomenon, though with a difference in the nature and extent of subordination across countries. Gender role ideology does not only create duality of femininity and masculinity, it also places them in hierarchal fashion in which female sex is generally valued less than male sex because of their socially ascribed roles in reproductive sphere. The gender status quo is maintained through low resource allocation to women's human development by the state, society and the family. This is reflected in the social indicators which reflect varying degrees of gender disparities in education, health, employment, ownership of productive resources and politics in all countries.

Additionally gender is mediated through class, caste and ethnicity that structure access to resources and opportunities. The socio-cultural dependence of women is one of the key detrimental factors to their political participation in public political domain. Women also find it hard to participate in politics due to limited time available to them because of their dual roles in the productive and reproductive spheres. With their primary roles as mothers and wives and competing domestic responsibilities and care work, they are left with little time to participate in politics. In some of the countries, particularly in South Asia, women also face cultural constraints on their mobility. The mechanisms of sex segregation and *purdah* are used to restrict their mobility. Politics requires women's exposure to interact with male and female constituents and address public meeting.

Economic Factors

Politics is increasingly becoming commercialized. More and more money is needed to participate in politics. Women lack access to and ownership of productive resource, limiting the scope of their political work.

Lack of Social Capital and Political Capacities

Women often lack social capital because they are often not head of communities, tribes or kinship groups, resulting in the absence of constituency base for them and means of political participation such as political skills, economic resources, education, training and access to information.

Strategies for Women's Political Participation

Due to non-availability of comparative data and time constraint this section is unable to assess comprehensively the successful strategies for promote women's political participation. The paper will focus only on two strategies: gender quotas and women's experience of networking.

Quotas

Gender quotas emerged as a global fast tract strategy to redress the historic exclusion of women from the formal arena of politics. Over the last half of the 20th Century, many countries have instituted gender quotas either voluntarily or through legislation. The gender quota is marred with discursive controversy. Without debating the two distinct opposing views, this section summarizes some of the issues highlighted in comparative studies on gender quotas. There is a clear consensus in literature that gender quota is an effective tool in addressing women's exclusion and ensuring their presence in formal structure of politics. However, the controversy starts around the vital question as to what extent women's presence in political structures has led to an effective mainstreaming of gender concerns in politics.

This has raised issues on the nature and modalities of gender quotas and its limitation to empower women in politics. Gender quotas are instituted within the context of gender disparities, which are structural and systemic. Without addressing the structural constraints to women's political exclusion, their inclusion through gender quota cannot lead to an effective representation. Rai (2005) has emphasized the same point by arguing that "while quotas are important in addressing the exclusion of women from the public political sphere, they can only form one part of a multi-facetted strategy for empowering women, which must together with increased political participation also involve a redistribution of socio-economic resources within societies."

Women who lack civil and economic rights are unable to exercise their political rights fully. The gender quotas, therefore, need to be linked with the social and economic redistributive justice in the society. Gender quotas are also riddled with essentialist assumptions of women as a distinct group with a distinct perspective and the universalization of women as a category. Women are not homogeneous groups. They are divided along the line of class, ethnicity, religion and rural/urban background. The domination of elite women in political structures due to state quotas calls for locating the gender quota within the framework of diversity and difference to ensure women's political empowerment.

The gender gap in politics cannot be redressed simply by bringing more women in the system. It is also a policy and outcome issue, which cannot be addressed unless supportive mechanisms are put in place and provided with an enabling environment to work effectively. This makes the nature and process of quotas systems central to an affirmative action measures. Experience shows that quota modalities must be direct, empowering and enable women to develop their constituency. Lastly the wider context of politics and democracy is equally important to determine the success of gender quota.

Quota debates are globally located within the framework of liberal democracy and citizenship. The extension of citizenship to all, irrespective of their color, creed and gender, has become the basis of modern liberal democracies. In the elite form of representative democracy being practiced in many countries, the electorates are not free to exercise their right to vote. Voting behavior of the large majority of electorate continues to be determined by primordial loyalties and patriarchal relations.

Within this political context when gender quotas are instituted, they do not necessarily bring gender equality because this is a way some these states negotiate with modernity and pluralism by bringing marginalized to the mainstream on the terms of male patriarchal elite. When women enter through quotas in politics on these terms, they are unable to transcend the public-private divide and are compelled to do politics only in the public arena.

Women in politics have failed to make family a part of pubic arena, despite the fact that when they enter public space of politics they do not cease to be private individuals. My contention is that within this patriarchal context of modern democracies when women enter politics through gender quotas, they are unable to transform the sexual politics in the state institutions. Rather they are forced to play on male's terms. Therefore, it is concluded that without the transformation of the wider politics, gender quotas cannot lead to women's political empowerment.

NETWORKING OF WOMEN POLITICIANS

There is an extensive documentation on experiences of collective power through networking. From the field of politics, lets share a success story from Pakistan where women councilors formed a network and later an election alliance. Women's representation in governance structures has been extremely low during the fifty-five years of Pakistan's history. In the last National Assembly, women's representation was merely 3.2 percent. Within this context of exclusion and marginalization, affirmative action measure is seen and promoted as the key strategy to redress gender imbalance in politics.

The past regime of Parvez Musharaff took a landmark decision and ensured women's representation in political structures of the country through the reservation of 33% seats for them in all three tiers of local government and 17% in the national and provincial legislatures. Reserved seats for women are filled through direct election at the union council level and indirect election at the *tehsil* and district level. At the national and provincial level, proportional representation system has been adopted to fill the reserved seats for women. The reservation of seats for women brought more than 40,000 women to the local government institutions and 205 in the national and provincial assemblies and the Senate. A majority of women who entered local government were the first time entrants in local politics. They had no prior affiliation with political parties, women's groups or civil society organizations. They also lacked political understanding of Local Government Ordinance/System. Women councilors across the three tiers of local government faced similar institutional and social constraints to perform their roles effectively despite differences among them along the lines of class, rural/urban divide and political affiliations. They shared the commonality of experience of patriarchal resistance they met from male members of district, *tehsil* and union councils.

The way male members ignored women councilors, treated them with contempt, denied them development funds and expected them to confine themselves only to women's issues created a strong oppositional consciousness among women councilors. This resulted into increased awareness among them of their own gender identities as women. They were able to clearly see the interconnection between public and private patriarchy. Their gender consciousness, which has evolved not necessarily within any feminist framework, has brought them together as women. They realized that a lot of the problems/constraints they faced as councilors in order to perform their political role more effectively is primarily due to their gender identity as women.

Therefore, women belonging to different political parties decided to create a common forum where women councilors could come together to combat these problems, share their experiences, learn from each other, find ways to become more effective in their newly assigned political roles, resist patriarchal backlash and assert themselves to have their right to access political power. With the help of a NGO Pattan Development Organization, women councilors formed a common platform with the name of Women Councilors Network (WCN) at the provincial level to institutionalize the support functions and use it to negotiate for better working environment for women councilors. The WCN had chapters in 16 districts in the province of Punjab with a membership of more than 2,000 councilors from UC, *tehsil* and district levels.

The WCN worked effectively with its democratically elected working committees at district and provincial levels to articulate the problems faced by women councilors on various public fora. They resisted the reduction of seats at the UC level and raised voice against the gender biases of their male colleagues. In the absence of constituency for *tehsil* and district councilor, WCN as a collective body provided them with a power base. In the process, WCN helped raised the political profile of its members. In the local government election of 2005, WCN decided to negotiate maximum seats and support from male politicians and political parties. The WCN formed an election alliance with the name of Women Unity Group.

The main purpose of the establishment of election platform was to enhance women's bargaining power at the local level to negotiate with political parties and the local power elite to take women more seriously as political actors and give them more slots in the category of general and *nazims* seats. The four point agenda of the Group included:

- To work on violence against women.
- To work for the repeal of all legislation that discriminates against women.
- To work for the elimination of poverty and to work for women's economic empowerment.
- To promote peace in inter-personal relations at family, community, national and ?international levels and to fight extremism.

There were more than 500 women who joined the Group and contested election in the first and second phase of election from this platform. Thirteen of them contested on the seats of *nazim* (head of local council). One of the electoral panels fielded by the Group comprised all women just to get the point across that women are entitled to contest on all seats in the local institution. Nearly 65% women contested on general seats on the platform of KIG won. This group of women can play a leading role in the present local government system.

ENABLING ENVIRONMENT FOR WOMEN PARTICIPATION IN POLITICS AND DEVELOPMENT

In the interconnected world of today, external factors such as globalization, international trade and economic polices impact the development policies of the nation-states. Therefore, the creation of enabling environment for women's participation in politics and in development cannot be viewed only within the boundaries of a country. It must be linked with global factors. Thus, the responsibility to create supportive environment for gender equality and advancement of women as shared responsibility falls equally on the national and international communities. Interlocking layer of gender inequalities are rooted in the power structures at the national and international levels.

Development and the globalization policies have led to increased poverty, exclusion and marginalization. Structural forces must be challenged and transform by linking them with the rights of people. Without changing socio-cultural, political and economic structural barriers at the national and international levels, the goal of gender equality or women's equal participation in politics and development will remain impossible to attain. Another important element in the enabling environment relates to the nature of democracy and the level of democratization in society. The participative and decentralized form of governance creates greater space for citizens to participate in governance processes and structures.

It also creates space for greater interaction between the state and the society. Human capacities are dependent on the availability of resources such as education, health and employment that build capabilities and enlarge human choices. Access to education, health and employment is directly linked with women's ability to create space for themselves in politics and development. Women's consciousness of their political rights is another critical element for women's individual and collective agency. Political consciousness through building transformative communities is the sustainable way to transform politics and development. A strong women's movement and civil society is another condition of enabling environment that can influence the direction of politics and development in favor of women.

Triple roles of women in productive, reproductive and community management spheres must inform the efforts for creating supportive environment for women's political participation. Provision of childcare and care work is vital to enabling women to participate in the development processes.

POLICY RECOMMENDATIONS

The United Nation should play its role to humanize globalization processes by advocating legislation that addresses imperfection of the market. The UN should develop a system of incentives for countries that work towards narrowing the gender gap in education, health and employment. Clear guidelines for modalities and implementation of affirmative measures that lead to empowering women and creating their ability to critically engage with the state and the society for a social change and gender equality should be developed. Research, documentation and dissemination of successful experiences in the world is needed to promote women's participation in politics and development.

5

Sexual Abuse of Women and Exploitation of Children

Sexual abuse and exploitation of children and youth occurs when an older child, adolescent or adult takes advantage of a younger child or youth for sexual purposes, including for participation in prostitution, pornographic performances and in the production of pornography. Sexual abuse and exploitation is perpetrated on children of all ages, from infancy to adolescence. Sexual activity includes all sexual contact ranging from sexual touching to sexual intercourse. Except for a narrow close in age exception, all sexual activity with a child under the age of 14 is a criminal offence, regardless of the child's consent.

Youth between the ages of 14 and 17 also cannot legally consent to sexual activity with a person in a position of trust or authority or with whom the youth is in a relationship of dependency. In such cases, sexual activity with 14 to 17 year olds is a criminal offence, notwithstanding their consent. There are many overlapping dimensions to the sexual abuse and exploitation of children and youth. A child or youth may be sexually abused and exploited by one or more family members or by others outside the family, including by others known to the child or youth or by a stranger. The perpetrator may be acting alone or in an organized group or network.

The perpetrator may be either the same or the opposite sex as the victim although current data suggest that the majority of perpetrators are male. Regardless, however, of where and how it occurs, or who commits it, or whether the child or youth consents, the sexual abuse and exploitation of children and youth is a betrayal of trust and an abuse of power.

TYPES OF SEXUALLY ABUSIVE OR EXPLOITIVE BEHAVIOR

The sexual abuse and exploitation of children and youth may involve a range of behaviours. Non-contact sexual abuse may involve making sexual comments to the child or youth, exposing intimate body parts, voyeurism, having a sexual fixation on a child or youth's clothing or body parts, luring, making sexually related phone calls and engaging in sexually related correspondence through the Internet. Contact sexual abuse may involve making the child or youth participate in acts such as touching (fondling) or digital or object penetration of intimate body parts.

Sexual exploitation may involve prostitution as well as making children and youth participate in pornographic acts or performances for personal or commercial use. There is an increasing international dimension to the sexual exploitation of children through sex tourism and also through the Internet. In Canada, acts of sexual abuse and exploitation against children and youth are crimes. Child sexual abuse and exploitation is a serious violation of the basic human rights of the child.

DYNAMICS OF SEXUAL ABUSE AND EXPLOITATION

Perpetrators may use various tactics to gain access to, isolate, manipulate and control their young victims. Typically there is a power differential between the perpetrator and the victim. Perpetrators tend to be older than their victims and are likely to be more knowledgeable about sexual activity. They may spend a lot of time befriending and grooming their victims. They may use threats, physical force, bribery, trickery or other forms of psychological coercion to gain access to, and make their victims compliant. Sexual abuse or exploitation may be a single act, or repeated acts. These acts may become more serious, frequent and intrusive over time. Victims may experience lifetime negative effects.

Although child sexual abuse and exploitation has occurred throughout history, it was not publicly recognized as a societal problem in Canada until the 1984 publication of *The Badgely Report*. Although there have been a number of studies on child sexual abuse and exploitation, it is not possible to know the extent of the problem within Canada because victims may not disclose, or known incidents may not be reported to authorities. In addition, some forms of sexual abuse and exploitation against children and youth may not be fully reflected in national-level crime reporting, and in provincial/territorial child protection reporting mechanisms. However, the available national data indicates that sexual abuse and exploitation of children and youth is disturbingly common in Canada.

EXTENT OF SEXUAL ABUSE AND EXPLOITATION

In 2002, 8,800 sexual assaults against children and youth were reported to a subset of 94 police departments in Canada. This included 2,863 sexual assaults against children and youth by family members. According to the Canadian Incidence Study of Reported Child Abuse and Neglect (CIS) - the first national study of the incidence of child abuse and neglect reported to and investigated by child welfare authorities in Canada - sexual abuse was the primary reason for investigation in 10% of all child maltreatment referrals to social services agencies in 1998. Thirty-eight percent of these cases were substantiated.

There are many different reasons why victims may keep the abuse secret:

- *Age and/or developmental stage:* In some cases, they may be too young (developmentally, cognitively or emotionally) to articulate what happened to them.
- *Feelings of powerlessness:* Some victims may feel trapped

by circumstances or have been threatened that harm will come to them, or someone close to them if they disclose.

- *Dependency:* They may be in a situation of dependency on the perpetrator.
- *Fear:* They may fear that they will not be believed. They may fear that they will be stigmatized, and that their sexual identity will be called into question. They may be afraid of the perpetrator's reprisals or other negative consequences of telling others. They may want to protect family members (including the perpetrator).
- *Conflicting emotions:* They may feel conflicted and suffer confusion or shame. They may believe that the abuse is their fault.

Even in cases where victims tell others about the abuse, the recipient may not report the abuse to authorities for reasons such as disbelief, shame, fear of and dependency on the perpetrator.

TYPES OF SEXUAL ABUSE

According to the CIS, the most common form of substantiated child sexual abuse in child protection cases was touching and fondling of the genitals (68% of cases), while attempted and completed intercourse accounted for 35% of cases. An adult exposing genitals to a child accounted for 12% of the substantiated cases of child sexual abuse. Six percent of cases involved an adult sexually exploiting a child for purposes of financial gain or other profit, and 4% of cases involved sexual harassment (including proposition, encouragement or suggestions of a sexual nature).

In 2002, according to the Incident-based Uniform Crime Reporting (UC2) Survey, children and youth accounted for 61% of the victims of sexual assaults reported to a subset of 94 police departments. This included crimes such as sexual assault, sexual assault with a weapon, aggravated sexual assault and a range of other sexual crimes including sexual interference, sexual touching, sexual exploitation and incest.

PERPETRATORS

Perpetrators are more often individuals who know the victim, rather than strangers. About half (51%) of sexual assaults against children and youth reported to a sub-set of police departments in 2002 involved friends or acquaintances, while a quarter of these assaults (25%) involved family members. About 18% involved assaults by strangers. Most (but not all) are male. According to the CIS, most alleged perpetrators of sexual abuse were either "other" (non-parental) relatives (44% of cases) or non-relatives (29%), and only very few (2%) of substantiated cases of sexual abuse involved a stranger.

Alleged perpetrators who were related to the victim were equally likely to be a biological father or step-father and less likely to be the child's biological mother or a foster or adoptive parent. Individual factors associated with sexual offending are complex, however, some of the common elements that child sexual abuse offenders may share are family histories marked by physical, sexual and emotional abuse as well as frequent experiences of failure, problems in social functioning and unsatisfactory peer relationships. Some perpetrators use child and/or adult pornography and others do not.

ROLE IN SEXUAL ABUSE AND EXPLOITATION OF CHILDREN AND YOUTH

Many factors may play a role in the sexual abuse and exploitation of children and youth. At the societal level, the dynamics of socialization as well as society's collective history of denial of child sexual abuse and exploitation may contribute to environments in which opportunities for abuse and exploitation can occur. At the community level, the absence of adequate safety precautions and educational supports in spiritual, cultural, recreational, child care, educational, residential and therapeutic care settings may place children and youth in situations of risk. Inter-generational patterns of abuse within the family, as well as family problems such as substance abuse and inadequate supervision are also considerations.

At the individual level, the developmental age and gender of the child may also contribute to risk. While any child or young person is potentially at risk, the interactions between various risk factors can be complex. Some children and youth may be more vulnerable due to factors that isolate and marginalize them in their homes and communities, such as poverty, disability, racism and other forms of discrimination. For Aboriginal peoples, the experience and devastating consequences of colonization - in particular the undermining of traditional beliefs and values and family and community structures through the residential school system - have contributed to social problems (including sexual abuse and exploitation) experienced within some Aboriginal communities today.

Gender of Child Sexual Abuse Victims

Both police-reported data and the CIS findings indicate that the majority of victims of child sexual abuse are young females. In 2002, 81% of the victims of family-related sexual assaults reported to a subset of police departments were girls. The rate of reported family-related sexual assault for young females was nearly four times higher than that of males. Similarly, according to the CIS, girls were the victims in 69% and boys in 31% of substantiated sexual abuse cases.

Age of Child Sexual Abuse Victims

There is evidence that the risk of child sexual abuse may differ for females and males at specific ages:

- For girls, the risk may be highest either when they are very young or when they are in their pre and early adolescence. According to the CIS, girls aged 4-7 and 12-15 were the victims in about twice as many cases of sexual abuse as girls aged 0-3 or 8-11. In 2002, the rates of sexual offences reported to police were highest among girls between the ages of 11 and 14, with the highest rate at 13 (165 per 100,000 females).
- For boys, the risk may be highest when they are very young. According to the CIS, 4-7 year old boys accounted

for three times more cases than other age groups of boys. Among boys, rates of family-related sexual assault reported to police in 2002 were highest for those between the ages of 3 and 7.

It is important to remember that the signs of sexual abuse and exploitation may vary based on factors such as the victim's age and developmental stage, gender, their experience of abuse, family functioning and community support. Moreover, current research suggests that approximately one-third of victims do not show signs of abuse (even when they have disclosed the abuse). Criminal justice practitioners and professional clinicians employ various investigative and assessment strategies to determine the possibility of sexual abuse and/or exploitation and to address its impacts.

Sexually abused and/or exploited children and youth who do show signs of sexual abuse and exploitation may, for example:

- Express sexual statements or demonstrate sexual behaviours when they are not typically old enough to possess that knowledge (for example, in cases where they have not received any sex education, or are unlikely to have peers who might have exposed them to sexual materials, and are unlikely to be sexually active).
- Express sexual aggression towards younger or more naïve children.
- Make verbal or behavioural sexual advances towards older individuals.
- Engage in promiscuous behaviour as a consequence of their victimization (for example, they may have low-self esteem and perceive sex as a way to gain acceptance and acquire relationships).

They may also show a range of non-sexual signs, however many of these signs may also be responses to other types of abuse (such as psychological or physical abuse). They may show:

- Physical signs, such as sleeping problems, eating problems (in particular anorexia or bulimia) and bowel and bladder problems. There may be physical evidence of trauma to their oral, genital and/or anal areas.

- Emotional signs, such as becoming quiet and depressed, preoccupied, hyperactive or anxious.
- Behavioural problems, such as physical aggression, running away, suicidal behaviour, substance abuse.
- Developmental signs, such as lags in their cognitive development and school performance.

Being sexually abused and exploited may have immediate impacts on a young person's experiences of childhood and personal development. According to the CIS, children who are sexually abused may experience disruptions in their developing view of themselves and the world. These disruptions can result in significant emotional and behavioural changes as they find ways to cope with these events. Their sense of personal integrity, safety and security is violated. They may experience shame and guilt.

Opportunities to play, learn and have healthy social interactions with others may be lost. They may try to cope with the abuse by acting in a secretive manner and behaving in a helpless way. They may delay disclosure, or disclose in conflicting and unconvincing ways. They may retract their statements. The impact of sexual abuse and exploitation may have far-reaching effects that may not be apparent until later in the individual's life. For example, some research suggests that child sexual abuse experiences may (among other factors) also contribute to a young person's later experiences of sexual exploitation. Many young people who are sexually exploited ran away or were abandoned at an early age from home environments that frequently included physical, sexual and emotional abuse.

The impacts of sexual abuse and exploitation may persist into adulthood. Adolescent and adult women sexually molested as children are more likely than non-victims to suffer from both physical and psychological problems. Research indicates that women who have a history of child sexual abuse are also significantly more likely than non-victims to experience a subsequent sexual re-victimization. Although the research on male victims of child/youth sexual abuse and exploitation is limited compared with research on female victims, it also indicates that male victims are also more likely than non-victims to experience physical and psychological problems. They may suffer from depression, anxiety and suicidal thoughts and behaviour and adopt poor coping strategies, such as substance abuse.

Impacts on Families

Non-offending family members may also experience negative consequences when a child or sibling is sexually abused or exploited. These consequences may vary by factors such as the nature of their relationship with and dependency on the perpetrator. For example, they may feel shame, anger and guilt about their failure to protect the child.

Impacts on Perpetrators

Perpetrators may experience negative consequences of their behaviour - including criminal sanctions and incarceration. They may experience shame, personal rejection and social condemnation. Many were victims of sexual abuse and exploitation as children and youth. Few seek treatment on their own initiative. Clinicians may conduct non-forensic and forensic assessments of offenders who enter the criminal justice system, to assist in determining appropriate sentencing and treatment options.

Costs to Society

Although it is not possible to measure the personal and social costs of sexual abuse and exploitation of children and youth, most people would agree they are enormous. There are also financial costs to society as a whole. According to the Day model, which measures the judicial, social services, education, health, employment and personal costs of violence, the total costs of child abuse (including child sexual abuse) are estimated to be $15,705,910,947 annually.

Though no one representative trafficking narrative exists, this true account incorporates elements common to many cases of trafficking for sexual exploitation. The victims, mostly women and children, are often deceived about the true nature of the work. They are exploited in slavery-like conditions. The traffickers grow rich, but the victims are held in debt bondage. Throughout the world, human trafficking of this nature continues with near impunity. It is a high-profit and low-risk endeavor for the traffickers, in many cases carrying penalties far less severe than drug trafficking.

However, it is not low- risk for the millions of women and children trafficked and exploited in the sex industry. Poverty, gender-based discrimination in employment and a history of sexual and physical violence are all factors that can make women and children vulnerable to traffickers. Some are abducted and sold, some are deceived into consenting by the promise of a better life or a better job, and some feel that entrusting themselves to traffickers is the only economically viable option. Regardless of the route of entry, most women and children trafficked for sexual exploitation suffer extreme violations of their human rights, including the right to liberty, the right to dignity and security of person, the right not to be held in slavery or involuntary servitude, the right to be free from cruel and inhumane treatment, the right to be free from violence, and the right to health.

Some trafficking victims are physically imprisoned by locks, bars or guards. Those with apparent freedom to leave are controlled by other means. Physical, sexual and psychological violence are employed against them effectively. Former trafficking victims report being beaten, in some cases with iron rods, for refusing clients, attempting escape, or "causing trouble." Others have reported being drugged or forced to consume alcohol, some to the extent that they became addicted.

Many women are "free to go"- as soon as they pay off a debt that grows each day. Traffickers threaten to have victims arrested, or their family members harmed, if they misbehave or tell anyone. Traffickers take care to instill an acute fear of police and immigration officials, to silence the women and smother their hope of escape. In one case, women were so terrified when police raided their brothel that they hid in the closet. The complex mixture of fear, intimidation and violence used by traffickers and brothel owners effectively immobilizes the victims.

TRAFFICKING AND HEALTH

The trafficking of women and children for sexual exploitation is accompanied by potentially lifelong and/or life-threatening health consequences. It prevents victims from attaining the highest possible level of physical, mental and social well- being. The World Health Organization is currently drafting recommendations for action to address the health implications of trafficking. Numerous reports of accidents and deaths have caused the International Organization for Migration to identify trafficking as the most dangerous form of migration. Clandestine transportation puts migrants at risk of drowning, freezing, or suffocating, so that the trafficking process itself becomes a health hazard. Victims' health is further endangered in situations of sexual exploitation. Available data suggest several areas of concern:

- Violence: The consequences of psychological, physical and sexual violence associated with trafficking and sexual exploitation include depression, suicidal thoughts and attempts, and physical injuries such as bruises, broken bones, head wounds, stab wounds, mouth and teeth injuries, and even death.
- Reproductive Health: Involvement in the sex industry is associated with an increased risk of sexually transmitted infections (STIs). Pregnancy and forced or unsafe abortions are primary health concerns, exacerbated by lack of access to health care.
- HIV/AIDS: HIV risk is heightened in situations where victims do not have access to condoms, or where they are not in a position to negotiate condom use. The risk is

further increased by cuts and tears in vaginal and anal tissue due to rough sex, rape and STI-related ulcers.

- Substance Abuse: Many women and children in the sex industry use drugs and/or alcohol as a coping mechanism. Both voluntary and forced use commonly leads to addiction and its attendant health consequences.
- Access to Health Care: Fear of detection and deportation can leave undocumented women reluctant to access social services. In situations of debt bondage, women may not be able to pay for care. Those forcibly kept in brothels may not be allowed to leave to seek health care. Because their access to care is so restricted, trafficking victims are at high risk of complications arising from undiagnosed and untreated infections, such as pelvic inflammatory disease, chronic pelvic pain, ectopic pregnancy, and sterility.
- Children: Often lacking accurate information and the skills, power and ability to negotiate condom use, children are at greater risk of HIV infection. Due to their immature reproductive tracts, girls are especially vulnerable to sexually transmitted infections and are more likely to suffer long term damage from them. The traumatic sexualization, betrayal, powerlessness and stigmatization involved in sexual exploitation are particularly damaging to child and adolescent development, and can lead to various types of psychiatric morbidity and an impaired ability to form attachments and successful interpersonal relationships.

TRAFFICKING IN THE AMERICA

Lack of information on trafficking in the America should not be mistaken for the absence of large-scale trafficking activity. A growing number of reports from non-governmental organizations, the media, and legal cases indicate that trafficking in women and children for sexual exploitation is a significant problem in the America. Available data show that women and children are trafficked to, from and within the region, with accounts reported in nearly every country.

Political instability and social unrest in some areas have created environments conducive to trafficking. Victims in the America are sexually exploited through brothels, bars, massage parlors, street prostitution, and pornography. The popularity of Latin America as a destination for sex tourists, which has increased since Asia began measures to reduce sex tourism, is particularly alarming. Growth of the sex industry and the demand for commercial sex assure that, without action, the incidence of trafficking will only increase.

CASE OF BOSNIA AND HERZEGOVINA AND DEMOCRATIC REPUBLIC OF CONGO

The United Nations Organization Mission in the Democratic Republic of the Congo (hereinafter MONUC) is on going mission while the United Nations Mission in Bosnia and Herzegovina (hereinafter UNMIBH) is terminated almost three years ago. Although scandalized with involvement of peacekeepers in trafficking in women and wide sexual abuse, the UNMIBH is graded by international community with a top mark: successful. After the mission was over, peacekeepers changed locations and countries, in following a war torn societies in need of peace. Still, the crimes perpetuated by peacekeepers against those in need, particularly women and children, did not change. Moreover, it looks like they exacerbated.

No doubt, the topic of sexual exploitation has always been "sexy" topic which attracts journalists but also readers around the globe. Moreover, if sexual abuse could be related in any way with the United Nations (hereinafter the UN) and its personnel, that is even more "interesting". However, media seems to be not very interested in, for example, economic opportunities mission could bring for local people such as possibility of their employment within the UN system. Indeed, curiosity to highlight positive outcomes that mission might bring to the host country rather then only failures is rarely of any one interest, except of the UN. In addition, the more shocking a title and story the greater is a sense of outrage and disappointment in overall UN system by a common public.

People are always disturbed when someone is sexually abused but why particularly when it comes to peacekeepers? Is it about the prefix UN in front of them? Is it because they should be "saviors" of the "vulnerable" population not their abusers? Or we like to confirm what we know well: not everything nor everyone is "perfect" as the UN always likes to leave impression on the worldwide population.

Attempt to observe if there were any improvements since 1995 when the UN peacekeeping mission came to Bosnia and Herzegovina and allegations on their involvement in sexual abuse and trafficking in women began to surface. How did UNMIBH respond to these allegations? What mechanisms for protection and prosecution were then and are now in place, if any? Has MONUC learnt a lesson from UNMIBH? 'Or Boys will be Boys' no matter what steps are taken to prevent such occurrences.

UNMIBH AND MONUC: PAST AND CURRENT MISSION

DRC and five regional states signed the Lusaka Ceasefire agreement in July 1999. To maintain liaison with the parties and carry out other tasks, the Security Council (hereinafter SC) set up MONUC on 30 November 1999, incorporating personnel authorized in its earlier resolutions. On 24 February 2000, the SC expended its size and mandate. After that time the SC extended its mandate several times. The current mandate is mostly provided by Resolution 1493, dated 28 July 2003, whereby the SC, acting under the Chapter VII of the UN Charter, authorized the increase of MONUCs military strength to 10,800. However, although war was declared over, hostilities persist to this day.

Set up in 1995, UNMIBH exercised wide range of functions particularly regarded police reform and law enforcement activities. Both of the missions, UNMIBH and MONUC have had quite similar mandates: disarmaments, demining, human rights, elections, reform of security forces and reestablishing the rule of law. After seven years, following the successful conclusion of its mandate, UNMIBH was terminated on 31 December 2002. Although they might be regarded as successful for some activities in their missions they both failed in the same: maintaining discipline and conduct of peacekeepers. And misconduct primarily affects (affected in the case of UNMIBH) women population as well as children in both countries.

DRC is country of almost 55 million of people while Bosnia and Herzegovina is 13 times smaller with around 4 million of inhabitants. However, in terms of casualties they both lost almost equal percentage of their population due to war. We do not have gender-segregated data so we do not know how many women lost their lives in those conflicts. What we do know is that almost 75% of Congolese refugees and international displaced persons (IDPs) comprise women and children. Almost the same percentage of women refugees and IDPs was in Bosnia and Herzegovina which confirms world statistical data which says that almost 80% of all refugees and IDPs embrace children and women. Still, this statistic does not say anything about percentage of women as it assumes that "women and children" are one homogeneous group of people. But, we know they are not.

PEACEKEEPING MISSIONS: FERTILE SOIL FOR SEXUAL ABUSE

What could be regard as a common feature to both missions is that they have triggered shocking reports on sexual abuse and rape. Although cases of sexual abuse and violence, which has become almost universal characteristic in peacekeeping context, were present (and in case of MONUC are still on going) in both missions, the nature of abuse between these two missions is different. For example, while trafficking in women boomed with shipping ten of thousands predominantly male peacekeepers in Bosnia and Herzegovina in 1995, in DRC there are no cases (at least not transparent and publicly known) of involvement of peacekeepers in transnational crime of trafficking in women. DRC is rather source country for women and children trafficked for sexual exploitation, forced labor and soldiering. However, "lack of information does not mean absence of trafficking in women and children in Congo." Hence, even if transnational crime of trafficking might not exist currently it could become problem and DRC should be prepared to punish those who might be involved in future trafficking networks. Since Penal Code in DRC "does not have specific provision against Trafficking in Women and Children", it should not wait to criminalize trafficking in humans after it becomes overloaded with cases or when it lose such necessity what exactly happened in Bosnia and Herzegovina.

In both missions peacekeepers use imbalance of power and have had sex with minors or adults for bizarre amount of money or in exchange for food or other goods. Cases of rape by peacekeepers in Bosnia and Herzegovina were not transparent and particularly known while in DRC they are wide spread. Sharp distinction in welfare between host population and peacekeepers drives opportunity to exercise power and authority over vulnerable population. However, in Bosnia and Herzegovina despite few cases where peacekeepers were sexually abused local minors, the main target were foreign women, victims of trafficking. This is another distinction between MONUC where sexual abuse involves peacekeepers and local girls/women/children while UNMBIH peacekeepers were mainly involved in sexual abuse of alien women.

Brothels in Bosnia and Herzegovina were established close to military bases with predominantly women from Romania, Ukraine and Moldova. Having had limited freedom of movement and lots of spare time might be a reason for turning to the nearest brothels and night bars crowded with foreign women. Nonetheless, even the cases, which were actually rumors of a sexual abuse of Bosnia and Herzegovina minors, had as a spot places those just outside the fence of military bases. The stories that had been circling among local population were about local girls mainly from high schools performing oral sex for 5-10 euros in the front of military bases even (some said) through a fence wire.

It is difficult to confirm that girls had performed sex for survival in Bosnia and Herzegovina or some other reasons were behind it. However, it is well known that women who were performing sex activities with peacekeepers, with exception of trafficked women, were driven by poverty and lack of alternative ways to secure basic human needs for them and their family. Although there are no existing cases of transnational trafficking in DRC, some cases of internal trafficking have been recognized as such. Young local boys act as pimps for MONUC personnel, procuring girls for prostitution. Congo boys earn on average 1US$ for each girl or they end up not being paid at all. These young boys are predominantly minors age 8-18, former child soldiers from whom very few attend the school. The majority of identified female victims were poor village children between 12 and 16 years of age.

Finally, noticed that Pakistani peacekeepers are one of the nationalities involved in serious allegations in Bosnia and Herzegovina in trafficking (purchasing) of women, in DRC in obstructing efforts to investigate sexual abuse but also in other recent peacekeeping operations (hereinafter PKOs). It would be valuable to do more serious research on possible assumption that some nationalities tend to be more involved in sexual abuse of women than others. That could be valuable in terms of "keeping an eye" on potential "trouble makers" but also to work with them more regarding preventive measures.

WOMEN STATUS IN BOSNIA AND HERZEGOVINA AND DRC

Status of women before PKO arrive in a host country should be analyzed and taken into account. Paul Higate as one of explanations for bad attitude towards Congolese women by peacekeepers see in already established imbalance and inequality of gender in DRC itself. In other words, if women are not respected by their "own men" how and why would you expect them to be respected by male foreign peacekeepers? Also, Higate is addressing the issue of racism by saying that "male peacekeepers find Congolese women different from white, educated women back to their home countries".

While Bosnia and Herzegovina and Congolese women both live in patriarchal society situation with Congolese women is much different. Bosnia and Herzegovina women before war enjoyed relatively good status and were able to exercise their social and economic rights. Also, women had a high level of literacy, were well educated and employed before war. On the contrary, Congolese women were treated as a "second class citizens" even before war. Moreover, "the law as well social norms defined the role of women and girls as subordinated to men." The Family Code in DRC requires women to obey their husbands who are recognized as heads of households. This is not to say that this is the reason for women to prostitute themselves but I think that previous social status and role of women might be important.

Low self esteem of women, high levels of sexual violence during the conflict coupled with a widespread domestic violence and social and law norm that subordinate women to men could lead to "a degree of local acceptance of violent and/ or exploitative behavior against women and girls". Also, we must keep in mind that DRC was a colony of "white men" for more than 60 years and therefore "white men" could be still seen as a "superior" race that should be obeyed. Furthermore, particularly after the war, the burden of survival and securing the survival of the family fall profoundly on Congolese women.

Hence, survival sex might create "a context in which abusive sexual relationships are more accepted, and in which many men-whether civilian or combatant-regard sex as a "service" [on which he has "natural" right that comes from his "natural" needs for performing sex whenever he feels need to do so] easy to get with the use of pressure." This could explain the attitude of victims who "were on the whole not aware of having been exploited or victimized, unless the act involved violence such as rape." Yet, even in the cases of rape by accepting the money from the perpetrator, many women "settled" cases in this way and may even think that they cooperated with abuser by the fact they accepted the money.

After this act women might feel guilty and find they do

not have any reason to report case of abuse. By giving money or goods in exchange peacekeepers cover up exploitation and rape. It is being done on purpose to show "mutual consent" and willingness of both sides in the case women speak up and try to prove case of unconsentual sex. Along with stigma, and fear a major factor is also high illiteracy rate among girls which does not make them capable of reading name tags on uniforms of peacekeepers. In this regard, it will be very difficult to expect women to report incidents of sexual abuse and particularly to identify perpetrators. A combination of fear and stigma from her immediate community as well as illiteracy and absence of awareness that she is a victim of serious crime makes the situation very complex.

Therefore, the civil society must play an important role as it did in the case of Bosnia and Herzegovina. They should make raising awareness campaigns, open SOS hotlines and try to provide alternatives for women. For Bosnia and Herzegovina women non governmental organizations (NGOs) played enormous role and helped hundreds of women who were trapped in brothels around the country by constant public campaigns, public discussions and statements and as a result of their open attempts to help women very often exposed themselves to life threatening situations.

However, peacekeepers have looked upon women as inferior race in any case. Although it might be true that they are particularly violent towards black women, in Bosnia and Herzegovina they were involved in sexual abuse and trafficking of women from the former Soviet Union who are all white. In Bosnia and Herzegovina we did not have black victims of trafficking. Therefore, I believe that real source of violence is masculinity, in particular military ones, and the attitude it brings toward women in general. As one senior male peacekeeper suggested "subordinate status [of women] was linked to their gender and .... following from this, men could exercise certain sexual rights over them, particularly when they had to share the same accommodation." Truly, Congolese women share "the same accommodation" since they share the same country as a common place for living with peacekeepers.

If peacekeepers share opinion of their senior staff then their level of hostility towards women should not surprise us. In addition, since peacekeepers are military men they are trained to dehumanize the "other" in order to be able to go into battle without emotional involvement. In the case of rape and sexual exploitation, foreign women are treated by peacekeepers as "others". They are not looked upon as human beings with equal values and needs who deserve absolute respect of universal human rights. Prejudices and stereotypes about women of different color, race, social and educational status might be something to consider of importance to be addresses with peacekeepers before their arrival in a host country.

How else is it possible to explain that a man who does not have a record of rape or any other crime in his country of origin and maybe never even thought of raping "his woman" will do all kinds of sexual abuse and exploitation (hereinafter SEA) and humiliate women in "other" countries? In addition, according to the study done by the UN Division for the Advancement of Women (DAW) it has been found that "the incidents of rape…fall significantly with just a token female presence…men behave better when in the presence of women from their own culture." This might explain difference in a treatment and respect of men towards their "own" and "other" women. As Jack Paul Clain said in the documentary "Boys will be boys" "those people [referring to women victims of trafficking by peacekeepers in Bosnia and Herzegovina] will tell you anything" accusing them of lying and making false statements. The attitude of devaluation and disrespect some peacekeepers have towards foreign females when they arrive on a mission might be a cause for future potential abuses.

It seems that West Africa "had to happen" to move things on in terms of bringing new policies. Bosnia and Herzegovina scandals of involvement of peacekeepers in sexual abuse were not "good enough" to put the policies on SEA in their much needed place. Only after the disgrace which came with UNHCR/SC UK report, the UN decided it was a time to do something. Although, sexual exploitation and abuse were always prohibited by the UN Staff Rules and Regulations it seems that very few of the UN staff have been taken this prohibition seriously.

Also, the Policy Planning Unit of Department of Peacekeeping Operations (hereinafter DPKO) has issued the Ten Rules-Code of Conduct for Blue Helmets which promulgate expected behavior of every military person taking part in a peacekeeping mission in its paragraph 4 prohibits "immoral acts of sexual, physical or psychological abuse or exploitation of the local population or United Nations staff, especially women and children." Beside these general rules which apply to all military peacekeepers wherever they are on the mission, there are also country-specific codes of conduct developed *if* a mission has some specific concerns to address. In-country codes of conduct are designed to draw attention to particular problems which have been acknowledged during the mission and are perceived by the mission as highly important to be addressed.

MONUCs Code of Conduct has being developed and pronounced in April 2003 and it "strictly prohibits...any act of sexual abuse and/or exploitation of members of local community, including children." Still, these rules had to be reinforced and repeated once more by administrative instructions of Secretary General in bulletin on "Special measures for protection from sexual exploitation and sexual abuse" released in October 2003, almost a year after the Bosnia and Herzegovina mission was over.

Also DPKO issued the Compilation of Guidance and Directives on Disciplinary Issues of Personnel Serving in United Nations Peacekeeping and Other Field Missions in 2002 with an aim to reinforce disciplinary procedures. In 2004 the Office of Internal Oversight Services launched an investigation into allegations and published a report on 7 January 2005 which identified 72 allegations of SEA by MONUC peacekeepers. Other measures have also been undertaken to eliminate SEA such as the establishment of non-fraternization policy, comprehensive training and awareness-raising and the installation of a curfew for military contingents.

Only 3 years after MONUC had been established, gender issues started to receive attention and action has been taken. Peacekeepers in Bosnia and Herzegovina might have had an "excuse" since SC Resolution 1325 on Women, Peace and Security (hereinafter SC Resolution 1325) had passed in October 2000, however the precedent for mainstreaming gender into peacekeeping operations had already been established in 1995 in The Beijing Declaration and Platform for Action. Also, throughout 1990s, the language of the UN began to include promoting gender balance in all professional posts and adoption of a strategy called "gender mainstreaming".

However, UNMIBH beside attempts to work on gender balance did not really work on gender mainstreaming nor did it have a Gender Unit within its mission. We can say that formal inclusion of gender perspectives into peacekeeping operations is therefore an emerging phenomenon. In this regard, prior to adoption of SC Resolution 1325, gender units were established only in two peacekeeping missions. Although MONUC was deployed in 1999, it was only in 2002 that the Gender Unit was set up. In addition, the Code of Conduct Officer was established as a new mechanism for fighting cases on SEA.

What certainly did not happen in UNMIBH and was in MONUC is training on gender issues. In MONUC training is done in cooperation with civil society, using both men and women in its delivering. So far, this training has had successful results. One of the UNMIBH tasks was also to closely monitor allegations of local police involvement, and to ensure that the local police internal investigations have been properly conducted. But one might ask who had "closely monitored allegations" of international police and UN personnel involved in sex abuse and trafficking?

Local police were monitored by international police and international police monitored themselves? Moreover those international police officers who were brave enough to speak up about crimes of their fellow officers have been removed from their jobs. Therefore, if allegations or evidence existed about UNMIBH civilian or civilian police involvement, the mission would conduct its own internal investigation and, "if necessary, take appropriate measures". Yet, appropriate measures are not defined. The case is the same with MONUC. If a MONUC staff member violates the Code of Conduct the sanction violating these rules would include: "summary dismissal and repatriation if applicable."

The language of sanctions is too weak and too loose and it seems too much freedom has been allowed to contributing countries for undertaking disciplinary action if necessary. Victims are sure that action is necessary but does anyone ask them? In addition, the member states enjoy absolute autonomy in responding in the ways they consider appropriate. What if a member state's notion of "appropriate" does not overlap with the wider idea of prosecution and justice but rather with narrow political interests? In majority of cases, "appropriate" means absolute impunity. Power dynamics and lack of political will by contributing member states to prosecute its citizens do not allow impartiality and justice to take place.

Only between 1999 and 2001, UNMIBH took action to protect the human rights of trafficked persons, particularly through the support of the International Organization for Migration (IOM) program of victim protection and creation of anti-trafficking law enforcement units. Six UN policemen in Bosnia and Herzegovina were sent home in 2000 for involvement in prostitution and trafficking of women and therefore "exceeding the mandate" of IPTF. In July 2001, UNMIBH spokesman said that twenty-four officers had been fired for offenses ranging from bribery to sexual impropriety.

In November 2002, UNIMBH gave a statement on the involvement of eleven police officers who were found to have violated codes of professional conduct when frequenting night clubs, and for using sexual services in these establishments. These eleven cases of removal of provisional authorization are the result of the relentless efforts of the IPTF STOP teams in their fight against human trafficking in Bosnia and Herzegovina. However, none of the repatriated police officers have been prosecuted by their country of origin after repatriation from mission. Their immunity was interpreted as absolute impunity for the crimes they committed in the country where the mission was taking place. Fortunately, the situation is progressing, and in the case of DRC member states, more action is taking place with regard to prosecution of their nationals. However, this is not enough, and we have to make sure that "the protection of some member states reputation [does not] take precedence over issues such as gender".

We are just at the beginning of the "gender road" and there is still a lot to be done on the path to achieving gender equality. Although gender units have started to be set up in the last few years they still lack support from the UN in both budget and human resources. There is also a lack of political will within the UN system to fully support work and activities of gender units. In addition, problem of SEA is complex and we should look at its root causes when trying to develop and implement new strategies and also our attention should be equally divided between perpetrator and victim as without simultaneously working with both of them the problem will not be solved. Therefore, following suggestions to be done in the future:

1. Develop programs which will target peacekeepers, but which will also address women victims of sexual abuse as well as children. Civil society organization s of the host country should be given the task to raise awareness before peacekeepers come to the country, and to continue the campaigns after their arrival. They should inform the population, in particular women, what might happen with their arrival, especially with regard to SEA. The UN should cooperate closely with civil society and work together to combat SEA. They have to build up confidence within the host country's population and develop cooperation to combat SEA.

2. Since it is much easier to control the UN military personnel (as they live in military bases) than civilian personnel, the UN should develop controlling mechanisms which will be able to follow more closely the UN civilian's life. Civilians live in apartments in cities, they have more freedom of movement and as such it is easier from them to get involved in criminal activities without fear of discovery. Some of them have even had sex slaves living with them in their residences without being discovered for a long time, and some of these cases will never be discovered.
3. Local NGOs as well as UN missions should open SOS hotlines where they will be able to receive anonymous telephone calls, both from victims but also from peacekeepers who know that their colleagues are involved in SEA. People who work in SOS hotlines should be trained and gender-sensitive. SOS hotlines should be confidential and anonymous so there is no fear that someone will be removed from their position as a result of blowing the whistle.
4. An ombudsman position or body should be established outside the UN machinery, which then could receive complaints from civilian population as well as peacekeepers. Such body should (hopefully) also be impartial and composed of people with strong human rights backgrounds.
5. The immunity of peacekeepers should be narrowed and not cover serious violations of human rights, regardless of whether they happen during the mandate of peacekeeping or not. No one should be immune from murder, rape or sexual abuse. These activities (!) are certainly not "necessary for the independent exercise of their functions."
6. Member states must, both more states and in more individual cases, start waiving the immunity of their citizens if they commit serious crimes while taking part in a peacekeeping mission. Their political interests and

reputation must be "sacrificed" in the name of accountability and justice. The Secretary General also has to start waiving the immunity of peacekeepers in order to enable local courts to exercise their jurisdiction. I am convinced that if we start waiving immunity in each case that has legal grounds for immunity to be waived, we would have fewer cases of crimes taking place by peacekeepers during peacekeeping missions.

7. Transparency must exist in all cases. More specifically, peacekeepers should be named, and the cases themselves should receive high publicity and coverage. Follow-up on proceedings in peacekeepers' home countries, and subsequent reporting back to the local population on what actions have been taken to address the crimes committed are crucial.
8. Reparation to victims of SEA must involve individual peacekeepers and a high financial compenzation benchmark should be established. Since money is their main motivator (if not the only one) to join peacekeeping missions we should seriously consider establishing financial punishment. The amount should be significant and be paid directly from the individual peacekeeper's account. This should take place in addition to the peacekeeper's dismissal from the operation, his repatriation, and subsequent appearance before a court in his home country, or alternatively in the mission country's local court in the cases where immunity is waived by the Secretary General. Money paid as a punitive measure by the peacekeeper should go directly to the victim.
9. Trainings on gender and SEA undertaken by civil society organizations, with trainers of both sexes, should utilize lessons learnt from UMNIC in developing training for all subsequent missions, and these changes in training should be implemented as soon as possible.
10. We need to put more emphasis on the cultural context of host country in relation to the peacekeeper's country

of origin. Peacekeepers should be trained not to be only gender-sensitive but also culturally-sensitive. They should also receive training on prejudices, racism and stereotypes.

11. I do agree that peacekeepers should have some short courses (maybe on culture of host country) or sport activities. Their cultural life must be enriched while on mission and not become a case of wasting time.
12. More women should be present in investigation teams in cases of SEA.
13. Civil society and government with support of UN mission should provide alternatives to vulnerable women and develop vocational trainings in their combating prostitution and sexual abuse.
14. Gender training should be broken down into several separate issues which will deal specifically with, for example, children's rights and abuse of children, women's rights and abuse of women while also highlighting sanctions that will take place in cases of violation. Workshops and discussion groups with small number of men should be developed. Men might be more open and honest in smaller groups. I do not believe that in one training session you can cover all issues. Also, some issues do not necessarily need (maybe it is not possible due to time restriction) to be covered during an induction course, but such issues can be addressed later during the mission. This can be done by using audio-visual materials (e.g. movies). This can ensure as much as possible that an interactive discussion takes place.
15. Identify future trainers since we do not have enough staff to deliver the gender training required. The trainers must also include men who are more gender sensitive and understand the issues involved. They might at the beginning, for example, be modestly financially awarded for their willingness to be involved in training for trainers. This is particularly important because of language barriers. Therefore, until we convince member

states to provide pre-deployment gender training, peacekeepers from different nationalities involved in the training can be of help.

16. Push for pre-deployment gender training. Since language is barrier and not everyone can be trained in the country of mission, it should be considered an obligation by the member states to organise pre-deployment gender training.
17. Bring in local civil society organizations to run training sessions, or bring in experts working outside of the UN to run the sessions who have experience in gender issues.
18. Decrease the age of experience for employment with UN civilian police for women. Women who have 8 years or more of experience have much more difficulty in leaving their families to go and work abroad. It is crucial to give opportunities to younger women, eager to learn and prove themselves. They are more willing to travel and do not usually have as many family obligations.
19. Training sessions should be culturally adjusted, both pre-deployment or in-mission. It is not the same to talk about gender to a guy from Norway and from Pakistan. Training should be designed from the prospective of their home country as well as their host country. Peacekeepers should know what they should expect to see in the mission country before they depart.
20. Distribution of condoms during the mission and at the same time prohibiting sexual intercourse sends a confusing message. Under this confused state of affairs, it is impossible to address the issue of safe sex, or to analyze to what extent peacekeepers use condoms for sexual activities, or to even inform them why is may be important to use them in a particular country.
21. The UN must take responsibility for children who were sexually abused, as well as for women. They must take part in the rehabilitation process of the victim and particularly for "peace babies" who are a result of peacekeepers' sexual abuse.

22. More financial and human resources must be dedicated to activities related to mainstreaming gender.
23. Decreasing the number of military personnel in peacekeeping operations and increasing the number of civilian personnel and other staff. Having 'military boys' maintaining peace has not proved successful so far, so it is time to start considering changing the strategy for the effective keeping of peace in a country.
24. If there are more cases of SEA committed by some nationalities, more work should be done with those particular groups of peacekeepers in identifying why this might be the case. This would help for designing better strategy in combating and prevention of SEA in overall peacekeeping missions.

Too much attention has recently been focused on SEA cases in DRC, and the danger is that this exclusive focus results in potential cases of SEA in other missions being ignored. Spotlight on MONUC could be misused for better cover up of the same abuses which as a result could be going unnoticed. Also, if we already know that it is almost inevitable that with the arrival of thousands of predominantly male peacekeepers into a country, the sex industry will boom, it is high time to put all our efforts on prevention measures which will target both: local women and peacekeepers. However, it is a positive development that for the first time more emphasis is being placed on sanctions that will follow misconduct of peacekeepers. In addition, there is now much more publicity on sanctions imposed by member states on their citizens who were repatriated to their home countries for misbehavior. Despite all obstacles on the way to justice, it seems that things are moving in the right direction and that slowly, hopefully, impunity will be translated into accountability and prosecution. This is certainly a big positive step forward in comparison with the UNMIBH.

6

Gender-Based Violence in Refugee Camps

The unequal status of women and girls in society generally increases sharply their vulnerability to gender-based violence during humanitarian crises. All too often, they suffer or must flee the risk of sexual violence in situations of armed conflict. They may also encounter violence while traveling to safety. In refugee camps, disruptions to community support structures, unsafe physical surroundings, separation from families, and patriarchal governing structures often heighten women and children's vulnerability to gender-based violence. Problems with camp location and design may exacerbate these problems. For example, many Burundian refugee women and girls in Tanzania were raped while traveling long distances to collect firewood. In protracted refugee situations, additional factors contribute to gender-based violence. Refugees are often frustrated by their long-term refugee status and unemployment. Rates of alcoholism as well as anxiety and depression may be high.

Competing international crises and seemingly intractable refugee situations may result in "donor fatigue." In some cases, as funding and international attention has decreased, the combination of scarce resources and male-dominated camp leadership and distribution structures has exposed refugee women and girls to exploitative situations where they exchanged sexual favors for aid supplies. The longer a refugee situation persists, the more entrenched refugee-run management structures may become, and the presence of international NGOs and UNHCR often diminishes. Empowering refugees in camp administration is often a desired and positive outcome, but, in many cases, their governing structures involve harmful traditional practices and conflict-resolution methods that perpetuate gender-based violence. In these situations, victims frequently cannot access support services or seek remedies for violations of their rights.

Sexual exploitation in refugee camps received international attention after the release of a report by UNHCR and Save the Children-UK in 2002 that detailed the widespread practice of refugee children exchanging sex with humanitarian aid workers in order to access food, housing supplies, and other goods in refugee camps in Guinea, Liberia, and Sierra Leone. If appropriate preventive and remedial mechanisms are not in place, refugees may be vulnerable to sexual exploitation by humanitarian aid workers, police, and government officials. Discriminatory practices reducing women's participation and leadership in refugee settings and women and girls' unequal social, legal, and economic status place them at particular risk of sexual exploitation.

GUIDELINES FOR PREVENTING AND RESPONDING TO GENDER-BASED VIOLENCE

The West Africa "sexual exploitation" scandal provided impetus for a re-evaluation of United Nations and NGO employee codes of conduct as well as methodologies for addressing gender-based violence in humanitarian crises. The Inter- Agency Standing Committee (IASC), a body of U.N. agencies and NGO invitees, established a Task Force on Protection from Sexual Exploitation and Abuse in Humanitarian Crises (IASC Task Force) in March 2002. The IASC Task Force's mandate was "to make recommendations to eliminate sexual exploitation and abuse by humanitarian personnel and the misuse of humanitarian assistance for sexual purposes." The IASC Task Force identified core principles for a code of conduct for all humanitarian workers in its Plan of Action.

UNHCR has independently developed a number of guidelines and manuals to ensure the protection of refugees, internally displaced people, and returnees. Among the most important guidelines for the protection of refugee women are the 1991 *Guidelines for the Protection of Refugee Women* and the 2003 *Sexual and Gender-Based Violence Against Refugees, Returnees, and Internally-Displaced Persons: Guidelines for Prevention and Response.* UNHCR also integrated the core principles delineated by the IASC Task Force into its own code of conduct.

UNHCR and its implementing partners use the following definition for gender-based violence:

[G]ender-based violence is violence that is directed against a person on the basis of gender or sex. It includes acts that inflict physical, mental or sexual harm or suffering, threats of such acts, coercion and other deprivations of liberty. While women, men, boys and girls can be victims of gender-based violence, women and girls are the main victims.

[Gender-based violence] shall be understood to encompass, but not be limited to the following:

1. Physical, sexual and psychological violence occurring in the family, including battering, sexual exploitation, sexual abuse of children in the household, dowry-related violence, marital rape, female genital mutilation and other traditional practices harmful to women, non-spousal violence and violence related to exploitation.
2. Physical, sexual and psychological violence occurring within the general community, including rape, sexual abuse, sexual harassment and intimidation at work, in educational institutions and elsewhere, trafficking in women and forced prostitution.
3. Physical, sexual and psychological violence perpetrated or condoned by the State and institutions, wherever it occurs.

The 2003 Guidelines outline key risk factors for gender-based violence in refugee situations, such as the collapse of social and family support structures; location in a high crime area; poor design of services and discriminatory social structures in the camp; predominantly male camp leadership, unavailability of food, fuel, and income generation opportunities; lack of police protection and security patrols; lack of UNHCR and NGO presence in the camp; lack of individual registration and identity cards; and hostility of the local population. These factors, in combination with individual vulnerabilities, armed conflict, discriminatory cultural practices, and weak and gender-biased legal systems set the stage for gender-based violence.

GENDER-BASED VIOLENCE IN NEPAL'S REFUGEE CAMPS

The problem of gender-based violence in the Bhutanese refugee camps punctured the camps' image as a "model" in late 2002, when UNHCR received reports about sexual exploitation of refugee children and requested its Inspector General's Office (IGO) to review the allegations and examine the conduct of UNHCR offices in Nepal. The results of the investigation team's findings became public in November 2002, documenting eighteen cases of sexual exploitation, including rape and sexual harassment, of refugee women and children. The perpetrators were two Nepalese government officials whose salaries were paid by UNHCR and fifteen refugee men (mostly school teachers) working for NGO implementing partners. Refugee girls comprised the vast majority of victims in these cases.

In addition to sexual exploitation by refugee aid workers and officials, the team discovered many other cases of gender-based violence within the refugee community, including rape, attempted rape, sexual assault, child marriage, forced marriage, and domestic violence. A humanitarian aid worker told Human Rights Watch that the two government officials involved in the sexual exploitation cases were a police officer stationed in one of the camps and an RCU official not stationed in the camps. The police officer encouraged a local man to rape a refugee woman in early 2002, and allegedly received a bribe to rape her himself. He did not rape the woman, but beat her at her home and then again at the police station, where he threatened to charge her with prostitution. The aid worker told Human Rights Watch:

The official, who was in a managerial position, was sexually harassing refugee women in his office. There was a case of a [repeated] rape of a disabled girl, this was by an aid worker. There were many cases of teachers being involved with their students. They would impregnate the girls, who were then kicked out of school. Nothing would happen to the teachers, they would continue to teach and went out with other girls. A young refugee woman emphasized the impact of the school-based sexual exploitation cases: "In one case a twenty-five-year-old teacher made a fourteen-year-old student pregnant. The community does not like it because then they will feel afraid to send girls to school." In some cases, the camp management committees or the parents of the student and teacher would "settle" the case by encouraging their marriage.

Attention to the sexual exploitation cases illuminated the broader and more pervasive problem of gender-based violence in the camps. The UNHCR investigation team also found that refugee women and girls suffered sexual assault and domestic violence perpetrated by other refugees, local Nepalese residents, and intimate partners. In such cases, refugee women and girls were doubly victimized first by their assailants, and then by the minimal response by the government of Nepal and UNHCR. They received inadequate and even harmful settlements meted out by the refugee camp management committees. Whether perpetrators were refugee aid workers, other refugees, or members of the local Nepalese community, the victims of gender-based violence had few avenues for redress. Refugees were forced to navigate a bureaucratic and male-dominated camp management system in which they first had to approach the refugee subsector head, who, if unable to resolve a situation, would refer the issue to the sector head, who might then pass the case on to the camp secretary, RCU, or police.

These two bodies might then refer it to the refugee-run counseling board, a conflict-resolution body that is part of the elected camp management committee. The camp management committee did not regularly refer cases to UNHCR. The camp management committees and counseling board did not have the appropriate training, gender-sensitivity, or legal authority to resolve gender-based violence cases. They often responded to domestic violence cases by dismissing women's complaints and advising them to live happily with their husbands, detaining abusive husbands for one night as punishment, or creating written agreements for the couple to commit to changing their behavior. These methods left refugee women with few options for finding safety and often reinforced cycles of abuse.

Deep social stigma inhibited many women from reporting domestic violence, and in the cases where they dared to seek help, the response by the camp management committee could compound the injustices women faced. Radhika S., who along with her co-wife had suffered chronic emotional abuse and threats of murder from her husband, started to live separately from him. She remembers the shame she felt about how her case was handled:

They [the camp management committee and counseling board] assumed our problems were because we were not having sexual relations. They advised my husband to spend fifteen days with each wife. But I didn't want that, I just wanted him to care for me. They told me if I want a husband, I need to cook food for him. He came to me because he was forced, he was angry, and I wanted a happy atmosphere. We shared a bed but we didn't have sex. And people laughed at this situation, they laughed at me, saying that I wanted sex.

When the case was taken to the counseling board, they said we have to stay together. I didn't agree because I knew everything would just repeat. I told my story first, we argued there [in front of the counseling board], and he denied everything. The sector head was there, the subsector head was there, there were lots of people listening. For them it is a comedy. A refugee whose case was not lost at the subsector or sector-level and who appeared before the counseling board could expect to tell her story in front of large crowds and to receive little redress.

The hearings and final judgments often humiliated and further traumatized victims. The UNHCR investigation team discovered cases where rape victims, including children as young as five years old, were given public apologies and a token compenzation of only ten rupees (U.S. $0.13). One aid worker told Human Rights Watch that there were "many cases where young girls were raped and these cases were settled by turning them into early marriages. Parents often felt they had no other option. It was regularized into a social situation. [There were] more than thirty cases where rape victims were forced to marry their assailant."

Survivors of gender-based violence were often unable to obtain appropriate medical assistance, legal aid, or counseling services. Staff at the Asian Medical Doctors Association (AMDA) hospital issued a medical certificate citing "internal damage" to a five-year-old girl raped by a seventeen-year-old boy instead of sending her to a government hospital where she could get a legally admissible medical report. Refugees and aid workers with inadequate training were often responsible for providing therapy and counseling for victims. In one camp, an aid worker relied upon tranquilizers for treating patients. In other cases, the counseling provided to victims exposed them to danger, as in one woman who was advised to stay with her husband despite severe and repeated physical and sexual violence.

A CASE OF NEGLIGENCE

The government of Nepal and UNHCR did not have adequate complaint mechanisms for reporting gender-based violence, and often failed to provide protection when refugees brought cases to their attention. UNHCR did not implement programs for effective prevention and response despite several indications about the problems confronting women and girls in the camps. UNHCR had an insufficient presence in the refugee camps and visited them irregularly, contributing to the denial of justice and protection for those who suffered gender-based violence. As one observer noted, UNHCR and implementing partners felt that since "refugees were electing their leaders, they were legitimate leaders to whom responsibility for camp protection and administration of justice could fully be delegated." Refugee camp management committee members did not have appropriate skills for addressing gender-based violence cases.

Furthermore, the refugee leadership's political priorities and male-dominated composition translated into injustices against survivors of gender-based violence. Many refugee women told Human Rights Watch that their abuser's friendship with their subsector head or sector head prevented them from obtaining help. In one case, a student raped by a refugee aid worker felt she had no options for protection. She and her friends were afraid to report the case because the perpetrator was related to a powerful figure in the camp management committee.

The absence of response mechanisms obstructed survivors' access to legal and medical assistance. The Nepalese camp police, whose positions are funded by UNHCR, were often unwilling to record complaints, and some posts did not even have log books. Police sometimes beat alleged perpetrators of violence. The police, AMDA, and UNHCR did not have a coordinated referral system to handle gender-based violence cases requiring medical assistance, including access to the AMDA ambulance. One source told Human Rights Watch that refugees had to pay for their travel expenses to the hospital. AMDA had no medical report form for gender-based violence cases, and there were few female health care workers to accompany or provide medical services to victims.

Although the three Nepal offices of UNHCR received several indications of gender-based violence in the camps for almost two years, they failed to act. In December 2000, OXFAM, which had been working in the camps for several years, conducted a survey of refugee women that suggested alarming levels of domestic violence. The report stated that Bhutanese refugee women "are subject to harassment and abuses by refugee male members and also host communities." The report noted complaints that Bhutanese refugee women are "sometimes also sexually abused by male staff of service delivery agencies." Several other organizations also warned of gender-based violence in the camps to no avail. Even after UNHCR headquarters issued recommendations about the appropriate measures to take regarding sexual and gender-based violence in the wake of the West Africa "sexual exploitation" scandal, the Nepal country offices failed to implement any real reforms.

UNHCR did not take significant action to address gender-based violence on an individual or camp-wide basis even when refugees approached them directly. In a UNHCR-facilitated consultation with refugee representatives and NGOs in July 2001, refugees raised their concerns about girl trafficking, rape, suicide, discrimination, and child marriage. The refugees highlighted alcoholism and its links with quarrels between married couples and the sale of rations, polygamy-related problems, and the widespread occurrence of domestic violence coupled with social sanctions against reporting such cases. They also perceived a rising incidence of rape cases. UNHCR also documented individual cases of gender-based violence as early as October 2001 and during the summer of 2002.

UNHCR did not refer any cases of gender-based violence for legal prosecution, instead relying upon the settlements meted out by the counseling boards. Senior international staff in Nepal were aware that the counseling boards "resolved" some gender-based violence cases by ordering apologies and token compenzation but still failed to take action. As one source told Human Rights Watch, "Cases came before UNHCR brought by refugees all sorts of SGBV [sexual and gender-based violence] cases, [including] rape of children. The response was not totally absent, but it was inadequate. There was no follow-up with perpetrators, or with victims in terms of psychosocial care, legal help. In many cases, UNHCR did not meet with victims directly. The CMC structures were failing [refugees], for example there were rapists who were repeat offenders."

Citing the terms of its agreement with Nepal, UNHCR decided to end or reduce funding in September 2002 for "informal" refugee organizations operating in the camps. Three of these organizations had been vocal about gender-based violence and child abuse in the camps. As grassroots networks, the Bhutanese Refugee Women's Forum (BRWF) and the Children's Forum often identified and supported women and children survivors of violence. The Children's Forum monitored the camps for child abuse and forwarded cases to The Lutheran World Federation. If cases reached UNHCR, the staff had no system to forward them to the Bhadrapur office and failed to respond to many cases.

The third organization, Bhutanese Refugees Aiding Victims of Violence (BRAVVE), provided training in weaving and other income-generating activities to economically and socially marginalized groups like widows, women heads of households, and people with disabilities. Eliminating funding for these groups would have likely meant that many incidents of violence would remain unreported, limiting survivors' access to support services and gravely undermining efforts to improve women and children's status in the camps. In the context of instituting reforms in the camps in late 2002, UNHCR addressed the problem by incorporating BRWF, the Children's Forum, BRAVVE, and other refugee organizations as "activities" under existing sub agreements with organizations like LWF and AMDA.

THE NATURE, EXTENT AND EFFECTS OF SEXUAL VIOLENCE

There are various forms of sexual violence. Rape, the most often cited form of sexual violence, is defined in many societies as sexual intercourse with another person without his/ her consent. Rape is committed when the victim's resistance is overwhelmed by force or fear or other coercive means.

However, the term sexual and gender-based violence encompasses a wide variety of abuses that includes sexual threats, exploitation, humiliation, assaults, molestation, domestic violence, incest, involuntary prostitution (sexual bartering), torture, insertion of objects into genital openings and attempted rape.

Female genital mutilation and other harmful traditional practices (including early marriage, which substantially increases maternal morbidity and mortality) are forms of sexual and gender-based violence against women which cannot be overlooked nor justified on the grounds of tradition, culture or social conformity. Since perpetrators of sexual and gender-based violence are often motivated by a desire for power and domination, rape is common in situations of armed conflict and internal strife. An act of forced sexual behaviour can threaten the victim's life. Like other forms of torture, it is often meant to hurt, control and humiliate, while violating a person's physical and mental integrity.

Perpetrators may include fellow refugees, members of other clans, villages, religious or ethnic groups, military personnel, relief workers and members of the host population, or family members (for example, when a parent is sexually abusing a child). The enormous pressures of refugee life, such has having to live in closed camps, can often lead to domestic violence. In many cases of sexual violence, the victim knows the perpetrator. Because incidents of sexual and gender-based violence are under-reported, the true scale of the problem is unknown. The World Bank estimates that less than 10 per cent of sexual violence cases in non-refugee situations are reported.

Two principal types of under-reporting are found in refugee situations:

- under-reporting by the victims, which can lead to distorted figures that suggest there is no problem; and
- an absence of figures relating to sexual violence within official statistics.

It is essential to know that the problem of sexual violence is serious. Reporting and interviewing techniques should be adapted to encourage both victims and relief workers to report and document incidents. Reporting and follow-up must be sensitive, discreet and confidential so no further suffering is caused and lives are not further endangered. In reporting, it is recommended that definitions (such as confirmed rape cases or sexual violence, in general) are provided and a rate calculated (for example, the number of reported cases per 10,000 people over a given period of time). This rate would allow for monitoring of trends and comparisons with other areas.

Sexual and gender-based violence has acute physical, psychological and social consequences. Survivors often experience psychological trauma: depression, terror, guilt, shame, loss of self-esteem. They may be rejected by spouses and families, ostracised, subjected to further exploitation or to punishment. They may also suffer from unwanted pregnancy, unsafe abortion, sexually transmitted diseases (including HIV), sexual dysfunction, trauma to the reproductive tract, and chronic infections leading to pelvic inflammatory disease and infertility.

CAUSES AND CIRCUMSTANCES OF SEXUAL VIOLENCE

Sexual and gender-based violence can occur during all phases of a refugee situation: prior to flight, during flight, while in the country of asylum, during repatriation and reintegration. Prevention and response measures must be adapted to suit the different circumstances of each phase. In conflict situations, sexual violence may be politically motivated-when, for example, mass rape is used to dominate or sexual torture is used as a method of interrogation. It may result from long-standing tensions and feuds and the collapse of traditional societal support. In situations in which the refugees are considered to be materially privileged compared to the local population, neighbouring groups may attack the refugees.

The psychological strains of refugee life may aggravate aggressive behaviour towards women. Male disrespect towards women may be reinforced in refugee situations where unaccompanied women and girls may be regarded by camp guards and male refugees as common sexual property. If men are responsible for distributing goods and necessities, women may be subject to sexual exploitation. Those women without proper personal documentation for collecting food rations or shelter material are especially vulnerable.

Women may have to travel to remote distribution points for food, water and fuel; their living quarters may be far from latrines and washing facilities; their sleeping quarters may be unlocked and unprotected. Lack of police protection and lawlessness also contribute to an increase in sexual violence. Police officers, military personnel, relief workers, camp administrators or other government officers may themselves be involved in acts of abuse or exploitation. If there are no independent organization s, such as UNHCR or NGOs, to ensure personal security within a camp, the number of attacks often increases.

PREVENTION OF SEXUAL AND GENDER-BASED VIOLENCE IN REFUGEE SITUATIONS

A multi-sectoral team approach is required to prevent and respond appropriately to sexual and gender-based violence. A committee or task force should be formed to design, implement and evaluate sexual violence programming at the field level. Refugee representatives, UNHCR, UN partners, NGOs and government authorities should be members of this task force. Each member of the task force, representing relevant sectors/ partners (such as protection, health, education, community services, security/ police, site planning, etc.), should identify his/ her role and responsibilities in preventing and responding to sexual and gender-based violence.

INVOLVEMENT OF REFUGEES, ESPECIALLY REFUGEE WOMEN

The most effective measures require that the refugee community participates in promoting a safe environment for all. Women leaders need to be involved; and women's refugee committees and groups should be established to represent women's interests and to help identify and protect those most vulnerable to sexual violence. Traditional birth attendants (TBAs) can be a valuable source of information and a channel for disseminating protection messages.

It is important to have at least one trained female protection officer at the site. Host countries and international relief organizations have a responsibility to provide the refugee community with funding, technical assistance and the safety measures necessary to allow the refugees to design and implement responses to the problem. Experience has shown that community-based groups, commonly called anti-rape or crisis intervention teams, should be established. These groups can help raise awareness of the problem, identify preventive measures and be at the forefront of providing assistance to survivors.

INFORMATION, EDUCATION AND COMMUNICATION

Public information campaigns on the subject of sexual violence should be launched (while respecting cultural sensitivities). Topics could include preventive measures, seeking assistance, laws prohibiting sexual violence, and sanctions and penalties for perpetrators. Pamphlets, posters, newsletters, radio and other mass media programmes, videos and community entertainment can all be used to transmit information about preventing sexual violence. The refugee community and health workers must understand the importance of the problem and have the confidence to report all cases of sexual violence as soon as possible.

Design, Location and Practical Arrangements

Refugee camps can be designed to enhance physical security. Alternatives to closed camps should always be sought. When designing and organising camp facilities, help protect refugees by:

- locating latrines, water points and fuel collection areas in accessible places;
- making special arrangements for housing unaccompanied women, girls and lone heads of households;

- locking washing facilities;
- providing adequate lighting on paths used at night;
- providing security patrols; and by
- avoiding shared communal living space with unrelated families.

Distribution of Food, Materials for Shelter and Assistance

Essential items, such as food, non-food and shelter materials, should be distributed directly to women. That way, women will not have to exchange sexual favours for these items. Women should be involved in, if not administer, the food distribution system.

Protection of Detainees

Women and men should not be detained together unless they are family members. Appropriate organizations must be allowed access to detainees to monitor their safety and living conditions.

Social and Psychological Factors

Life in refugee camps can lead to a breakdown of traditional social structures, frustration, boredom, alcohol and drug abuse, and feelings of powerlessness that may contribute to aggression and sexual violence. Therefore, educational, recreational and income-generating activities must be promoted.

Responding to Sexual Violence

The response to each incident of sexual violence must include protection, medical care and psychosocial treatment.

Protection

Immediately following an incident of sexual violence, the physical safety of the survivor must be ensured. All actions must be guided by the best interests of the survivor and her wishes must be respected at all times. Wherever possible, the identity of the survivor should be kept secret and all information kept locked and secure from outsiders. Health workers should give the survivor as much privacy as she needs and reassure her about her safety. She may want a family member or friend to accompany her throughout the procedures.

She should not be pressured to talk or be left alone for long periods. If the incident occurred recently, medical care may be required. The survivor should then be escorted to the appropriate medical facilities. It also may be necessary to contact the police, if the survivor so decides. The likely course of events and all the procedures that may follow should be carefully explained to her to ensure informed consent and preparedness.

MEDICAL CARE

The key elements of a medical response to sexual violence are described below. Health care professionals must be specially trained to undertake post-sexual violence medical care. Psychosocial support should begin from the very first encounter with the survivor. A protocol should be adopted to guide the medical and psychosocial care provided to survivors.

A doctor (or qualified health worker) of the same sex should conduct the initial examination and follow-up. The survivor should be prepared for the physical examination and perhaps accompanied (if she so wishes) by a staff member who is familiar with the proceedings, or by a family member or friend. Strict confidentiality is essential. Staff dealing with the survivor must be sensitive, discreet and compassionate.

Take a Complete History and Do a Physical Examination

The survivor should not shower or bathe, urinate or defecate, or change clothes before the medical examination, as evidence may be destroyed. A detailed history of the attack should be documented, including the nature of the penetration, if any, whether ejaculation occurred, recent menstrual and contraceptive history, and the mental state of the survivor. Procedures for medical examination after rape should be established and follow national laws, where they exist.

The results of the physical examination, the condition of clothing, any foreign material adhering to the body, any evidence of trauma, however minor, scratches, bite marks, tender spots, etc., and results of a pelvic examination should be documented. Health workers should collect materials that might serve as evidence, such as hair, fingernail scrapings, sperm, saliva and blood samples.

Perform the Tests and Treatments as Indicated

The following tests may be indicated to establish pre-existing conditions: syphilis blood test, pregnancy test and HIV test. Treatment for common sexually transmitted diseases (STDs), such as syphilis, gonorrhoea and chlamydia, may be indicated. A tetanus vaccination should be considered.

Provide Emergency Contraception, if Appropriate, Along with Comprehensive Counselling:

1. Emergency contraceptive pills (ECPs) can prevent unwanted pregnancies if used within 72 hours of the rape. As described by WHO "emergency contraceptive pills (ECPs) work by interrupting a woman's reproductive cycle-by delaying or inhibiting ovulation, blocking fertilization or preventing implantation of the ovum. ECPs do not interrupt pregnancy and thus are not considered a method of abortion." WHO acknowledges that this description does not command consensus and that some believe that ECPs are abortifacients. Women and health workers holding such belief may be precluded from using this treatment and women who request this service need to be offered counselling so as to reach an informed decision. ECPs should not be seen as a substitute for regular use of contraceptive methods. Women should be counselled concerning their future contraceptive needs and choices.
2. Copper-bearing IUDs can be used as a method of

emergency contraception. They may be appropriate for some women who wish to retain the IUD for long-term contraception and who meet the strict screening requirements for regular IUD use. When inserted within five days, an IUD is an effective method of emergency contraception. However, IUD insertion requires a much higher degree of training and clinical supervision than ECPs. Clients must be screened to eliminate those who are pregnant, have reproductive tract infections, or are at risk of STDs, including HIV/ AIDS. As for ECPs, some women and health workers may be precluded from using this treatment and women who request this service need to be offered counselling so as to reach an informed decision.

Provide Follow-up Medical Care

A woman should be counselled to return for follow-up examinations one to two weeks after receiving initial medical care. Health care providers should monitor her follow-up care. Further tests and treatment, such as testing for or treatment of STDs or referral to other RH services, may be indicated during follow-up. Further visits may also be required for pregnancy and HIV testing.

Psychosocial Care

Survivors of sexual violence commonly feel fear, guilt, shame and anger. They may adopt strong defense mechanisms that include forgetting, denial and deep repression of the events. Reactions vary from minor depression, grief, anxiety, phobia, and somatic problems to serious and chronic mental conditions. Extreme reactions to sexual violence may result in suicide or, in the case of pregnancy, physical abandonment or elimination of the child. Children and youth are especially vulnerable to trauma. Health care providers, relief workers and protection officers should devote special attention to their psychosocial needs.

Survivors should be treated with empathy, care and support. In the long term, and in most cultural settings, the support of family and friends is likely to be the most important factor in overcoming the trauma of sexual violence. Community-based activities are most effective in helping to relieve trauma. Such activities may include:

- Identifying and training traditional, community-based support workers,
- Developing women's support groups or support groups specifically designed for survivors of sexual violence and their families, and
- Creating special drop-in centres for survivors where they can receive confidential and compassionate care.

These activities must be culturally appropriate and must be developed in close cooperation with community members. They will need ongoing financial and logistical support and, where appropriate, training and supervision. Quality counselling by trained workers, such as counsellors, nurses, social workers, psychologists or psychiatrists-preferably from the same background as the survivor should also be provided as soon after the attack as possible. Reassurance, kindness and total confidentiality are vital elements of counselling. Counsellors should also offer support if the survivor experiences any post-traumatic disturbances, if she has difficulty dealing with family and community reactions, and as she goes through any legal procedures.

The objectives of counselling are to help survivors:

- Understand what they have experienced,
- Overcome guilt,
- Express their anger,
- Realise they are not responsible for the attack,
- Know that they are not alone, and
- Access support networks and services.

SPECIAL ISSUES

Sexual Violence in Domestic Situations

Caution should be exercised before intervening in domestic situations because the survivor and/or other relatives could be subjected to further harm. If the survivor has to return to the abuser, retaliation may follow, especially if the abuser learns that the matter has been reported. Each situation needs to be individually assessed in close cooperation with colleagues to determine the most appropriate response. Health care providers may choose to refer the matter to a disciplinary committee, inform the authorities, or provide discreet advice to the survivor about her options.

Children Born as a Result of Rape

These children may be mistreated or even abandoned by their mothers and families. They must be closely monitored and support should be offered to the mother. It is important to ensure that the family and the community do not stigmatise either the child or the mother. Foster placement and, later, adoption should be considered if the child is rejected, neglected or otherwise mistreated.

LEGAL ASPECTS

The government on whose territory the sexual attack occurred is responsible for taking remedial measures, including conducting a thorough investigation into the crime, identifying and prosecuting those responsible and protecting survivors from reprisal. In all cases, the wishes of the survivor should be respected when pursuing the legal aspects of the case. Confidentiality must be ensured. All agencies should advocate the enactment and/ or enforcement of national laws against sexual violence in accordance with international legal obligations. These should include prosecution of offenders and the implementation of legal measures to protect the survivor.

The local UNHCR Protection Officer must be familiar with the national criminal and civil law on the subject of rape and sexual violence before an incident occurs so he/ she will know what procedural steps should be taken and what advice should be given to survivors.

Monitoring

Monitoring cases of sexual violence should be a routine

task of health care providers, protection officers and others, as appropriate. In addition, there should be regular assessments of the providers' ability to offer comprehensive medical and psychosocial care for rape survivors. Ideally, care should be given as soon after a rape as possible.

FUEL PROVISION AND GENDER-BASED VIOLENCE

The specific needs of women and girls in displaced settings, whether as refugees or as internally displaced persons (IDPs), have been the subject of growing levels of concern, and are attracting more focused responses since the mid-1990s. As practitioners, advocates and researchers have focused their attention on the needs and roles of women refugees and IDPs, the literature documenting the link between women's changing roles during their displacement and the increased complexity of conflict has also improved. One area of particular concern is the link between women's roles in the provision of fuel for the household and their vulnerability to gender-based violence (GBV). But more needs to be known not only about the prevalence of GBV outside of camps, but also about the broader security impact of fuel-related violence within camps.

The following desk review is intended to provide a summary of literature relating to the provision of fuel and GBV in displaced settings and add to a growing knowledge-base on the subject among researchers and practitioners. It is also intended to identify key gaps and obstacles in the knowledge on fuel-related issues for displaced people and women in particular. The more comprehensive studies conducted have approached fuel provision and fuel-efficiency from the perspective of environmental sustainability and reducing environmental degradation. Specific literature linking these two issues is limited, and some of the information available may lead to erroneous conclusions about the link between fuel provision and GBV.

In reviewing the related literature, this desk review will identify and summarize the relevant international guidelines and principles on fuel provision and GBV, review two case studies and identify what can be learned from these contexts. Finally, it will seek to identify potential strategic entry points for UNIFEM's Peace and Security programming on the prevention and response to gender-based violence in conflict and post-conflict contexts. The research and analysis undertaken in this review have pointed to several key gaps or obstacles, as well as potential opportunities and recommendations for further exploration. In summary, the gaps identified in this review around both fuel provision and GBV are the following: Specific literature on fuel provision focuses on environmental impact and not on security.

The causes of and vulnerabilities to GBV in this context are poorly understood. Direct fuel provision has been unsustainable and costly. There has been lack of coordination in the provision of fuel alternatives. There is greater potential for coordinated response to and prevention of GBV as it relates to fuel provision. The findings and recommendations of this review indicate that the following strategies may provide sustainable means to address the link between GBV and fuel provision: Developing firewood conservation protocols increasing the use of policing strategies Using confidence building and rule of law training in GBV as a response strategy. Fostering collaboration between local research capacities, community organizations and national institutions.

The violence experienced by women in conflict does not happen in isolation. Disparities in rights, limited access to recourse, and restricted autonomy which exist in times of peace exacerbate the impact of violence on women in conflict. This continuum of violence extends into conflict-induced displacement, whether it is among IDPs or refugees. Between 1992 and 1993, much-publicized incidents of rape within Kenyan refugee camps brought the issue of GBV into stark relief for the international community, especially with regard to fuel and fodder provision.

Most recently this same issue has reappeared in both the media as well as the international aid community as a point of concern in the Darfur regions of Sudan. Over the last twelve years, progress has been made in better understanding the connection between GBV, security and assistance. Until very recently, emergency response plans did not consider GBV protection in their earliest phases. As cross-sectoral collaboration has increased and GBV is better understood, guidelines and guiding principles have begun to outline GBV prevention and response in the earliest phases of planning. The following section will: review the relevant guidelines and policies, summarize strategies used to address GBV and fuel provision, and finally provide two case studies that illustrate both the innovations and shortcomings in fuel related programming and knowledge.

Guidelines and Policies

As early as 1993, UNHCR issued guidelines on sexual violence among refugees. This first set of guidelines was titled Sexual Violence Against Refugees: Guidelines on Prevention and Response. Where mentioned, fuel provision was noted as a security issue when women left camps. At about the same time, UNHCR implemented specific programming to address GBV. One such initiative was titled "Women Victims of Violence Project" (WVVP). In both the WVVP and Guidelines, the GBV focus rested mainly on sexual violence rather than a more broadly defined GBV response.

Beginning in 2001, the RHRC advocated for the inclusion of sexual violence under the umbrella of GBV, laying the groundwork for programming based on multi-sectoral approaches (using legal, physical and social mechanisms). In recent years, UNHCR has begun to include fuel provision as an explicit cause or risk factor for GBV. It has noted that scarcity of food, fuel and income generation opportunities may cause women to venture into isolated areas, leading to potential insecurity. Researchers and practitioners are increasingly advocating for approaching protection within refugee and IDP setting from a broader perspective, as well as asking that threats to security be seen as part of a spectrum rather than narrow definitions.

According to this research, the solutions to this type of security risk would be most successful if they were multi-sectoral in order to reflect the issue's breadth. Beginning with the WVVP, a number of approaches have been used to address the intersection of fuel and fodder provision with refugee and IDP women's security. In many IDP and refugee settings, the primary cooking system used is "an open fire surrounded by three stones on which cooking materials rest. Simple, but inefficient in terms of energy loss, the result, in some instances, has been an excessively high consumption of firewood, with consequent environmental damage." Because of the visible environmental degradation caused by this method, the most common approaches to addressing excessive firewood collection have focused on fuel-efficiency.

The four main strategies used have been: new fuel-efficient technologies, alternative fuels, camp location and size, cultivation and/or reforestation of local vegetation. Each of these fuel-efficiency techniques has been employed in a variety of instances with varied results and lessons learned. Of these four groups of strategies, the first two have been used most often when refugee and IDP security has been compromised. The latter have been more common when resources around refugee camps have been limited. In the past, the use of fuel-efficient technologies has included new types of stoves or stoves that use replaceable fuels such as kerosene. Strategies have also included the introduction of fast-cooking food staples, such as rice and potatoes. The use of existing yet potentially inefficient materials such as biomass, dung, and human energy as fuel has provided creative solutions in insecure or resource-poor environments.

The first situation is when an "unacceptable amount of time and labour to secure sufficient energy" is required to cook the minimum rations, and when specific groups, such as women and girls, are targeted for banditry and assault. This handbook asks that those responsible for assessing a particular situation note the differential between the security threats posed outside of the camps and the security situation within the camps. They state, "fuel supply is not the easy solution to security problems that have more deep- rooted causes," noting that fuel supply programs are very difficult to scale down once they have been implemented. This caution may have been in response to criticism leveled against the costliness of direct firewood provision programs.

It is also important to note that the scarcity of consolidated, specific, GBV-related data in individual camps may also lead to misjudgments regarding the relationship between GBV and fuel provision. In contexts where firewood projects have been implemented to address incidents of rape occurring outside of the camps, there has not necessarily been an overall long-term reduction in GBV. As part of an exhaustive review of GBV among displaced settings it was noted in one particular case, "the greatest majority of reported rapes occurred in residential areas of the camps, not outside while survivors collected firewood, as is commonly believed." By better understanding where incidents of GBV take place, it would be easier to correlate fuel provision and GBV.

According to the Guidelines for Gender-based Violence Interventions in Humanitarian Settings (2005), a key consideration for any fuel distribution and collection initiative must be the generally high cost involved, as well as how sustainable the initiative might be, both in terms of duration as well as environmental impact. The Guidelines state that the following actions should be taken when considering the implementation of a fuel provision initiative:

1. Assess and analyse information about the location(s), routes, means, and personal safety for collecting cooking and heating fuel. Participate in the coordinated situational analysis.
2. Reduce fuel consumption by implementing saving measures.
3. Implement strategies to increase safety and security during fuel collection.
4. When feasible and appropriate, request and ensure

adequate funding to meet temporary fuel needs during the early stages of an emergency and/or to provide fuel to community members unable to collect their own fuel.

5. Coordinate with the GBV working group, which includes providing information to security authorities and the community, about the location and circumstances of reported cases of sexual violence during fuel collection. Information shared must be done in accordance with the guiding principle of confidentiality and anonymity for survivors/victims.

FUEL PROVISION STRATEGIES

Some of the more comprehensive studies conducted relating to fuel-efficiency have stemmed from the perspective of reducing environmental damage, rather than from a specific security concern for women and girls. One such report noted however, that some of the coping mechanisms IDPs have developed were not due to concern for the environment; rather these environmental alternatives acted as measures for increasing security. One particular study focused on the resettlement of largely urban IDPs in Angola to a rural setting. The resettlement did not take into account the availability of natural resources, including fuel wood. While firewood was one particular potential use, fuel wood may have also been used for shelter or tools, neither of which was provided to the IDP population.

The subsequent security threats to women were numerous: walking long distances, the threat of assault, exhaustion, organizing the supervision of children while they were away, not being able to participate in food-for-work programs, and the threat of landmines. The result was complex. Women asked for an increase in the provision of either non- food items or support for agricultural production which would both garner a higher yield in both the market and in the fields. This not only created a misleading impression that there was a reduced demand for fuel wood within the camps, but it also created fuel wood scarcity on the local market.

Within this context, the recommendations were to increase women's education on efficient cooking techniques, providing appropriate cooking devices to IDPs, and demonstrating tangible benefits to sustainability. This particular author also called for a better understanding of the complex relationship between "peoples' needs and behaviour and the local environment." Perhaps the most streamlined statement on GBV and displaced populations is outlined in Action Sheet 7.3 of the IASC Guidelines (2005).

As mentioned in the previous section, this most recent set of recommendations not only explicitly states that fuel collection can create an environment where GBV is likely to take place, but also that "local/host communities may not want or permit displaced people to take fuel wood from nearby areas, or there may be other concerns related to environmental degradation.

Some displaced women collect and sell fuel wood to make an income; a free fuel distribution system will adversely affect these people." The GBV working group of the IASC observed that by promoting the training of women to construct their own fuel-efficient stoves, they were able to reduce the amount of firewood ultimately needed for their cooking. In reducing the necessary firewood, they were able to cut down on the amount of time and distance travelled while collecting firewood. Problems with security and access delayed extending this project to all IDPs in this particular case.

To supplement these strategies, the IASC provided four examples of fuel collection initiatives which responded to a demonstrated need for GBV response or protection. The four cases were in Darfur (Sudan), Dadaab Refugee Camps (Kenya), Kasulu Refugee Camp (Tanzania), and Bhutanese Refugee Camps (Nepal). The following measures were taken to respond to instances of GBV relating to the provision of firewood in each of the following instances:

- Darfur, Sudan -The African Union conducted patrols along "commonly used firewood collection routes."
- Dadaab Refugee Camps, Kenya -30% of household

firewood was distributed through a general ration to all registered households.

- Kasulu Refugee Camp, Tanzania -"Refugees were transported by truck to collect firewood."
- Bhutanese Refugee Camps, Nepal -Kerosene was distributed to households within the refugee camps.

For the purposes of illustrating promising current initiatives, in addition to the above programming examples, Oxfam International and Relief International have worked in Kebkabiya, Sudan (Darfur) on fuel-efficient stove alternatives. They piloted a mud stove program in early 2005. According to their reports, as recently as May 2005 over 2,500 women had learned to make these alternative stoves out of mud, clay, water, and donkey dung. Kebkabiya experienced an influx of over 60,000 IDPs leading to firewood shortages and subsequent security problems for women as they ventured further away from town to gather fuel.

According to Oxfam, the new stoves, which are small enough to be carried by one person, have allowed women to use half the normal amount of firewood, leading to fewer trips outside of town. The process of making the stoves takes roughly three weeks and includes both a course in stove construction and fuel-efficient cooking techniques. The project is seen as having a secondary benefit -reducing the impact of IDPs on the environment.

SELECTED CASE STUDIES

This desk review looked at a variety of materials, but the following two case studies are useful in illustrating both the development of innovations to address GBV and fuel provision, and the gaps which have emerged from these contexts. The following case studies illustrate two specific displacement contexts, one refugee and the other IDP, in which GBV and fuel provision programming has been implemented and in the case of the Dadaab camps, evaluated.

While these two cases by no means represent the entire range of fuel related programming, they share characteristics of a number of other contexts in which vulnerable populations seek refuge and fuel. Both sets of camps are located in remote, desert-like environment which has proven problematic in both accessing the displaced populations as well as in planning for sustainable solutions to a very resource-poor terrain. The Dadaab camps provide a long-term view of GBV efficiency related projects, while the Darfur context provides a timely evolving example of lessons learned over the last ten years.

Dadaab Refugee Camps, Kenya

In 1991 three refugee camps were established in northern Kenya to accommodate Somali refugees, as well as refugees from Uganda, Sudan and Ethiopia. Publicity about rapes occurring when women and girls left the camps to gather firewood raised international awareness of the banditry and assault taking place. Interestingly, the alarm over the number of rapes was raised not by the refugees; rather it was the intensified medical assistance requested which brought the issue to the attention of camp administrators. As a result, in 1993 UNHCR implemented a camp security initiative which also encompassed anti-violence programming.

This programme was the previously mentioned WVVP. In 1995 UNHCR passed this programme on to Care International, which steadily increased programming to include social services and gender-sensitivity training and community mobilization. Following an evaluation of UNHCR's WVVP in 1996, the United States government funded a firewood collection initiative to be implemented by German Technical Cooperation (GTZ). The project aimed to both rehabilitate the environment surrounding the camps as well as reduce conflicts about resources between local communities and the refugee population. According to the Independent Assessment conducted by the Women's Commission for Refugee Women and Children (UNHCR Policy on Refugee Women and Guidelines on their Protection: An Assessment of Ten Years of Implementation), the Firewood Project "tended to view firewood as a 'cause' of rape, rather than a convenient context" in which GBV could occur.

One of the stated objectives of the programme was to prevent further violence from occurring. This approach failed to deal with sexual violence within a broader context and instead treated fuel provision as a "technical fix." An observation made in the Review noted that while measures taken to increase women's security outside of the camp were moderately successful, they achieved "little progress in addressing the overwhelmingly gender- and age-specific protection problems occurring outside the camp." According to this Review, the cultural requirements around who collects firewood and who herds goats created obstacles to developing alternative solutions. While the highest numbers of documented rapes in the Dadaab camps occurred between 1992 and 1993, approximately 90% of rapes reported between 1996 and 1997 took place while the survivors were gathering firewood or tending to livestock.

Rapes continued to be reported through 1998. There are now three camps located in the Dadaab region of Kenya which have continued to receive international assistance from a range of international actors over the last 13 years, and women's security has continued to be an issue of concern to camps residents as well as those providing assistance. As recently as mid-2004 refugees in the Dadaab camps were receiving prototypes of solar cookers to test the viability of using this technology in areas were firewood was scarce. According to a press brief, the newest prototype was one of almost ten that have been introduced over the last couple of decades. Preliminary results noted that the new solar-cookers were widely accepted among refugees, but also indicated that there would be resistance to unfamiliar technology. The long-term benefits of the cookers have yet to be determined.

The costs incurred in delivery, training, and awareness-raising need to be evaluated. The focus of the programming continues to rest on environmental impact, rather than on GBV or women's security. According to UNHCR, "the cookers on their own cannot completely eliminate the problems of deforestation and the risks to refugees of firewood collection.

But used in conjunction with other traditional techniques such as tree planting and selective logging, UNHCR hopes the cookers can have a positive impact on the environment and lessen the impact of large scale refugee influxes."

Darfur, Sudan

An estimated 1.6 million people have been displaced as a result of conflict in the Darfur region of Sudan. As is well known, livelihood strategies of displaced people -whether refugees or IDPs -are interrupted by conflict. Over the last two years, the conflict in Darfur has drawn the attention of the international community; with some focus on conflict-related GBV taking place both prior to and after displacement. As with the Dadaab camps in Kenya, media and international organization attention has also been drawn to incidents of GBV and sexual violence occurring when individuals leave camps to collect firewood, fuel and to tend to livestock. Many women and girls experienced GBV while fleeing attacks on their homes, so the threat to their security extended from the initial flight to their arrival in the camps.

Many have been retraumatised once they reach their refuge site. Traditionally, the provision of firewood and fuel has been the responsibility of women. This has remained true among refugee and IDP communities. Women have also shouldered much of the burden of travelling to nearby markets despite threats to their security. As a number of reports noted, "Difficult household decisions have been made that select the least risk strategy -better to risk being raped than being killed."

A large number of IDPs rely almost completely on assistance through rations and often find that begging and firewood collection are the only livelihood strategies available to them. Firewood collection (either for personal use or for sale) constitutes a security risk for both men and women. Once outside the camp or town perimeter, men may face physical assault or death and women sexual assault. For some of the IDPs in Darfur it had been relatively safe to venture into surrounding *wadis* to search for firewood and straw, but as the surrounding vegetation was increasingly depleted, women found that they had to venture further away, once again raising the risk of GBV.

At least one NGO was reportedly considering introducing alternative fuels in mid-2004. As mentioned earlier, the relationship between the provisioning of firewood and other fuels may not directly reflect the actual need for the fuel. It is possible that IDPs gather firewood and straw for resale. This may reflect a fear of current or future food insecurity, or a deficiency in some other portion of what is included in the IDP rations. Even if women are able to gather firewood for resale, one report indicated that they may be prevented from accessing the market because of exclusionary sourcing practices in the local marketplace which favor local residents over displaced persons.

It is reasonable to assume that some individuals may take the risk of gathering firewood in order to resell it, no matter the security consequences. However, this does not preclude those charged with GBV prevention and response from trying to establish initiatives that may make the risk tolerable as long as the benefits remain appealing enough. Both the recent report issued jointly by researchers from the Feinstein International Famine Center at Tufts University and Aḥfad University for Women in Sudan and field reports from UNIFEM on Darfur, noted the imperative of registering women heads of household (WHH).

Given the reliance on rations, WHH need to be as visible as possible so that they too might receive rations appropriate for themselves and those entrusted to their care. While the Feinstein/Ahfad study focused primarily on livelihood strategies, and not on GBV specifically, the issues are clearly connected. An estimated 60% of IDP households are female-headed.

By extension, the segment of the population most vulnerable to GBV now also constitutes the majority of those responsible for sustaining the livelihood of their families. Some IDPs may fear the threat of future loss of livelihood strategies, such as the death or theft of livestock, and try to curtail this loss by venturing into firewood collection for resale. Given this complex economic and humanitarian relationship, if a sustainable solution to fuel provision-related GBV is to be reached, it must take into consideration both a comprehensive understanding of security as well as viable IDP and refugee livelihood strategies.

KNOWLEDGE GAPS

As has already been mentioned in this chapter, a number of gaps in current GBV and fuel provision programming strategies have been identified over the last fifteen years: the specific literature on fuel provision focusing on environmental impact and not on security, the poorly understood causes of and vulnerabilities to GBV, the unsustainable and costly nature of fuel provision programming, and the lack of coordination in providing fuel alternatives. A contributing factor to programming gaps may be often-conflicting priorities in assessing programming impact such as the choice of using quantitative or qualitative measures.

As Beth Vann pointed out in Gender-Based Violence: Emerging Issues in Programs Serving Displaced Populations, when data on GBV is scarce or inaccurate, it can be difficult to arrive at a complete assessment of a particular security threat. In the instance cited by Vann from Tanzania, the data available on rape incidents indicated that the primary threat to women in this particular case did not necessarily come from gathering firewood as had been thought; rather it came from within the camp itself. Vann recommended that GBV coordinators use information on the location of GBV incidents to develop better monitoring and evaluation techniques for the purposes of assessing GBV prevention and response programming.

Although this report has focused primarily on GBV threats outside of camp perimeters, part of what Vann implies in this criticism of data is that the link between GBV and firewood does not exist entirely outside the camps. Shifting responsibilities within camp settings and high levels of anxiety may raise the risk of refugee or IDP perpetrated GBV. In particularly dangerous instances, UNHCR has provided firewood directly to refugee families as a short-term intervention. This has been done in order to address serious security threats to women but as has been noted before, this solution is far from sustainable. The costs incurred by this kind of provision are very expensive and do not necessarily address the larger issue nor do they contribute to broad-based prevention strategies.

Given the cost involved, Patricia Weiss Fagen noted that the sustainability gap might be addressed through more community-based initiatives, such as having men accompany women as they gather firewood. This strategy may have been successful in some instances, but as in the case mentioned before in Darfur, men face the threat of being killed if they venture out of a protected environment. In this case the risk of GBV is considered to be lesser than that of death. On the subject of fuel-efficiency, Fagen cautions that some alternative fuels and technologies require extensive training which can require more dedicated staff, translating into higher programming costs. In a recent article on new solar cookers tested in the Dadaab camps in Kenya, UNHCR was optimistic about their effectiveness.

The new prototype took less time to assemble than previous versions. According to the article, integrating the cookers into daily life requires considerable effort on the part of staff and can be quite costly to initiate. The measured success of these cookers in Kenya is mostly linked in part to the persistent severe shortage of firewood and the continued threat of GBV. Working to integrate new technology would be less effective if firewood were abundant in the area surrounding the camps. As the preceding case studies and background literature illustrate, steps have been taken by a variety of actors to address the link between GBV and fuel provision. The two case studies used in this desk review are perhaps the two most well-documented instances of the link between fuel provision and GBV.

Unfortunately, they also serve to illustrate the complexity of this relationship and the considerable challenges in the way of effective protection of women and prevention of GBV. It was over ten years ago that the direct link between firewood and rape was extensively documented, and yet it persists today as a serious security issue not only in more recent humanitarian crises, but also among the very same refugee and IDP populations in which it first emerged. Women's physical and psychological well-being continues to be compromised as they seek to sustain themselves and those in their care even as they are uprooted from their homes. The protracted security threat faced by women and girls in the Dadaab camps threatens to be echoed among displaced populations in both Darfur and Chad, but most particularly in the IDP camps in Darfur.

The mud stove initiative undertaken by Oxfam and Relief International, combined with the push toward greater inter-agency coordination may help to control how persistent a security risk fuel provision remains. It was as recent as February 2005 that the Inter-Agency Evaluation of the Humanitarian Response to the Darfur Crisis suggested fuel-efficient stoves as a prevention measure. The Oxfam/ Relief International programme began that same month. In March 2005, the United Kingdom's House of Commons published a report titled Darfur, Sudan: The Responsibility to Protect in which it outlined concerns about gaps in humanitarian coordination, specifically with regard to IDP camp management.

This observation was in contrast with the confidence held in UNHCR's coordination of the refugee camps in Chad. The concerns articulated about the IDP camps were in relation to threats of violence faced by IDPs once they reached the camps, and specifically the threat of rape and GBV of women and girls. This report highlighted again the risk evaluation undertaken by displaced persons in choosing between the greater threat - rape or death. According to this report, police patrols along firewood routes had been effective in at least one camp (Al Sherif). Broadly speaking, innovation in fuel technologies and strategies to manage fuel usage seem to have been studied primarily for their potential environmental sustainability.

The criticism of firewood collection programmes has focused on their apparent one- dimensional prescription for a specific type of GBV, such as rape. This was the case with the criticism leveled at the firewood collection program in the Dadaab camps. The idea of integrating local community knowledge and resources with expertise provided by international actors is not new. Local capacity building initiatives were suggested in Burundi as a way of integrating fuel-efficiency and security. Other suggestions combining women's skill and knowledge capacity have included the use of teaching new cooking techniques, such as using lids on pots, using metal pots, and extinguishing fires after use.

The more recent research relating to IDPs in Darfur and refugees in Chad seems to indicate that international actors, as well as community groups, are seeking to develop more robust approaches to GBV prevention and response. Strategies not covered in the examples listed by the IASC include firewood conservation protocols, policing strategies, and using confidence building and rule of law training as a strategy for responding to GBV. In 1998 two Refugees International researchers advocated for the development of firewood conservation protocols which would set standards for how firewood would be used in IDP or refugee camps. The implementation of these protocols was not elaborated, but the implication was that the protocols would be put into practice in the earliest stages of a humanitarian response.

The protocols would include prevention measures such as conservation-oriented cooking techniques not unlike some of the techniques listed above. In Darfur, the African Union has been engaged in patrolling frequently used firewood collection routes. If there is a sufficient security force presence, an expanded policing strategy might provide a deterrent to would-be attackers as women collect firewood for camp use or transport firewood to market. In Darfur, the United Nations Development Program (UNDP) and the International Rescue

Committee have been engaged in a human rights and rule of law programme initiative since September 2004. One of the stated objectives of this programme is to build confidence between the IDP community and local authorities.

To achieve these objectives, the programme aims at educating potential victims, survivors and perpetrators of human rights violations on basic human rights principles. Members of the police force, legal community, unions (students and women), university professors and teachers, and business owners, all participated in the programme. Through building trust between these groups, UNDP and IRC hoped to increase IDP security as well as work to prevent further instances of GBV through prevention measures. According to the interim report: One of the main purposes of this training is to address the immediate threats to displaced women and to promote access to justice and accountability, particularly with respect to SGBV. To serve this purpose, the training makes specific provision for the inclusion of female law-enforcement and judiciary officials.

While a worthy end in itself, building the capacity of educated Sudanese women working in Rule of Law institutions may also serve to defend and protect female IDPs and returnees. The RHRC report from 2002 and the Feinstein/ Ahfad study completed in February 2005 both suggest using national-level strategies to confront the link between GBV and fuel provision. The majority of the programming initiatives highlighted throughout this report focus on coordination between international actors and the displaced community. As suggested by the Feinstein/Ahfad study, there may be an opportunity in Darfur in particular to use national level mechanisms such as the Forestry Department of the Ministry of Agriculture to coordinate more sustainable, long-term institutionalized response to the problem of firewood scarcity.

This kind of collaboration may foster trust, as emphasized in the UNDP/IRC programme, between governmental authority and displaced communities. As demonstrated by the UNDP/IRC programme and the Feinstein/Ahfad study, the potential of harnessing local research capacity, community organizations like the Sudan Women's Union, and international expertise may prevent a long-term GBV crisis. UNIFEM is uniquely positioned to lend this kind of leadership of development expertise on the ground. Using its relationships with local and national women's organizations, both within the public sector and among NGOs, and its position among international actors, UNIFEM has a comparative advantage in working at the intersection of multi- sectoral and multi-lateral coordination.

Through both UNIFEM's comprehensive understanding of how women are impacted by conflict, especially with regard to GBV, and connections already established with women's organization s through the North- South dialogues in Sudan, finding dynamic solutions to GBV prevention and response in Darfur is possible. Capacity building potential coupled with the research conducted on fuel alternatives could be implemented in other areas, and not exclusively in the context of Darfur.

This concept is not without precedent. UNIFEM's support of the African Women in Crisis programme (AFWIC) was catalytic not only in supporting the needs of Burundian refugees in Tanzania, but also in ensuring that women's voices were included in the peace process. Using the lessons learned from years of GBV and fuel-efficiency programming in Kenya, as well as innovative techniques such as those undertaken by Oxfam and Relief International in Darfur implies that durable solutions to the threat of GBV are possible in the near-future.

7

Globalizing the Sexual Exploitation of Women

Globalization involves widespread political and economic restructuring among many countries and regions around the world. It involves large shifts in wealth, employment, and populations in a complex set of processes that frees corporate power from local and even national regulation and control. Supranational corporations and international banking institutions that are richer and larger than most countries, and organized crime syndicates that are richer than some countries, are no longer accountable to any national government. In fact, the largest most powerful governments support and foster the globalization of corporate power.

In this milieu, women and children are increasingly becoming commodities to be bought, sold and consumed by tourists, military personnel, organized crime rings, traffickers, pimps, and men seeking sexual entertainment or non-threatening marriage partners. Around the world today, women and children are increasingly vulnerable to sexual exploitation when they are refugees or migrants, and when they are suffering from the effects of poverty, racism, and caste systems. Women and children are compelled into sex industries by varying degrees of violence, ranging from prior victimization and lack of economic alternatives, to deception, debt bondage, and enslavement. The trafficking of women and girls has reached crisis proportions around the world, and is a human rights disaster. Accompanying and facilitating globalization is a revolution in communication and information technologies. The computer based telecommunications system known as the Internet can send text, images, audio and video files around the world in seconds. Significantly, the cost of access to this global communications network is within the financial reach of most people in wealthier nations. Within the last five years this network with its worldwide audience has been undergoing commercialization. Some of the commodities being bought and sold are women and children.

Technology has given the sex industry new means of exploiting, marketing and delivering women and children, as commodities, to male buyers. A general principle to remember is: When a new technology is introduced into a system of exploitation it enables those with power to intensify the harm and expand the exploitation. This characterizes what is happening as predators and pimps move to the Internet to stalk and market girls and women.

The growth and expansion of the Internet industry is closely intertwined with the sex industry. In the early years of the industrialization of the sex industry, the sex industry followed new technological innovations, later it assisted the public adoption of new technology, but recently, the success of commercial technology, such as the Internet, is dependent on the sex industry.

Through financial and technological interdependence, the sex industry and the Internet industry have become partners in the globalization of sexual exploitation. In 2000, there were an estimated 280,000 sex industry sites on the Internet. Last year, the online "adult entertainment industry" as the sexual exploitation industry is called, made US$1.7 billion dollars, with several Web sites making over US$150 million each.

The Internet is used in multiple ways to promote and engage in the sexual exploitation and trafficking of women. Pimps use the Internet to advertise prostitution tours to men from industrialized countries. The men then travel to poorer countries to meet and buy girls and women in prostitution.

Traffickers recruiting women from the Baltic States use the Web to post advertisements for unlikely jobs in Western Europe, such as waitress or nanny. Information on where and how to find girls and women in prostitution in cities all over the world is posted on commercial Web sites and non-commercial newsgroups.

New technologies and high speed transmission on the Internet enables live video chat, which is used to transmit strip shows, live sex shows, and live Web cams (continuous transmission of live images). These new technologies enhance the capacity of pimps and buyers to sexually exploit women in several ways. The ability of men to buy private interactive sex shows so that they can masturbate in the privacy of their homes or offices, creates a form of online prostitution. Fast transnational transmission of live shows enables traffickers and pimps to exploit women and girls in their home countries where law and/or law enforcement is weak. Women and girls do not have to be trafficked across national borders to provide sexual gratification to buyers and money for pimps.

In 1999, an American man living in Phnom Penh, Cambodia set up a pay-per-view Web site. The content was to be the rape and torture of Asian women for the sexual pleasure of Western men. More recently, live sex shows are being made in Latvia for the consumption of men elsewhere. The women sign contracts in which they are required to work 10 hours per day, six days a week. The women are required to live in a house with three to five live broadcasting cameras in each room, including bathroom, and doing approximately 5 hours per day of "private shows" for online viewers.

The women may not terminate their contracts before the end date, although the "producer" can terminate it at any time. If the women do not perform to the satisfaction of the "producer" they have to pay him damages. They must follow all posted rules or be fined. The "producer" has full rights to all images or videos that are made of them women to use them in the future in any way he chooses. Although a contract gives the appearance of legality, this is a highly exploitative situation in which the "producer" has power and control over the women. It is a typical pimp or brothel set up in which women have little control and are likely to face many "fines" which result in less money.

Trafficking and sexual exploitation of women and children through the Internet offer grave challenges to society, from law makers, to law enforcement, to NGOs. The policy decision that hinders actions to combat sexual exploitation on the Internet is that Western countries that benefit commercially from the Internet industry -the same ones that benefit from corporate globalization -have made the economic growth and development of the Internet a priority. Their laws, policies, and proposed international agreements do nothing to impede e-commerce and it's partnership with the sex industry.

TECHNOLOGY, GLOBALIZATION AND SYSTEMS OF EXPLOITATION

When those with power introduce a new technology into a system of oppression and exploitation, it enables the powerful to intensify the harm and expand the exploitation. This characterizes what is happening as predators and pimps, who stalk, buy and exploit women and children, have moved to Internet sites and forums for advertising, documenting and engaging in sexual exploitation. Sexual abuse and exploitation are indigenous to all patriarchal cultures, institutions and nations, but the recent, rapid economic and political restructuring in many regions of the world has escalated the trafficking of women and children. There are approximately 200 million people around the world are forced to live as sexual or economic slaves.

The widespread political and economic restructuring, referred to as globalization, involves large shifts in wealth, employment and populations in a complex set of processes that is freeing those with power from local and even national regulation and control. Supranational corporations and international banking institutions that are richer and larger than most countries, and organized crime syndicates that are richer and larger than some countries, are setting the pace and are no longer accountable to any national government. In this milieu, women and children are increasingly becoming commodities to be bought, sold and consumed by tourists, military personnel, organized crime rings, traffickers, pimps, and men seeking sexual entertainment or non-threatening marriage partners.

The global sexual exploitation of women and children that is accompanying globalization is a human rights disaster. Pino Arlacckі, who heads United Nations efforts to fight organized crime said, "Slavery is one of the most undesirable consequences of globalization." He added, "We regret this is not considered as a priority by any country at the moment." Accompanying and facilitating globalization is a revolution in communications and technology. The computer based telecommunications system known as the Internet can send text, images, audio and video files around the world in milliseconds.

Significantly, the cost of access to this global communications network is within the financial reach of most people in wealthier nations. Within the last five years this network with its worldwide audience has been undergoing commercialization. Some of the commodities are women and children. The Internet has accelerated and deepened the marketing of women for the purposes of sexual exploitation. Forums on the Internet have become meeting grounds for pimps selling women, predators buying women or stalking victims. Web sites and newsgroups have become show rooms and bragging spaces for every type of violence perpetrated against women and children.

Like other powerful constituents of globalization, the Internet is almost without any regulation. Its international reach and new technologies have made local and national laws and standards either obsolete or unenforceable. Nicholas Negroponte, Director of the Media Laboratory at the Massachusetts Institute of Technology, and founder of Wired magazine said, "As we interconnect ourselves, many of the values of a nation-state will give way to those of both larger and smaller electronic communities."

With Internet technology and communications pimps and predators can access global markets and unsuspecting victims. Pimps can locate their computer servers in countries with the most libertarian laws and operate outside the reach of regulations in all other countries. The Internet allows pimps and predators to create their own culture outside community standards or interference. The technology of computer based communication also provides a high degree of privacy and anonymity for men to engage is stalking, viewing and buying of women and children in acts of sexual exploitation.

THE REPORT ON PIMPS AND PREDATORS ON THE INTERNET

This report will examine how men are using the Internet to engage in and promote the global sexual exploitation of women and children. As a non-commercial communication medium the Internet is used by predators and amateur pimps to exchange information on where to go buy women and girls in prostitution, exchange pornographic images and videos, and even, broadcast in real time the sexual abuse of children. Predators use the Internet to contact victims and display their abuse of women and children. Pimps are using the Internet as a commercial venue to advertise and sell several types of sexual exploitation of women and children.

Commercial prostitution tours are advertised and arranged. Mail-order-brides are displayed and contact information sold to men seeking wives or sexual partners, followed by "romance tours" to meet women. Advertisements and sites for pornographic images and videos, strip shows and live sex shows saturate the web. This report also documents police efforts to stop predators from using the Internet to engage in the sexual abuse and exploitation of children. A number of specialized units have been set up to catch predators of children. In several cases there has been unparalleled international cooperation among police units to break-up international child pornography and abuse rings.

The Internet has received so much bad publicity for the amount of illegal and offensive materials that can be obtained that the Internet industry has responded with efforts at self-regulation. Several of these self-regulatory programs, their goals and results are reviewed in this report. Frustrated by the lack will or ability of the Internet industry and the police to stop predator's use of the Internet for the purposes of sexual abuse, especially child sexual abuse, vigilante groups have formed to impose their own form of ethics and standards on the Internet. A few of these groups and their activities are described. Finally, the connection between the sex industry and the Internet industry is examined. The symbiotic relationship between the two enables us to see that the commodification and exploitation of women and children is an integral part of globalization.

SEXUAL EXPLOITATION

A practice by which a person achieves sexual gratification, financial gain or advancement through the abuse or exploitation of a person's sexuality by abrogating that person's human right to dignity, equality, autonomy, and physical and mental well-being; i.e. trafficking, prostitution, prostitution tourism, mail-order-bride trade, pornography, stripping, battering, incest, rape and sexual harassment. Sexual exploitation preys on women and children made vulnerable by poverty and economic development policies and practices; refugee and displaced persons; and on women in the migrating process. Sexual exploitation eroticizes women's inequality and is a vehicle for racism and "first world" domination, disproportionately victimizing minority and "third world" women. Sexual exploitation violates the human rights of anyone subjected to it, whether female or male, adult or child, Northern or Southern.

NEGATIVE IMPACT OF GLOBALIZATION

Migration, trafficking and customary practices (marriage, etc.) are the institutionalized channels of exploitation of women since centuries. Globalization has accelerated the pace and chances of institutionalized exploitation of women due to free movements of and electronic transactions by transnational crime syndicates. Migration Related with the flesh trade and labour force, trafficking and migration of women are the two important factors that seem to be negatively affecting the status of women causing institutionalized exploitation.

A recent study on migration of women speaks of institutionalized exploitation of women in the name of migration. It says: "There is clear evidence of abuse and exploitation in all parts of the global migration system, not surprisingly these tend to be found where women are most vulnerable and are in illegal and low paying jobs. Women are often overworked and live in unhealthy environments with low rates of pay and few benefits."

Despite such abuse, very large numbers of women mostly from the Philippines, Thailand and other Asian countries opt to migrate to join labour markets in the Middle East, Europe and other developed regions as they feel that they could improve their livelihoods options and living condition and could better support their families back home. The study also finds that while migration could indeed thrust women into exploitation overseas, it could also remove them from servile and abusive conditions at home.

If we look at this situation, we find that both at home and overseas these women are being exploited. Their exploitation both at home and abroad is of different nature but institutionalized. They are supposed to be abused physically, mentally and sometime sexually while they are at home in a small and closed circle and after being migrated, they are vulnerable in another sense where they are open to a range of different people including their foreign masters, their colleagues and customers.

After being migrated to labour market or trafficked to flesh trade or home based work, women look like the exploited prisoners who are shifted from a mini prison to a large prison. On the fear of being exploited, we could not limit the migration option. It should be an open option for the people, especially the women but certain security mechanism should be provided to them so that they could protect them against any exploitation. Globalization is being defined differently and has been one of the most used and abused terminologies of the 1990s.

It speaks of transition towards a global community with common norms and an institutional framework that facilitates international cooperation. Globalization is a free flow of capital, technology, information and people. But free flow of the people is neither as fast nor easy as goods and capital do. Barriers are being erected to the free movement of labour at a time when the world labour market is expanding and creating more demand for labour. In this background, we should not limit or discourage migration as migration could increase the range of options open for women and could prove to be a powerful force for their empowerment.

What we really need is to provide women a protective mechanism that could save them from negative impacts of globalization and provide them space to benefit from it. Though migration of women, both legal and illegal, is rampant across Asia and Pacific and women from the poor Asian countries migrate to Australia and the developed countries of Asia on the count of labour market and marriage or accompanying their families, such a large number of migration of women is not reported from countries such as Pakistan and other South Asian countries.

Mostly the women from South Asian countries are trafficked and we could find only a few migrant women workers in the labour market in the developed countries, particularly in the Middle East. Migration is a legal right of the people on various counts, though it is not all negative but the way it is being dealt with turns this otherwise humanly activity as a punitive trend. Thus, it causes institutionalized exploitation of women migrant workers as a negative impact of globalization against the real spirit of globalization that allows free movement of the people across regions. There are sad stories attached to migrations as well.

On June 14, 2001, New York based Human Rights Watch released a report on the plight of Migrant Domestic Workers who Face Abuse in the U.S. The special visas granted to foreigners who work as household domestics in the U.S. leave them vulnerable to serious abuse, Human Rights Watch charged in the report. Thousands of these migrant workers, typically women, enter the United States every year to work for diplomats, officials of international organizations, foreign business people and the U.S. citizens temporarily. In the 56-page report, Human Rights Watch documents the cases of dozens of workers, but believes that many more are exposed to some form of abuse.

"Often these employers come from a powerful, elite class, and they are abusing the rights of some of the most powerless," said Carol Pier, researcher for the U.S. Program of Human Rights Watch and author of the report. "This is a serious human rights abuse in the United States, but it has remained largely hidden from public view. This has to stop." The most effective recourse for workers in abusive employment relationships is to change jobs. But under U.S. law, these workers' visas are tied to their employers and in most cases they cannot legally change employers. If they leave, they lose immigration status and can be deported.

In about ten percent of the cases that Human Rights Watch reviewed, workers were the victims of trafficking. Employers lured the workers to the United States with false promises about their employment conditions and then held them in servitude. These women worked long hours, up to 19 per day, and were often paid less than $100 per month. They were rarely allowed outside and were prohibited from speaking to strangers. Some were physically or sexually abused. In the cases Human Rights Watch reviewed, the average hourly wage was $2.14, from which deductions for room and board might, according to U.S. law, still be made. The average workday was fourteen hours.

Most of the workers were not allowed to leave their employers' homes without permission, and most were only allowed to leave on their one day off per week- Sunday. The report sharply criticizes the structure of the special visa programs that allow these workers to enter the U.S. No government department or agency monitors the migrant domestic worker visa programs. No laws establish specific employment conditions that must be provided to these workers. Unless these workers publicly complain about employer's abuse, the U.S. government ignores them. Human Rights Watch called on the U.S. government to establish an effective monitoring mechanism for the visa programs, under the Department of Labor, and urged Congress to amend immigration law to include mandatory employment conditions for these workers and to allow them to transfer employers when their rights are violated.

All workers seeking justice against their employers should be allowed to stay in the U.S. to do so and to work during that time. Similar situations prevails in most of the Middle East and Gulf countries where migrant workers are not allowed to change employers, 'kafils' in case their rights are violated. Hence, this sort of exploitation of workers is institutionalized. Trafficking With this realization that trafficking in persons has been fast emerging as the third largest illegal trade after guns and drugs, the world seems perturbed over this growing menace. Several studies on trafficking in women and children in South Asia have been conducted.

The U.S. Department of State has, for the first time, come up with a global report on trafficking. The first Trafficking In Persons (TIP) Report 2001 is based on a worldwide survey on the state of trafficking. According to the TIP Report, as many as 700,000 persons are sold into labour each year against their will. They are forced to toil in sweatshops (mostly in the United States), construction sites, brothels and fields. There is a global concern that human trafficking with an annual turnover of US$7-13 billion at the cost of human souls is fast emerging as the third largest trade around the world after drugs and weapons. Though there is no consensus on definition of human trafficking, coercion is considered to be the key element behind trafficking in human beings.

CAUSES OF RISE IN TRAFFICKING OF WOMEN

The reasons for the increase in trafficking are many. The globalization of the world economy has relatively increased the movement of people across borders, legally and illegally, especially from poorer to wealthier countries. International organized crime syndicates have been taking advantage of the movement of the people and undertaking electronic transaction of money for such trade. The subordination of women continues in many societies, as reflected in economic, educational, and work opportunity disparities between men and women. Many societies still favour sons and view girls as an economic burden.

Desperate families in some of the most impoverished countries sell their daughters to brothels or traffickers for the immediate payoff and to avoid having to pay the dowry to marry off daughters. Lack of opportunity and eagerness for a better life abroad made many women and girls vulnerable to entrapment by traffickers. With the weakening of law enforcement in post- Communist societies, criminal organizations have grown and established themselves in the lucrative business of international trafficking. The growing demand, worldwide, for trafficked women and children for sex tourism, cheap sweatshop labour, and domestic work is also one of the reasons for rise in the trafficking. Traffickers are encouraged by large tax-free profits and continuing income from the same victims at very low risk. In effective and inadequate laws and law enforcement mechanisms are also a reason for growth of trafficking as an institutionalized activity based on exploitation of women. Prostitution is legal or tolerated in many countries, and widespread in most of the countries.

TRAFFICKING OF WOMEN: PAKISTAN

Trafficking of women, to which prostitution is directly related, is considered a social crime and is not tolerated by South Asian society. Major routes are known to exist between Pakistan, Nepal, Bangladesh, Sri Lanka and different parts of India, from where women are transported to Bombay.

Trafficking also takes place to the Gulf States from Sri Lanka, Pakistan and the Maldives, and Nepalese girls might also find their way to Hong Kong, Thailand, the United States of America, Australia and Europe.

There have been one million Bangladeshi and more than 200,000 Burmese women trafficked to Karachi, Pakistan. Majority of these women have been trafficked for the slave trade and prostitution. Some of these women were sold for marriage purposes. In Pakistan, where most of the trafficked Bengali women are sold, there are over 200,000 undocumented Bangladeshi women in Pakistan, including some 2,000 in jails and shelters. Bangladeshis comprise 80 percent, and Burmese 14 percent, of Karachi's undocumented immigrants. A Bengali or Burmese woman could be sold in Pakistan for US$1,500 - 2,500 - depending on age, looks, docility and virginity.

For each child or woman sold, the police claim a 15 to 20 percent commission." Women kidnapped at the Pakistan-Afghanistan border are being sold in the marketplace for Rs 600 per kilogram as of 1991. Auctions of girls are arranged for three kinds of buyers: rich visiting Arabs (sheiks, businessmen, visitors, state-financed medical and university students), the rich local gentry, and rural farmers. As many as 160,000 Nepalese women are in Indian brothels. Orphaned girls are sold as 'wives' to men who may resell them.

INSTITUTIONALIZED TECHNIQUES OF TRAFFICKING

Traffickers acquire their victims in a number of ways. Sometimes women are kidnapped outright in one country and taken forcibly to another. In other cases, victims are lured with job offers. Traffickers entice victims to migrate voluntarily with false promises of good paying jobs in foreign countries as models, dancers and domestic workers. Traffickers advertise these phony jobs, as well as marriage opportunities abroad in local newspapers.

Bangladeshi and Burmese women are being kidnapped, married off to agents by unsuspecting parents, trafficked under false pretenses, or enticed by prospects of a better life, into sex industry in Pakistan. Border police and other law enforcement agencies are well aware of the trafficking through entry points into Pakistan like Lahore, Kasur, Bahawalpur, Chhor and Badin. Nepalese and Bangladeshi woman and girls are trafficked under false pretenses, such as jobs, and then they are forced into prostitution in brothels in Pakistan.

A rise in trafficking of girls, aged 8-15, in Pakistan has occurred during this last decade. The human traffickers target mostly young women and children because they are vulnerable and most wanted for sex industry, forced or false marriage and adoptions. The global crime syndicates "catch their prey" from Russia and the other former Soviet republics, large parts of Asia and Central and South America.

Victims who in a bid to escape poverty in their home countries are lured fraudulently for a job in another comparatively prosper country. The victims are not directly recruited for flesh trade but are offered jobs like child-care, housekeeping or restaurant work. When they arrive in strange lands, they are forced into prostitution in deplorable conditions to pay off a phony smuggling debt of thousands of dollars. The traffickers snatch the victims' travel documents to deprive them of their identity or force them to remain in their dens and brothels. However, the trafficked women and girls are recycled and turned over from one brothel to another. Many of them return home only after contracting diseases such as HIV/AIDS. This is a heinous crime against humanity and an institutionalized exploitation of women that is growing with the trends of globalization.

TEMPORARY MARRIAGE

Arabs stationed for a short time in Pakistan take "temporary wives," abandoning the women and any children afterwards. A farcical *nikah* (registered marriage) takes place and the buyer actually marries the purchased woman, thus legalizing her enslavement. The husband then either sells her to someone else and makes a tidy profit for himself or keeps her in a brothel so that she may become a permanent source of income.

Alternatively, he may make her a labourer in the fields and the house. Trafficking of women to the Middle East from Pakistan is reportedly continuing in the garb of the so-called "temporary marriages" as the traffickers got a three-month 'wife visa'. During these three months, these trafficked women have to work day and night as sex workers and they have to artificially forego their menstrual cycle by taking drugs that damage them physically and emotionally. They have no option but to fight with the nature to pay off debts they owed for their families.

EXPLOITATION OF TRAFFICKED WOMEN IN AN INSTITUTIONALIZED MANNER

The police and the legal system further victimize trafficked women, which treat them as criminals. The women are booked under Pakistan's controversial 'Hudood Ordinances.' The Zina Ordinance, which comes under the Islamic Hudood Ordinance, makes adultery or sex outside marriage a crime against the state. Women and girls in prostitution are often charged with Zina ordinance. Sometimes, they are booked under the Passport Act. Either way, they have to spend long time in prison. For illegal immigration, the sentence is four years, but many women end up serving three or four years extra, either waiting for trial or to clear immigration formalities.

Occasionally, token police raids are made in which only the women and children are arrested and the real criminals of the trade, the pimps, go free. The arrested women and children are the ones usually harassed and victimized by the police. When authorities do crack down, it is against prostitutes and not the customers. Once imprisoned, most women are either charged under the Foreigners Act prohibiting illegal entry and/or incorrectly charged under the Zina section of the Hudood Ordinance, which specifically prohibits extra-marital sexual intercourse.

While the lawyers do not have access to the victims in jails, the pimps, with the aid of jail authorities, manage to see them regularly, harassing and directing threats at them. Confined in deplorable jail conditions where they are frequently abused and with no access to any other source of help, the women submit to the pimps' offers to get them released. Under duress and in sheer desperation, the women agree to the conditions of the pimps. Once released, they are forced to comply with the conditions, since it appears to be their only hope in the face of involvement of the law enforcement authorities on the one hand and the pimps' threats to revoke the bail on the other.

They are trapped. Furthermore, shame, fear and poverty force them to remain entrapped in the web of this trade, preventing them from returning to their country. The priority placed on stemming illegal immigration in many countries, including the United States, has resulted in the treatment of trafficking cases as a problem of illegal immigration, thus treating victims as criminals. When police raid brothels, women are often detained and punished, subjected to human rights abuses in jail, and swiftly deported. Few steps have been taken to provide support, health care, and access to justice. Few victims dare testify against the traffickers or those who hold them, fearing retribution for themselves and their families since most governments do not offer stays of deportation or adequate protection for witnesses.

The governments of Pakistan over the last three decades have established, three commissions of inquiry into the sexual exploitation of women. However, the successive governments did not implement in total the recommendations by these commissions and hence the trafficking has been the highly institutionalized exploitation of women in the country.

Recommendations There are two sets of recommendations. They are trafficking specific and migration and general on the well-being and empowerment of women so that they could protect them against any sort of institutionalized exploitation.

Since their exploitation is institutionalized, the remedy for their protection from exploitation also lies in the institutionalized protective mechanism as described in the following sets of recommendations.

Trafficking specific There is a dire need that the governments of sending, receiving and transit countries in conjunction with national, regional and international NGOs must wage a sincere and responsible campaign against agents involved in trafficking in connivance with certain border security guards and other law enforcement authorities. These governments must train and position law enforcement authorities to be ready to prosecute the trafficking agents under criminal and civil laws.

Trafficked women and children must be recognized as victims of trafficking and not as criminals. The victims of trafficking must be considered witnesses to the crime of trafficking. The rights of woman and child victims must be protected and the criminal agents must be prosecuted under existing domestic and international laws prohibiting trafficking. If and when victims testify against the agents, they must be afforded protection and their right to privacy must be upheld. The repatriation costs of victims of trafficking that wish to return to their country of nationality must be shared by the sending and receiving countries.

The Government of Pakistan must provide temporary, if not permanent, amnesty to those victims unwilling to be repatriated, with the option of permanently legalizing their status in Pakistan. Trafficked women must be protected as migrant workers under relevant ILO conventions. Governments and NGOs of sending, receiving and transit countries must institute an education campaign to minimize the social stigmatization of victims of trafficking. NGOs of these countries must be prepared and well positioned to provide training, job placement and financial assistance to rehabilitate survivors of trafficking to prevent further exploitation and to facilitate their self-determination.

GENERAL WELL-BEING AND EMPOWERMENT OF WOMEN

There is a need to affirm the principles of national sovereignty, strong democracy, social justice, sustainable development, and gender equality. Political governance must be guided and propelled by a critical and dynamic citizenship. Collective voices and views of the women should be transformed into a growing force that takes into account the intersecting gender and class issues at the macro and micro levels.

The process of globalization has pushed and legitimized reckless conversions of agricultural productive lands into industrial zones and business subdivisions. This has gravely threatened our food security and livelihood, which for women is the means by which they sustain their families and communities. Stop immediately the conversion of prime agricultural lands into commercial industrial sites. Support food production by putting in place the mechanism of price subsidy for basic food crops, such as wheat, corn, rice, etc. Provide credit facility with low interest rates to farmers, especially women who are engaged in domestic food production. The right to work must be assured.

The pursuit of neo-liberalization policies has resulted in the loss of jobs, casualization and contractualization, and the fall in workers' wages. Gender bias and unequal opportunities serve to make women more vulnerable in this context. Work conditions continue to ignore women's specific needs, thus, undermining their right to work. There is a need to formulate clear guidelines on contractualization to prevent abuses and unfair practices against labour, particularly the women workforce.

The social wage or non-wage benefits of workers such as social security, hospitalization and pension plans need to be taken care of. Ensure that the minimum labour standards and working conditions required by law are likewise implemented in special industrial zones where the overwhelming majority of the workers are women. Implement laws and codes to end Sexual Harassment at workplace to formulate and create mechanisms for monitoring sexual harassment in the workplace. As well, provide stricter sanctions for the non-compliance to the provisions of the law. Basic needs are basic rights. People have the right to shelter, education and health. However, the ideology of the market forces has eroded these rights. Government responsibility to provide for these services has given way to privatization and deregulation to the detriment of the welfare of women, children and men.

There is a need to launch such a pro-poor programme that must consider adequate and inexpensive housing, accessible employment for both women and men, infrastructures such as schools, health centers and roads, and public utilities like electricity and water. The government policy of exporting labor is recognized as the one single factor that has kept the economy afloat. This dependency of the economy on the demands of the global market cannot be sustained, however. There is a need to turn around this policy that has burdened the entire nation with a huge social cost and institutionalized exploitation and abuse. What we need are real jobs at home. Ensure the quick and sensitive response to the needs of women workers in distress whether on site or upon return.

Ensure the dissemination of community-based information on the many issues surrounding work and migration. Review and strengthen the existing programs and services for returning migrant workers and give special attention to "unsuccessful returnees" and those suffering from psychosocial trauma. Implement a policy that will affirm government responsibility over the plight of migrant workers by strictly regulating overseas employment and giving more attention to monitoring of recruitment agencies. For women and men to live full satisfying and self-determined lives is the vision and goal and society.

However, gender inequality and the sexual division of labour, in particular, have imprisoned both sexes into traditional masculine and feminine roles. This has constrained the exercise of reproductive and sexual rights, especially for women. This impacts on women's participation in the public sphere since central to the issue is the ability of women to make decisions related to their own fertility, sexuality and reproduction.

Reproductive and sexual self-determination, economic autonomy and political decision- making make up the triangle of women's political participation. The potential and ability of women to engage in the political arena will never be realized unless the space in each of the three areas is opened to women's decision-making. There is a need to appoint more women to top-level positions in monetary and fiscal institutions and agencies that determine the economic directions of the country. Adopt and implement a policy that will redress the marked discrepancy in the number of women and men occupying top-level positions in government. Neither gender should occupy lower than 40% or higher than 60% of these positions. Only through these institutionalized protective mechanisms, we could address the institutionalized exploitation of women in a nicer manner.

TRAFFICKING OF WOMEN FOR SEXUAL EXPLOITATION

"The trafficking of persons, particularly women and children, for forced and exploitative labor, including sexual exploitation, is one of the most egregious violations of human rights which the United Nations now confronts." So stated the United Nations Secretary- General Kofi Annan at a recent international conference on transnational crime. Experts disagree on the full scope of the problem, as figures are difficult to ascertain due to the illicit nature of the exploitation. However, it is generally accepted by the International Organization for Migration, agencies of the United Nations and other relevant organizations attempting to tackle the problem that trafficking in human beings is a rapidly expanding, and incredibly profitable, violation of human rights.

Human trafficking is the third most lucrative activity of organized crime groups worldwide, following the trafficking of arms and drugs. Trafficking for the purposes of sexual exploitation is also the least punished of the three above mentioned forms of trafficking; when human traffickers are made to serve time, which is rare, their sentences have been much lighter than those served by drug and arms traffickers. Although human trafficking has been the focus of world attention since the first international counter-trafficking treaty was signed in 1904, attention in the international arena has increased dramatically since the 1990s.

Regardless of the international commitments to diminishing trafficking in humans, studies show that the phenomenon is increasing as the disparity between wealth and poverty grows between and within countries. As poverty disproportionately affects women and their children, it is not surprising that, following trends in migration, women would be pushed to migrate in the hopes of acquiring economic security for themselves and their families. Although the push and pull factors of migration are similar for men and women, their migration experience can differ greatly. For millions of women this economic migration ends in sexual exploitation and debt bondage, with no international legal framework in place to address their protection needs. Although the majority of trafficked women could be safely repatriated, a number of trafficking survivors suffer a well-founded fear of persecution at the hands of their traffickers upon return to their country of origin.

Legislation to meet the protection needs of trafficked people is sparse and inconsistently implemented. The international refugee regime now in place could serve as a back-up protection mechanism for this particular social group, but at present trafficked women are rarely recognized as refugees. At a time when international organizations are stressing the importance of addressing the protection and human rights needs of trafficked women, European governments are striving to harmonize their migration and asylum laws. It is presently an opportune period for the European Union to consider an interpretation of asylum laws that respects the protection and human rights needs of women trafficked into prostitution against their will, which could also work in the favor of European governments by decreasing organized crime activity within their borders.

This chapter will examine the root causes of migration, and how migration and poverty are rapidly becoming feminized. It will consider how the uprooting caused by rural to urban migration can lead to international migration, and the vulnerability this can create in female migrants taking advantage of pre-existing migrant networks. It will analyze how the poverty of CIS/CEE countries following capitalist transition has contributed to the structural nature of trafficking. It will discuss recruitment of women for trafficking purposes, methods of trafficking, work conditions, and manners of exit. This chapter will further discuss characteristics of both traffickers and clients. Finally, it will detail protection concerns based on corruption and reprisals suffered by trafficked women and their families upon repatriation.

Although research has taken place regarding the refugee-trafficking nexus, these studies have uniformly concentrated on the trafficking of women who have already been granted refugee status. This chapter strives to address this junction from another perspective: that of granting refugee status to trafficked women with a well-founded fear of persecution. In so doing, this chapter will analyze the 1951 Geneva Convention and the 1967 New York Protocol, as well as the arguments for gender-based persecution as a determining factor for refugee status. International precedent for protection mechanisms addressing the needs of trafficked women, and alternatives to refugee status will be discussed.

Finally, this chapter will address the upcoming European harmonization, and will argue for European acceptance of gender-based persecution as a factor to access refugee determination proceedings. If one analyzes the current phenomenon of migration, the causes are not significantly different than those that have encouraged migration throughout human history. War, hunger, and the desire to better one's situation has always been a driving factor of migration. According to the International Organization for Migration, 2.5% of the world's populations are international migrants. Theories abound regarding why people migrate across national borders. One of these theories, belonging to the neoclassical school, speculates that migration is an individual decision, taken in the interest of maximizing the migrant's earning potential.

This theory assumes that due to unemployment, underemployment, low wages, poor working conditions and the absence of economic opportunities, migrants concerned with their personal betterment choose in a rational and calculated way the destination country which will reap the most benefit. A second economic theory of migration is the New Economics of Migration. In the interest of diversifying risk, families choose to gain different training for each worker in the family unit. Further, these workers may be sent abroad to test the opportunities in the country of destination, before advising the rest of the family to join him/her. This bypasses one of the criticisms of the neo-liberal model, which questions why the poorest of the poor in countries of origin do not tend to migrate. For economically disadvantaged families, according to the New Economics of Migration theory, the risk of migration is too high, without labor diversification and basic financial security.

Alternatively to the Individualist based approaches outlined above, Structuralist theory also attempts to explain the root causes of migration. Structuralist approaches focus upon the idea that people make their decisions to migrate based on political, social and economic forces that are out of their control. Therefore, the choice to migrate is not necessarily a logical, carefully weighed out, economically tested decision, but rather occurs as a result of circumstances over which the migrant has little power. According to the structuralist Dual Labor Market Theory, there are two tiers of jobs produced by a capitalist system.

The tier generally attractive to nationals of the destination country is one with jobs that are secure, permanent, well paid and require formed skills. The tier that is increasingly unattractive to nationals is one with jobs that are temporary, unclean, perilous and poorly paid. These positions have, in past generations, been filled by female or teenage labor. However, as countries have become more industrialized, educational patterns and population dynamics have changed. As each generation receives a better education than the last and has fewer children on average, receiving countries often find women and teenagers refusing or unable to fill these positions.

This could be remedied in part by raising salaries for these jobs; however, employers in destination countries are generally resistant to the idea of decreasing their profits. Therefore, to the benefit of employers and to the temporary benefit of migrants, these 3-D jobs (dirty, difficult and dangerous) are increasingly filled by foreign labor. A final structuralist approach, the World Systems Theory, claims that 'modern' economic development destabilizes populations. Annually, partially due to economic development policies supported by the current power of neoliberal economists at the World Bank and the International Monetary Fund, 30 million people migrate from the countryside to cities in their own countries. By 2025, 60% of the world's population will be living in cities, estimates the United Nations.

As employment and infrastructure in the world's cities are unable to absorb this mass migration, most of these workers find jobs in the informal sector, resulting in a global figure of 900 million underemployed. The disappointment of the lack of opportunities in the city, as well as the uprooting effect of the original rural- urban migration acts to break the psychological security barrier to migration abroad. While potential migrants develop networks of family members or acquaintances from home areas who have successfully relocated abroad, the possibility of an international move becomes increasingly attractive and less risky.

According to structuralists, a further element contributing to an increase in migration is what has been called the 'shock of the new'. The globalization of the media and telecommunications industries has acted to introduce populations worldwide to a romanticized version of the global north, and serves to make these destinations less alien, and therefore more secure for an impending move. The United Nations Development Program's Human Development Report of 2000, while discussing the increasing gap between the poor global south and the rich global north, has argued that the mounting inequalities should be classed as human rights violations.

As life expectancy is dropping in the global south and rising in the global north, and the wealth of the richest 200 people in the world is ten times that of the combined wealth of the 582,000,000 poorest, a transfer of funds from the rich global north to the poor global south is desperately needed. However, as documented in the HDR, there has been a massive shift away from a global-north to global-south allocation of development resources. While these global inequities exist, it is unlikely that we will see any great reduction of migration as citizens from less developed countries seek out economic opportunities.

Young women are subject to the same push-pull factors for migration as the rest of the population in poor countries. However, as will soon be argued, women can be particularly vulnerable while migrating. In some circumstances, this vulnerability can lead to trafficking for sexual exploitation. One must note that migration is not always a fully voluntary phenomenon, as seen with refugees and internally displaced persons. IOM estimates that there are more people in need of humanitarian assistance and protection than a decade ago, although the actual numbers of persons granted refugee status has decreased from 17 million in 1990 to 14 million in 2000. However, internally displaced persons have increased, outnumbering refugees by more than two to one. As the number of asylum seekers worldwide is multiplying, the number of people who are granted refugee status is falling. Of those granted refugee status, seven out of ten are hosted by low-income countries.

The decreasing number of recognized refugees in Europe is seen as a victory by some politicians, but in actuality seems to lead to more asylum seekers trying any means necessary, regular or irregular, to access European soil. As demonstrated in a 1998 UNHCR study, the nationalities of those most often smuggled or trafficked into the European Union closely corresponds to the nationalities most often given asylum worldwide. According to studies by refugee experts, the majority of asylum seekers arriving in the European Union have been either trafficked or smuggled. Whereas asylum seekers may utilize the services of human smugglers to assist their movement across borders, they may also face the exploitation of traffickers following their entry into European territory. In some cases, recognized refugees are also trafficked directly from refugee camps.

Worldwide, poverty is increasingly and disproportionately affecting women. Of the 1.3 billion absolute poor in the world today, 70% are women and their minor dependents. This poverty is due, in part, to women's lack of access to formal education and job opportunities in their countries of origin. Further, women fail to fully benefit from market 'reforms' of today's world economic regime due to the lack of economic power in their communities and families. At the same time, women are the principal segment of the population affected by the massive cuts in social spending by governments following structural adjustment or similar reforms. Due to gender inequities and relative powerlessness, 'people who have little to lose may be willing to take great risks'.

Women are also increasingly migrating to cities within their own countries. While this most often occurred in the past as women accompanied their partners, women are progressively migrating for economic reasons and finding that formal sector jobs are even more closed to them than to their male counterparts due to their lack of schooling or other discrimination. Therefore, patterns show that the informal sector is largely receiving female internal migrants, and women are taking jobs with a lack of job security or benefits. Female-headed households are also on the increase in the majority world of developing countries, and these households tend to be poorer and support more dependents than male-headed households.

This is resulting in what is being called the 'feminization of poverty'. The internal uprooting, lack of a support network, and increased financial responsibility adds to the vulnerability of women to be recruited by a trafficker, in the hopes of improving her family or personal economic situation. The European Commission contends that contributing factors to international female migration include female-focused unemployment, extreme poverty, and the marginalization of women in source countries. This is particularly true when analyzing countries in transition from a community-based to an individual-based economic system. Following the collapse of communism in the USSR, and in communist states supported by the USSR, economic controls were imposed that led to great unemployment, social and financial insecurity.

Those to be most affected by this economic transition were women. According to the U.S. Agency for International Development, between 70 and 80% of currently unemployed Russian workers are women. Similarly, in Ukraine and other Eastern European countries, women make up 70% of those involuntarily unemployed. This is equally true for Moldova, considered by IOM to be the main source of trafficked women for Western Europe, the Balkans and the Middle East. At a time when 25% of the workforce has immigrated internationally, news reports contend that the poorest Moldovans are selling their own organs, and 80% of households live below the poverty line. Not surprisingly, patterns have also emerged that as women are struggling with poverty and are internally displaced for economic reasons, international migration of women is also on the rise.

Not only is there a feminization of poverty, but a feminization of migration, as well. Female patterns of migration contribute to the overall patterns outlined previously; women, too are affected by unemployment and poverty, and depend on migrant networks for information regarding how best to migrate to the global north. When one adds into the equation the disproportionately higher levels of poverty among women worldwide, the family responsibility for both their children and elderly relatives, the lack of formal job opportunities in countries of origin and the lower levels of education available to women, it is not surprising that migrant streams which have typically been male are gradually becoming filled by women. In fact, according to IOM, over half of the world's migrants are women, and the numbers of unaccompanied women who migrate are on the increase.

The majority of women who migrate internationally do not succumb to traffickers. Discrimination against women continues to affect these migrants during their time outside their country; female migrants generally work in less favorable conditions for less pay than their male counterparts. However, they are able to aid their families financially, and their standings within their own communities tend to increase upon return to their countries of origin. Due to the relative success of female migrants, who depend upon migrant networks for contacts in their countries of destination, as well as housing, transportation and occasionally financial assistance, it is not surprising that other women would put themselves at risk for trafficking by attempting to follow a similar path. Further, due to the stigma attached to prostitution in most countries of origin, repatriated trafficked women discuss the exact nature of their experiences abroad with difficulty, so the risks are not fully understood by other women considering a similar relocation.

TRAFFICKING

In the UN Convention against Transnational Organized Crime (the Palermo Convention), adopted by the UN General Assembly in 2000, trafficking in persons was defined as 'the recruitment, transportation, transfer, harboring or receipt of persons, by means of the threat or use of force or other means of coercion, of abduction, of fraud, of deception, of the abuse of power or of a position of vulnerability… Exploitation shall include, at a minimum, the exploitation of the prostitution of others or other forms of sexual exploitation, forced labour or services, slavery or practices similar to slavery, servitude or the removal of organs.' Human trafficking for purposes of sexual exploitation has existed for many years.

The first International Convention on Trafficking was signed in 1904 to address British women being trafficked to brothels in Europe, and Europeans being trafficked to the United States. Although exact figures are impossible to acquire due to the illicit nature of trafficking, it is estimated that from 700,000 to 4 million people are trafficked across borders every year. Trafficking in human beings takes on many forms, such as forced labor, slavery or similar practices, indentured servitude, forced marriage or the sale of organs; and victimizes men, women, boys and girls. However, international attention has focused on the trafficking of women for sexual purposes. In fact, international law addressing trafficking, outlined in the Suppression of Traffic Convention, solely addresses trafficking for the purposes of commercial sexual activity. This has been criticized by anti-trafficking advocates, as the problem of human trafficking additionally involves other oppressed groups.

It is however important to address the phenomenon of women prostituted against their will for others' profit and pleasure, if nothing else than for the sheer number of exploited women, and to brace against the impending increase of their number and the corresponding international responsibility to fight against the barbarity of this human rights violation. Four hundred years of human trafficking from Africa enslaved 11.5 million people; the last 10 years of what is increasingly being called 'Modern Slavery' has produced 30 million victims of trafficking from Southeast Asia alone. Approximately 120,000 women and children are trafficked into the European Union every year, with half a million trafficked women currently residing in Western Europe. Of these women, 75% are under the age of 25, of whom a great number are teenagers.

The US Central Intelligence Agency estimates that traffickers earn approximately $250,000 in profit from the work of each trafficked prostituted woman. Prostituted women earn traffickers from $800 to $5,000 every time they are resold to another organized crime ring. Every country in the world is affected by trafficking, either as a country of destination, transit or origin, or in combination. With an ever widening gap between the rich and the poor both nationally and internationally, declining socioeconomic status of women in CEE/CIS countries of origin, increasing profits for traffickers, lack of government action and, in some cases, government complicity, the trafficking in women is on the increase. According to a UNHCR study, the CEE/CIS area is particularly affected as it has become the fastest growing source region for trafficked people.

Established trafficking routes are constantly changing as flexible traffickers change tactics and entry points in order to continue their exploitation of millions of people. Identified trafficking and smuggling routes from the CEE/CIS region to the European Union include:

- Albania and 'the Balkan Route'. Widely used by organized crime rings.
- The 'Eastern Route'. With transit in Moscow, Belarus and Poland. Mainly used by African and Asian migrants. Poland is a transit country.
- The 'Southern Route'. Used by Balkan residents and Romanians. Poland is a transit country.
- via Croatia and Slovenia. With Hungary as the most significant transit country into Austria;
- via the Czech and Slovak Republics: With transit through the Ukraine. Used by migrants from the Middle East, Far East and the Soviet Union;
- via Albania, Hungary or the Czech Republic: With Turkey, Bulgaria and Romania as significant transit countries;
- The Mediterranean 'Blue Route': crosses the Mediterranean. Migrants from Africa and Asia. Transit through North Africa to Europe via Greece, Italy, Spain and more recently Portugal;
- The 'Northern or Baltic' routes: with transit through Moscow and the Baltic States into Scandinavia.

An upcoming challenge for the European Union will be stemming the flow of trafficked people in new member States following European Union enlargement. With the Czech

Republic, Slovakia, Slovenia, Hungary, Poland, Cyprus, Malta, Estonia, Lithuania and Latvia set to join the European Union in 2004, and Romania, Bulgaria and Turkey anxious to join as well, observers fear the worst with a massive growth of trafficking activities within the newly defined borders. Countries that have had the role of areas of origin or transit may find themselves at the receiving end of human trafficking following European Union expansion.

A further challenge is the emerging phenomenon of trafficking through the Internet, with traffickers buying and selling their victims on-line. Both European Union expansion and the use of the Internet for the sex business are set to assist the growth of trafficking and affect trafficking routes in coming years. Although trafficking routes frequently change, the general direction of trafficking remains the same. As movements of raw materials flow from poorer countries to richer countries, so do movements of migrants, both legal and illegal. As stated at the UN World Conference against Racism in Durban, South Africa, "[Trafficking victims] are the commodities in a multi-billion dollar global industry, dominated by highly organized criminal groups operating with impunity." Mary Robinson, the UN High Commissioner for Human Rights continued by commenting, Not only does trafficking take place between separate nation states, but also occurs within a nation state.

This 'internal trafficking' has not been as much of a focus of intense international attention as cross-border trafficking, but remains a violation of the human rights of women that must be addressed. Internal trafficking also follows patterns of traditional migration flows, originating in the poorer countryside and concluding in the more affluent cities. Human exploitation in the form of trafficking is not limited only to adults. Unfortunately, children are targets of traffickers, as well. Two separate prototypes emerge in the trafficking of minors. Teenage girls are recruited and exploited in a similar manner to young adult women for the purposes of non-consensual sexual activity. It has been estimated that up to

80% of the females trafficked from Albania, for example, are minors. Reports from NGOs suggest that this number is lower for other CEE countries, making up between 10 and 30% of the total. It is important to keep in mind the distinction between adult trafficking and child trafficking. Female child victims of trafficking face a double vulnerability due to gender and age.

Although the focus of traffickers for sexual exploitation for the most part may be the gender of the victim rather than their age, prostituted children have radically different protection and reintegration needs than adults. A second pattern of child exploitation is the trafficking of young boys and girls under 12 for forced labor, as well as begging, adoption, prostitution, and pornography. As with other forms of trafficking, this happens both within the State and internationally. According to UNICEF, there are no specific protections or legal frameworks to address the specific needs of trafficked children.

TRAFFICKING AND SMUGGLING

Trafficking differs greatly from smuggling, as international bodies and non-governmental organizations are taking pains to point out. Whereas migration through smuggling rings is primarily voluntary and initiated by the potential migrant, trafficking is generally involuntary in nature; victims of trafficking are coerced, sold or at the most rare and extreme, kidnapped into their work. Coercion can take place through deceit, sexual abuse, torture, starvation, imprisonment, and threats of violence against family members, among some tactics used by traffickers. Although many of the women trafficked are aware that they will be migrating, they are deceived about the nature of the work they will be forced to perform, as well as their future working conditions.

An additional difference between smuggled and trafficked migrants lies in entry to the country of destination. Women who are trafficked to be prostituted enter the countries of transit and destination both through legal and illegal avenues.

Through the issuance of tourist and student visas, as well as forged documents, many of the women who will later be exploited pass borders through regular means, while accompanied by their exploiters. This differs greatly from the increasingly common picture of smuggling seen in Europe, with hundreds of immigrants being smuggled past borders by boat or truck. One of the most striking differences between smuggling and trafficking is that, in the vast majority of cases, smuggled adult migrants are male, while trafficked adult migrants are female. Further, the nature of the action is fundamentally different.

Whereas smuggling is an action with the intention to assist in the border crossing (albeit in a sometimes oppressive or life-threatening way, for exorbitant fees) the intention of trafficking is oppression of the victim and the ensuing financial gain following migration. Therefore, the focus of smuggling is entry into the destination country, while the focus of trafficking is the exploitation of the migrant upon arrival. Whereas smugglers have in recent years been demonized by governments as wholly exploitative, for many migrants and asylum-seekers, smugglers are seen as providers of an often expensive service. Past examples of well-known smugglers include Varian Fry, Oscar Schindler, Raoul Wallenberg, Frank Foley and Nicolas Winton, as well as various Danish fishermen who smuggled Jewish refugees for a fee to safe havens in the 1930s and 1940s. More recently, the 'Snakeheads', an organized crime ring in Asia, smuggled Tianamen Square activists out of China into Hong Kong with the knowledge of western governments. It is only recently that governments have focused upon the negative aspects of organized crime involvement with migration.

As detailed earlier, the root causes of migration are similar for both smuggled and trafficked migrants. When immigration is discouraged by governments through visa, financial or passport regulations, determined migrants can turn to illegal means, or are vulnerable to exploiters promising safe passage and opportunities abroad. For women wishing to better their economic situation, the push and pull factors of migration can lead them to accept the assistance of people who intend to exploit them. There is a great deal of overlap in the distinction between smuggled migrants and trafficked migrants. In some cases, trafficked migrants may be smuggled into the country of destination.

Additionally, smuggled migrants may be victims of abuse and exploitation similar to that which threatens trafficking victims. However, the general patterns that emerge suggest that different approaches are needed to tackle the problems facing smuggled migrants and trafficked migrants. As governments act to reinforce their commitments to impenetrable borders, policy is being developed to counteract illegal migration. However, due to the exploitation and deceit involved in the presence of trafficking survivors, as well as the substantial difference in their security needs, it is essential that decision makers develop policy that also acknowledges the human rights responsibilities of the host state.

There is an increasing presence of national and transnational organized crime groups in human trafficking. Human trafficking activities are often combined with other illegal activity, such as drug and arms trafficking, and profits from trafficking are partly used to procure equipment, legally invested, or used to further the illegal activity through corruption. Authorities have observed that organized crime groups have moved the focus of their activities from immovable goods such as real estate, to moveable goods such as drugs, arms, and human beings. Of moveable goods, humans are the least risky; traffickers in humans face little chance of prosecution, relatively lower fines, and a high resale value of the women they traffic for sexual exploitation.

As Brunson McKinley, Director General of IOM, recently wrote in the International Herald Tribune, 'The penalties are far less severe than for drugs, the up front investment much smaller, and the evidence has legs and tends to run away.' Women have little decision making power or recourse in being sold to another crime ring; this method is often used to break any ties the woman has made in the area where she is working, to increase her debt burden, or to disorient her so that escape is difficult. Repeated trafficking across national borders is also useful from the criminals' point of view, because if the victims are less able to communicate through language, then they are less independent and less likely to incriminate traffickers.

Although recruiting practices differ greatly from one country to another, some common patterns emerge, particularly within the CEE/CIS region. This area is dominated by criminal networks that have taken trafficking out of the hands of individual exploiters for massive financial gain. These crime rings, while previously remaining deeply divided by ethnic origin (including, in part, Albanian, Italian, Turkish and Russian organized crime networks) are now collaborating 'transnationally' to maximize their profits. Giusto Sciacchitano, the Italian Antimafia Deputy Prosecutor contends.

These organized crime groups function by first recruiting potential migrants in their own countries of origin. Trafficked women are often approached by members of their own communities, lured by deceitful promises of jobs in the service sector as waitresses, nannies, or caregivers for the elderly. As already outlined, non-exploitative migrant networks have traditionally served to assist acquaintances who wish to migrate. The approach by traffickers is quite similar to these traditional networks, by utilizing trustworthy members from the same or a similar community who have worked abroad, in order to make first contact with women for the purposes of recruitment. Although most traffickers are male, a growing number are female, and offer assurances of jobs in the global north, transportation and housing assistance, as well as financial help.

Following recruitment, the original group of traffickers often leaves their victims with other crime groups with whom they have working agreements, who assume responsibility for the transfer of the victims across borders. Collaborators also include government officials and businesses that have been corrupted by profits offered by the crime networks. Four main systems of exploitation of trafficked women have been identified by IOM in Italy, largely based on the country of origin of the controlling organized crime groups. The Albanian model, which encompasses Bosnian, Kosovar, Moldavian and Bulgarian organized crime rings, uses coercion and violence in order to maintain control over its victims.

This model also is strongly based on private ownership of the women under its control, and has been called a particularly brutal form of trafficking by the UN High Commissioner for Human Rights. A second model, the Nigerian model, including Jamaican, Camerunese, Liberian and Burundese prostituted women, relies on debt bondage. High debts and quickly accumulating interest are used to control its victims, with the faint hope of being able to pay off debts to gain freedom. Women are pressured through psychological and physical means to live up to their debt responsibilities. The Eastern-European model includes women originating from Poland, Hungary, Ukraine, the Baltic Republics, the Czech Republic and the Slovak Republic. This system is highly organized and highly mobile, with a defined contract period.

Finally, the Latin American model, involving women from Peru and Colombia, is semi-voluntary due to economic interests of the women trafficked, and is often part time. Although generalization of conditions of trafficked women is necessary on some level in order to comprehend the situation as a whole, it is also important to note that the conditions of trafficked women differ significantly, with a great deal of grey area existing between the slave-like conditions of some forced prostitutes and the semi-voluntary sex work of others. Once forced into prostitution, women are prohibited from leaving by a variety of methods. Traffickers typically assist victims to transfer abroad by providing for the costs of transportation, passport and visa acquisition. By accepting this arrangement, trafficking victims find themselves in a situation of debt bondage, owing what can be tens of thousands of dollars, once they arrive at the country of destination.

Traffickers typically force their victims to work until the debt is paid off, taking a cut of their profits while the victim's debt regularly mounts to cover the cost of clothing, medical expenses, housing and food, and victims rarely manage to pay off their debt. Traffickers frequently use threats against family members in the country of origin, brutal beatings and sexual violence to control women who have been trafficked for prostitution. Additionally, traffickers employ deceit, isolation, blackmail and psychological pressure to control the women they have prostituted. Although many trafficked women enter the country of destination legally, upon arrival their documents are taken by the trafficker for 'safekeeping'. Traffickers instill fear of the authorities on trafficked women due to their lack of working papers, further hindering contact with police.

This is particularly effective in destination countries in Western and Eastern Europe where prostitution is illegal and women are afraid of exposure. The trafficking and smuggling of women already engaged in sex work presents a challenge in the development of a fair and all-encompassing policy for trafficked women. The women's human rights lobby to the United Nations has long been divided on the issue of voluntary prostitution in what is characterized as the good-girl/bad-girl argument. While some feminists contend that all prostitution is forced, albeit financially, others believe that action should be concentrated on women who have been recruited into sex work through deceitful means.

This debate impacts the number of women defined as 'trafficked', for if the voluntary/forced prostitution argument is accepted, those considered having chosen to follow a career in sex work would be excluded from protection measures for trafficked women. The involuntary aspect of an informed choice to work abroad as a prostitute has been demonstrated in Ukraine. A 2002 Ukrainian report on the subject of trafficking contended that in Ukrainian cities the majority of those recruited for international sex work by organized crime rings were Ukrainians already involved in sex work. These sex workers were informed of their future positions and work conditions. However, the recruitment in the countryside involved targeting poor families with little to lose in the decision to migrate for purposes of prostitution.

As governments develop tactics to identify and prosecute traffickers, recent studies have shown that traffickers operating in Europe are changing their recruiting tactics. Many women find it difficult to identify themselves as survivors of trafficking, as they have established romantic relationships, even resulting in marriage, with their traffickers. Women trafficked by their 'boyfriends' are more apt to blame themselves for bad decision-making rather than recognize their victimization by a trafficking ring. Little is known about the clients creating the demand for young and 'exotic' sex workers, as studies focus more on the foreign supply of prostitutes than on domestic demand. It has been observed, however, that a great number of trafficked women seek and receive aid through their clients to escape their traffickers. In so far as Italy is concerned, there is much lower incidence of street-based sex work in the southern regions where men are under stronger social control.

Additionally, IOM contends that as the age of marriage is lower in southern Italy, there is less demand for sex services. According to the study The Sexual Behavior of Italians (2000) 9.0% of men and 0.4% of women in Italy buy sexual services. This activity is more concentrated in the north of Italy, in the cities, among older populations, and with holders of university degrees. The study Sex for Sale, further contends that a driving force behind the use of prostitutes by clients in Italy is inter-gender relations, erotic imagery and the construction of the sexual identity. Analysis of the symbolism of the relationship between the prostituted woman and her client can be quite enlightening.

The poor, uneducated, young, and oppressed female from the global south is involuntarily servicing the older, rich, educated and privileged male from the industrialized global north at her peril for his gratification and well being. As one considers the current trade and resource relationship between the developing and industrialized countries, the symbolism of this relationship is quite striking. According to this anthropological study, the rationale by male clients for frequenting prostitutes can be generalized into four separate approaches. 'Consumers' approach prostitutes as objects to be bought, and see themselves as the rightful consumers of their services. 'Insecure' clients use prostitution to confirm their sexual ability.

A category Leonini describes as 'romantic' are driven by a need to have a female sexual conquest. Others, categorized as 'blasé', recognize the harm done by their actions, but prefer not to cease their purchase of sexual favors due to a general acceptance of the use of prostitutes by their peers, or out of boredom. A final category, the 'faithful', uses prostitutes to augment their sexually unfulfilling romantic relationships. According to the study, female clients generally pay for sexual services due to their lack of a partner and an unfulfilling sexual life. Although many of the information campaigns and projects currently in place throughout Europe target female victims of trafficking, few European countries are targeting the users of sexual services.

Sweden, however, is taking a stand much different from its fellow European countries, in suggesting that rather than only focus on limiting the supply of prostitutes, countries should also look at their own residents and focus campaigns on the clients. By addressing issues such as the image of women in the media, male-female power and control, and the damage caused by clients' actions, States could act to minimize demand, as well. This could be particularly important for some destination countries such as Greece, where it is estimated that one third of sexually active males regularly purchase sexual services from prostitutes

PROTECTION NEEDS

A factor relevant to trafficking survivors is their need for safeguarding, as the organized crime groups increasingly in control of human trafficking regularly threaten the lives of the women who are able to flee from sex work upon their return home. Further, government and/or police collaboration with wealthy traffickers in CEE and CIS countries of origin and transit is widespread, and adds to the fear of repatriation. In a radio address in the late 1990s, Russian President Boris Yeltsin warned that the Russian judicial system is 'defenseless against the pressure of criminal structures', particularly as many of the Russian *mafiya* members are former KGB agents with strong contacts within the government.

In Southeastern Europe, estimates are that 70% of trafficked women either cannot or do not intend to return home, due to a fear of persecution and the lack of trust in the local authorities to provide adequate protection. Corruption of local authorities and border guards by the moneyed criminal rings has a tremendous impact on the protection of women being trafficked or repatriated following trafficking. Reports by trafficked women include accounts of authorities ignoring the exploitation, delivering repatriated trafficked women back to traffickers, utilizing the sexual services of the women involved and even participating in the trafficking itself. Further, there has been some evidence of collusion by authorities in host governments, as with a Greek official in Moscow caught selling visas to traffickers.

The 2001 International Corruption Perceptions Index shows that most of the CEE or CIS countries of origin for trafficking victims included in the survey have a high level of official corruption, where corruption is defined as '...the misuse of entrusted power for private gain.' This corruption leads to a genuine fear, for some trafficked women, regarding the ability or willingness of the State to provide for their protection upon repatriation. According to a report co-sponsored by UNICEF, as governments often tie protection access to incrimination of traffickers and 'voluntary' repatriation, those who refuse to leave the host country or are fearful to turn in their traffickers are not identified as victims of trafficking by police. Without this identification, they are not referred to IOM or other organizations working to meet the needs of trafficked women.

This has resulted in numerous cases of trafficking survivors being labeled as illegal migrants and deported, only to be met at the border by their traffickers, and re-trafficked with additional debt burdens. Although a number of women escape trafficking rings by requesting the help of clients, a great quantity are arrested during police sweeps. Although this is often represented as a liberation of trafficked women by State authorities, it is not interpreted as such by many of the women who have been 'rescued'.

As many trafficked women do not see themselves as 'victims' but rather as people who have made bad decisions or bad contacts, they are not fully cooperative with the authorities they have been taught to avoid. This can lead to misinterpretation of their situation by authorities, and result in deportation. The grounds for survivor refusal of assisted return are numerous, but certainly include fear of personal persecution. These fears cannot be taken lightly. In Italy, a destination country where protection for trafficking survivors is a priority, 189 foreign sex workers were killed in 1999. However, witness protection programs, when accessible by trafficked women, are often unsuitable for this group as they are based on an assumption that the survivor to be protected can assimilate into a new environment.

There is little incentive for women who have been trafficked to cooperate with criminal investigations of their traffickers, as testifying often increases the risks of reprisal upon repatriation. As most countries offer little protection to trafficking survivors, and immediately arrange for their return to their countries of origin, even in the case of an ongoing trial, the benefits for trafficked women of incriminating their exploiters are minimal. The cases of reprisals are much more numerous and serious in countries of origin than countries of destination, as even the basic protection mechanisms are often missing. In cases where the protection of trafficking survivors is weak, traffickers have corrupted officials, and trafficking survivors retain debts to their traffickers or have testified against them, their fear of physical harm or further exploitation is palpable. In fact, in Eastern Europe, 30 -50% of trafficking survivors are eventually re-trafficked following repatriation. Family members of trafficked women are also subject to reprisals in countries of origin.

Children that trafficked women have been forced to leave behind with other family members are often the targets of organized crime rings seeking reprisals against women who have chosen to implicate them with authorities. Strong calls are being heard throughout Europe and other receiving areas for official reform of protection strategies for this particular social group, and some States, such as Italy, are heeding this call with stronger legislation to protect these survivors of human rights abuse. However, the implementation of such protection is discretionary, and largely depends on the government and officials in place at the time of first encounters with foreign sex workers, as trafficked women are rarely otherwise aware of the existing legal framework that could serve to aid them. IOM reported in 2000 that regardless of the legislation in place in Italy, in most cases the Italian police were continuing with immediate deportations of Albanian foreign sex workers. As seen in the Associated Press article below the targeting, apprehension and deportation of hundreds of prostitutes from the Balkans continues today.

SEEKING SOLUTIONS TO TRAFFICKING

The international community is striving to address the issues of trafficking through legal instruments, including most recently the commitments at the UN Millennium Summit to Fight Transnational Crime, including Trafficking in Human Beings; the UN Convention against Transnational Organized Crime; and the optional UN Protocol to Prevent, Suppress and Punish Trafficking in Persons, Especially Women. However, governments are too often pursuing strategies that target the legal and immigration-based issues of trafficking, but not fulfilling the human rights protection responsibilities of host states.

CONVENTIONS

International conventions and agreements regarding trafficking and other modern forms of slavery have been numerous, and include the following: Europe has seen a rise in recent years of negative popular opinion regarding immigrants from non-EU member states. This issue has come to the forefront in Britain, Germany, Austria, Spain, France, Italy, Greece, and the Netherlands. The reluctance toward receiving migrants and refugees occurs at a time when Europe is rapidly aging. The 'greying of Europe' could profoundly affect the European economy as a small working population struggles to meet the needs of a much larger retired population. Anti-foreign sentiment has grown in Europe since the attacks in the United States in September 2001, as governments in Europe have justified their anti-immigration and asylum measures with the renewed need to protect their States from terrorism. These measures have acutely affected the treatment of migrants and asylum seekers in Europe.

It is not surprising, therefore, that a strong focus has been put on migrants entering by irregular means into the European Union. Italy, as well as other Mediterranean countries of first entry, has received both internal pressure and external pressure to address the issue of irregular migration. As Italy is often a country of transit for irregular migration, other EU member states would like to assist Italy to stem the tide of Kurds, Albanians, Bangladeshis, and other undocumented migrants. Tackling both smuggling and trafficking has been the focus of considerable interest on the part of the European Union in the last decade.

This attention has been appreciated by advocates for the rights of trafficked women. However, many of the declarations, conventions, and treaties that have been reached since 1990 focus on the needs of the governments and their voters increasingly critical of immigration. While the need to fight the criminal rings is widely acknowledged, with strong legislation enacted in order to counter their migration activity, equally strong legislation is lacking regarding meeting the needs of those who have been victimized by these smugglers or traffickers. In addition, for societal solutions to be durable, governments must also focus their attention on changing societal attitudes. While some States have addressed the lack of EU common legislation on protection needs of trafficking survivors, a cohesive standard practice for dealing with the survivors of trafficking has not yet been reached, although initial discussion regarding this matter took place in December 2000 at the Palermo Convention against Transnational Organized Crime.

LEGALIZATION

Some States have adopted the legalization of sex-work as a protection measure. Advocates for legalization argue that if prostitution were legal, women would be able to more freely organize themselves into cooperatives or other work systems that would allow them to control their work on their own terms, reducing or eliminating the need for pimps. Further, legalization would enable sex-workers to participate in a work-based health system, reducing some professional health hazards. Finally, the State would benefit from legalization, due to increased tax revenues from the now recognized laborers. Many advocates of the rights of trafficked women, however, fiercely oppose legalization. The trafficking of women has actually increased in countries with legalized prostitution, according to studies conducted by the European Women's Lobby. Legalization has proven to increase the demand for sexual services by decreasing some of the social stigma and lowering the health risks for clients.

Further, women lacking working rights in destination countries would continue as illegal residents, even if their industry were legalized. Counter-trafficking advocates further contend that in a legalized context, trafficked women are less visible and therefore less accessible by those wishing to assist this exploited group, and pimps and other managers of sex work are given more legitimacy. Therefore, although legalization may improve the conditions of local women involved in sex work, international trafficked and prostituted women could experience deeper exploitation.

THE REFUGEE CONVENTION

In 1951, responding to the massive human rights violations and displacement of millions of people in Europe, official representatives met in Geneva, Switzerland to draft the UN Convention relating to the Status of Refugees. This convention, along with the 1967 New York Protocol establishes the right to asylum due to a well-founded fear of persecution based on five grounds. According to the Convention, a refugee is defined as 'a person who, owing to a well-founded fear of being persecuted for reasons of race, religion, nationality, membership of a particular social group or political opinion, is outside the country of his [sic] nationality and is unable or, owing to such fear, is unwilling to avail himself [sic] of the protection of that country.'

Therefore, it is not enough to prove a well-founded fear of persecution, but that persecution must be based on reasons of race, religion, nationality, political opinion or membership in a particular social group. Central to the Refugee Convention is the principle of 'non-refoulement', prohibiting governments from forcibly returning refugees subject to torture or death upon repatriation. The flexible Refugee Convention and 1967 Protocol, and the later 1969 OAU Convention and 1984 Cartagena Declaration, have been interpreted to safeguard those requiring international protection due to civil war, international war, conditions of generalized violence, or other serious strife, as humanitarian needs have changed.

GENDER-BASED PERSECUTION

The threshold of the five convention grounds has served as a filter to allow refugee determination proceedings to occur only in the cases of some people in need of international protection. People fleeing economic or environmental crises are generally excluded from the possibility of accessing the procedures leading to the granting of refugee status. Further, access to asylum has historically been guided by male protection needs. The gender-partial basis for defining the five convention grounds has recently become the focus of much analysis both within agencies working directly with refugees, and within legal and academic circles. To fully understand the concept of gender-based persecution, it is necessary to differentiate between the concepts of 'sex' and 'gender'.

Whereas sex is defined on a biological level, gender is a cultural construction taking into account power relationships between men and women. Gender is further defined by how power affects the identity, status, roles and responsibilities of both men and women. The idea of gender is not shared between all people, but holds social meaning for individual cultures, and is adapted as the culture changes. It is equally important to analyze the concept of 'persecution'. According to UNHCR, it is not necessary to prove that the government is the perpetrator of acts against the asylum seeker, but rather to show the systematic failure of State protection. Therefore, if the State fails to protect those put at serious risk due to gender, whether or not the State is the direct executor of harmful deeds, such acts can still be considered Gender-based persecution.

Those advocating for the inclusion of gender-based persecution as an entry point for refugee determination proceedings argue that there are specific forms of persecution based on gender-related claims which are not presently covered by the Refugee Convention. These claims have included, but are not limited to, persecution due to homosexuality, female genital mutilation, domestic violence, systematic rape, sexual slavery, forced pregnancy, enforced sterilization and human trafficking for prostitution. Focus upon the gaps in the refugee determination system, namely in the exclusion of gender-based persecution as a sixth ground for refugee recognition, is not entirely new. In 1984, a resolution was passed by the European Parliament asking States to allow women who violate religious or societal traditions access to refugee determination proceedings. According to the European Parliament, these women could be considered members of a particular social group, therefore allowing assessment of their need for international protection.

This groundbreaking resolution was followed by UNHCR conclusions and consultations on persecution specific to women. In the early nineties, it became increasingly accepted that gender-related claims could fall under the 1951 Convention. Recently, the understanding of the severity of gender-based persecution was underlined by the 1998 adoption of a statute by the International Criminal Court to adjudicate gender-related persecution, and the 2001 convictions of Bosnian Serb officers for crimes against humanity due to their use of systematic rape as a form of torture. However, States have adopted varying stances on gender-based persecution, and acceptance of gender-based claims is sporadic. An ever-growing number of organizations are calling for general recognition of gender- based persecution as the basis for refugee claim.

These advocates maintain that due to the fact that gender is not indicated as one of the five grounds laid out in the Refugee Convention, persecution particular to women is often overlooked. Therefore, they contend, women subject to gender-based persecution should be entitled to refugee status as members of a particular social group, if it is possible to prove a well-founded fear of harm and the lack of State protection.

ARGUMENTS AGAINST GENDER-BASED PERSECUTION

There is a considerable amount of resistance to the extension of refugee protection to survivors of gender-based persecution, as it is feared that granting asylum to those suffering severe forms of gender-based persecution would open the floodgates to a great number of women fleeing domestic violence, female genital mutilation, or other female centered violence that the State may consider a private domestic matter. However, gender-sensitive refugee determination would not automatically lead to a blanket acceptance of refugee status for all women suffering from systematic violence. In fact, in 1999 only one in four asylum seekers were granted refugee status in the European Union.

The Refugee Status Appeals Authority of New Zealand has stated that, 'The refugee claimant must still establish that the fear of persecution is well-founded, that the nature of the harm anticipated rises to the level of serious harm, that there will be a failure of state protection and that the well-founded fear of being persecuted is for reasons of race, religion, nationality, membership of a particular social group or political opinion. The refugee status inquiry is always individual; it is always particularized.' Recent political opinion in destination countries has swayed away from the responsibility- sharing of hosting asylum seekers. Intergovernmental organizations, such as UNHCR and IOM, have therefore been put in the difficult position of balancing the needs of migrants and refugees against the anti-foreigner sentiment rising in the global north. The additional burden of granting asylum to potentially thousands of women fleeing gender- based persecution is indeed a daunting prospect, and it would be difficult to convince host governments of their human rights responsibilities for women who have been trafficked into their States, and even more so toward women who are victims of internal trafficking in third States.

UNHCR, therefore, has made a number of public statements regarding repatriation for those not in needs of international protection in order to safeguard the commitments by the States to protect those already recognized as refugees. In doing so, UNHCR has singled out trafficked and smuggled migrants as among those who should be targeted for repatriation. UNHCR is presently developing a Conclusion providing direction to States regarding the establishment of complementary forms of protection for those trafficked or smuggled. This alternative to refugee status for those in need of international protection is meant to be compatible with protection provided as per the 1951 Convention. A further criticism of asylum for trafficked women concentrates on the difference in the needs between survivors of trafficking and other human-rights abuses leading to refugee status.

It has been argued that survivors of trafficking have needs different than those of refugees, including protection within the host country and legal redress of their traffickers, and, in some cases, resettlement in a safe, third country. In addition to safety concerns trafficked women often suffer when returning to their countries of origin, they also have specific needs due to the nature of their oppression, including often severe physical and psychological trauma. Some experts claim, therefore, that although protection should certainly be guaranteed to survivors of trafficking, protection and social assistance should take a different form than that currently secured by refugees. According to these counter-trafficking advocates, asylum for women fleeing gender-based persecution due to resistance to trafficking should be considered only as a last resort in States that have not developed their own comprehensive protection mechanisms for survivors of trafficking.

REFUGEE DETERMINATION PROCEEDINGS FOR TRAFFICKING SURVIVORS

UNHCR has taken a cautious stand on the issue of granting asylum to survivors of trafficking in need of international protection, in short writings located in various documents. UNHCR has stated that providing safe houses in countries of origin for survivors of trafficking should be pursued as much as possible in the interest of maintaining the integrity of the national asylum system producing an adequate substitute to the determination of refugee status. Whereas the UN refugee agency has said as recently as 2001 that status as a victim of trafficking should not by itself allow or deny access to refugee status determination, UNHCR has also encouraged governments to open their asylum processes to claims from individual trafficked persons.

In a joint report with the World Health Organization, UNHCR identified sexual violence as a form of torture, and has recently called for individual State introduction of gender and age-specific safeguards regarding female victims of torture and gender-based persecution. Whereas some of the statements issued by UNHCR have been guarded about the possibility of asylum, questioning its effect on the integrity of the international refugee regime, it has increasingly become supportive of the idea of case-by-case refugee determination proceedings for trafficking survivors. In Guidelines issued in spring 2002 on International Protection, UNHCR took up the question of refugee status for trafficking victims, arguing that survivors are entitled to refugee status if their country of origin is unable or unwilling to provide protection. Some progress has been made in the establishment of international gender guidelines, in a departure from the political focus of persecution that has favored male refugees in the past.

In 1985, UNHCR and the Executive Committee of the High Commissioner's Programme issued a report which called upon the High Commissioner to: Further, during the 1995 World Conference on Women in Beijing, China, official representatives drafted Strategic Objective E.5 in the Platform for Action. This item called for the recognition of women as refugees, if there is a well-founded fear of persecution due to sexual violence or other gender-related persecution. A number of State precedents exist that are steering the protection of trafficking survivors in the direction of refugee status. In 1996, a U.S. Immigration Judge in San Pedro, California granted asylum to a Chinese woman referred to as Ms. M. Having been internally trafficked in China with the collaboration of local police, Ms. M. managed to escape from the hair salon/brothel where she had been confined, and arranged to be smuggled into the United States.

Upon her apprehension by U.S. border officials for illegal entry, she sought asylum due to gender-based persecution. Although the U.S. Immigration and Naturalization Service (INS) appealed the decision granting her refugee status on these grounds, the highest level Board of Immigration Appeals later upheld the verdict, granting Ms. M asylum in the United States. Although advocates hoped that this case would establish precedent for asylum of human trafficking survivors with a well-founded fear of persecution upon repatriation, a U.S. Immigration Judge in 2000 denied a similar case (Ms. O) instead conferring temporary relief under article 3 of the Convention against Torture.

Although still protected by the U.S. government, Ms. O has no permanent status and her travel is restricted, therefore has received a more limited form of protection than would be the case if she had been granted asylum. This case was appealed by Ms. O's lawyers, and INS withdrew its opposition to the appeal in November 2001. Although not uniformly enforced, the U.S. Immigration and Naturalization Service adopted Considerations for Asylum Officers Adjudicating Asylum Claims from Women ('Gender Guidelines') that direct INS officials to recognize that gender-specific forms of persecution can be the basis of asylum claims. Additionally, the Gender Guidelines advise that if an asylum applicant can prove a well-founded fear of persecution, and the trafficking survivor cannot avail herself of protection from her own government, she can be considered a member of a particular social group and therefore meets one of the five grounds of the 1951 Geneva Convention.

As stated by Amnesty International, Canada has made legal judgments in favor of refugee status for survivors of trafficking, as well. In a recent case involving a Ukrainian survivor of trafficking, refugee status was granted on the basis of her membership in a particular social group. The board of the Canadian Convention Refugee Determination Division stated that Additionally, other States have begun to adopt provisions recognizing gender-based persecution in refugee determination, including Denmark, Germany, Ireland, Norway, Sweden, UK, and Australia. The gender guidelines and adopted legislation specifically address women who fall prey to systematic acts of violence.

Some States have indeed formally recognized non-state and gender specific persecution as grounds warranting international protection under the 1951 Refugee Convention, including most recently Germany, with legislation passed in 2002. At present, there is little incentive for governments in countries of origin to protect women from trafficking. As the women who are victimized by traffickers are often poor with little political power and low levels of education, they are frequently seen as more of a burden than a benefit to the national economy. In addition, as the traffickers are pulling in an astronomical profit, there is great opportunity for public officials to be bribed to turn a blind-eye to human trafficking. The censure of the government of origin by conferral of refugee status on their citizens abroad, implying the incapability of a government to protect its own people, could work to increase local protection and counter corruption. In the end this could benefit European destination countries by stemming the tide of trafficking victims into Western Europe.

As stated by the UNHCR Protection Department, '[The Refugee Convention] is the best we have, at an international level, to temper the behavior of States.' In cases where the well-founded fear of persecution exists, trafficking survivors, as members of a particular social group, should legally be entitled to enjoy the protection afforded to other persecuted groups through existing refugee mechanisms. In addition to putting pressure on countries of origin, if trafficking survivors are afforded the possibility of asylum in their host country, the benefits may extend to national governments, as trafficking survivors will not be identified solely based upon their willingness to testify and return home. With protection in place, more survivors may be willing to testify against their traffickers, which would have a significant impact on the numbers of future women trafficked into the countries of destination, as well as attack the growing strength of organized crime rings.

PROTECTION ALTERNATIVES TO REFUGEE STATUS

As seen in the U.S. case of Ms. O, other options to the protection guaranteed to refugees may be applied in the case of trafficking survivors. The recently approved 'T' visa in the United States is one such precedent, giving proven survivors of trafficking a status similar, although not identical, to refugees. The T-visa guarantees 'victims of severe forms of trafficking' access to shelters, social assistance, medical care, compenzation, residence, privacy and protection. However, this status is only granted to those who are willing to provide information on traffickers to police. Five thousand trafficking survivors may be granted T-status annually, and are entitled to many of the advantages of refugee status.

Additionally, responsibility for T visa holders falls within the Office for Refugee Resettlement. Italy has been in the forefront for enacting legislation to meet the needs of women who have been trafficked. Article 18 of the Alien Law departs from legislation in most of the other EU Member States by extending protection to trafficking survivors regardless of their collaboration with state authorities. The protection provided as part of Article 18 is a six-month temporary 'social protection residence permit', with the possibility of extension for up to eighteen months, as required. While under State protection, the holders of this residence permit are given access to social services. Following the expiration of this residence permit, trafficked women may be able to convert their status into a two-year residence permit for study or work.

The enactment of Article 18 is relatively new; residence permits on the basis of trafficked status have been in place for approximately three years. As per the Ministry of the Interior, as of early 2001 there were 726 holders of social protection residence permits, benefiting trafficking survivors from Albania, Moldova, Nigeria, Romania and Ukraine. With an estimated 35,000 to 50,000 foreign sex workers in Italy, the number of women receiving this form of protection is quite low, perhaps due to a reluctance on the part of the Italian police to grant social protection residence permits, particularly in Venice, Foggia and Palermo. Besides the obvious human rights benefits such a law has on women escaping oppression, a 2001 report by the Italian Ministry of the Interior has detailed the positive effect that these residence permits have had on the fight against organized crime, with an increase in the incrimination of traffickers from 664 traffickers in 1990, to 2866 in 2000.

Additionally, the percentage of foreign traffickers has also increased, from 24% of the total to 56% of the total of all incriminated traffickers. This has been attributed to the temporary protection offered by the Italian state. In addition to the Italian social protection residence permit, a number of other protection measures have been enacted in Italy, including the establishment of shelters, hotlines and social services to meet the needs of trafficked women. In addition, in Italy there are currently 49 non-governmental organizations working specifically with prostituted women, with activities ranging from street-based outreach to counseling to protection.

Following Italy's lead, Belgium, the Netherlands and Spain have adopted measures to provide temporary residence permits to trafficking survivors. However, they have taken the decision to limit these permits to those willing to incriminate their traffickers. If needed, the utilization of witness protection mechanisms, in place for domestic needs, may be considered for the protection of trafficked women in these States. Europe-wide, it is theoretically possible for trafficked women to qualify for residence permits on humanitarian grounds, but the implementation of residence permit distribution for survivors of trafficking is uneven and discretionary. According to the European Commission, the minority of European States that currently hold legislation addressing protection for survivors of trafficking have policy which is vastly divergent.

EUROPEAN HARMONIZATION OF ASYLUM LAWS

The Amsterdam treaty of the European Union came into force on the first of May, 1999. A key element of the Amsterdam treaty was European Union harmonization, including the harmonization of asylum law and policy. The European Union gave itself a deadline of 2004 to realize harmonization of asylum law, establishing common standards but not uniform procedures. Additionally, the Presidency Conclusions of the European Council in Tampere, Finland declared in 1999 that the EU must move past aiming toward the minimal standards of refugee protection and instead target a common asylum procedure and refugee status. As Europe studies and debates the commitments they are prepared to make as a union toward the people of the world with a proven well-founded fear of persecution, the analysis of precedents and human rights responsibilities toward the ever-growing phenomenon of trafficked women might be a timely and vital exercise.

Although some States, such as Italy or the United States, have developed their own measures to protect trafficking survivors, UNHCR contends that individual State protection measures may be discretionary or unevenly implemented, as seen in the recent deportations of foreign sex workers by the Berlusconi government in Italy, or the uneven immigration judgments in the United States concerning trafficked women. Adherence to an international standard would increase the regularity of implementation, particularly with a common geographical approach to asylum issues. Discussions in the European Union currently include proposals for short-term residence permits for survivors of trafficking. Studies show that States issuing temporary residence permits have a higher success rate of persecution of traffickers than States without such protective measures.

This is particularly true if residence permits are not restricted to willingness to testify against traffickers. Also contributing to successful persecution is a three-month 'reflection period' currently in place in the Netherlands and Belgium. This reflection time allows trafficked women to decide whether or not to testify, as well as to determine if they are willing to repatriate. This period is important to allow trafficked women to fully understand the consequences of testifying against their traffickers, as well as to consider the possible consequences of repatriation, such as further trafficking, reprisals by traffickers, and stigmatization. On a governmental level this waiting period is also important, as trafficked women can continue to be influenced by their traffickers immediately after apprehension.

The European Union proposal would, similarly to the Italian Article 18, allow short-term residence for trafficking survivors. Different from the protection given under Article 18, however, the Commission for European Communities proposes that this protection be offered as a reward for cooperation with police authorities and incrimination of traffickers following a reflection period. The Commission itself admits that 'The prime objective of the proposed Directive is to tighten up measures against illegal immigration by introducing a short-term residence permit for victims... who cooperate with authorities.'

By its own admission, the driving factor of proposed EU legislation regarding survivors of trafficking is protection of the integrity of its own borders, rather than its human rights responsibilities to women suffering 'the biggest violation of human rights in the world'. The Commissioner for Justice and Home Affairs for the European Commission, Antonio Vitorino, has himself called for further legislation targeting the human rights needs of trafficking survivors. '[This directive] is only one element of a comprehensive strategy which must strike a clear balance between the repressive aspect of fighting crime and respect for human rights and aid for victims.' Temporary protection for trafficking survivors with a well-founded fear of prosecution could be an inadequate form of protection, however.

Besides the obvious reservations regarding providing protection solely to those willing to testify against their traffickers, the European Council on Refugees and Exiles has documented that people receiving temporary protection in Europe have experienced mental health problems due to the insecure nature of the protection. Further, the lack of long-term status contributes to the social exclusion of those temporarily protected, particularly those suffering trauma from their experiences. Often temporary protection is not coupled with the right to family reunification, education, basic health care, national identification documents, and travel. Finally, respecting the binding principle of 'non-refoulement', European governments should avoid involuntary return for the trafficking survivor with an ongoing well-founded fear of persecution, if the Refugee Convention is applicable in her case. UNHCR states that temporary protection 'only complements and does not substitute for the wider protection measures, including refugee asylum, offered by the [Refugee] Convention.'

European Union harmonization in 2004 would be an appropriate occasion to adopt guidelines recognizing gender-based persecution, specifically addressing the need to offer international protection to trafficked women with a well-founded fear of persecution. If the EU took the opportunity to follow precedents set both within and outside of the borders of its member states, and expanded its interpretation of grounds leading to refugee determination procedures, the benefits would be two-fold. First, the European Union would be fulfilling its human rights responsibilities by extending protection to a growing vulnerable group. Second, it would be aiding in the struggle against organized crime and irregular entry into Europe by enabling victims to testify and seek justice against their exploiters without fear of retaliation.

Further, conferring refugee status on victims of trafficking would put pressure on countries of origin to decrease corruption and prosecute organized criminals. Protection of trafficked women is, at present, not a strong focus of destination governments who are concentrating their efforts on impenetrable borders. While authorities focus on economic interests and public order, the human rights of victims of trafficking tend to be a less pressing concern. By focusing on diminishing the activities of human smugglers and traffickers challenging the authority and ability of the State to keep unwanted irregular foreign nationals outside their borders, governments are pursuing policies to assuage their national pride, rather than analyzing their responsibilities to protect the human rights of those who have been abused during power struggles between the State and the ethnic mafias controlling trafficking rings.

However, as has been shown in countries implementing policy that strives to protect trafficking survivors, the success rate of apprehension of traffickers increases when States put an emphasis on protecting the human rights of trafficked women. The European Union has already taken a strong step toward safeguarding those in need of international protection by requiring that all States joining the European Union sign on to the 1951 Refugee Convention and 1967 Protocol. The

Convention, developed at a time of massive displacement due to ethnicity and political ideology, supports the modern idea that people with a well-founded fear of persecution should be able to seek safe haven.

As methods of oppression have changed to target victims based on gender, the application of the Convention should embrace massively targeted new groups, such as women with low socio-economic status being regularly sexually assaulted for others' financial gain.

At the very least, governments should guarantee the human rights of trafficked women through the Refugee Convention while developing more adequate protection measures specifically suited for this particular social group. In refugee-status determination proceedings, country experts would be necessary to determine survivors with legitimate claims to refugee status.

A case-by-case determination for trafficked women seems to be needed, particularly in light of claims that traffickers have manipulated aid agencies into assisting who they believe to be trafficked women, only to discover that those assisted were working for the trafficker as recruiters. In light of traffickers offering freedom to prostituted women if they recruit young women from their own communities, the problem of deception will need to be addressed by country specialists currently working with refugee determination proceedings.

This chapter is not a call for asylum for all trafficked women, but instead a call for a common understanding that women trafficked for forced sexual services are victims of gender-based persecution. As survivors of trafficking, women and girls who have been prostituted by force form membership of a particular social group.

With this classification, a trafficked woman should be entitled to entry into refugee-determination proceedings to assess whether, as an individual, she has a well-founded fear of persecution, and is in need of international protection. Although being a survivor of trafficking does not guarantee blanket refugee status, victims should be afforded the possibility to be heard for refugee status determination, having passed the threshold on one of the five convention grounds.

If trafficking survivors as members of a particular social group are afforded the possibility of asylum benefits may also extend to governments, as more survivors may be willing to testify against their traffickers and governments of origin may feel pressured to provide adequate protection of their citizens.

8

Political Status of Women

Political participation of Indian women, though in a miniature form, started with the freedom movement. Mahatma Gandhi was mostly instrumental for arousing political consciousness in the poor, illiterate women and making them take part in the freedom movement. Political participation may be defined as voluntary participation in political affairs through membership, voting and partaking in the activities of the political parties, legislative bodies and/or politically motivated movements. The Constitution of India guarantees adult franchise and provides the framework for women to participate actively in politics.

Article 15 of the Constitution prohibits discrimination on the grounds of religion, race, caste, sex or place of birth. It is a pity that women have not substantially availed of the constitutional provisions. The successive election statistics shows that the number of women who exercise their franchise has increased from election to election. For the last two decades almost equal numbers of men and women have gone to the polling booths to vote. The number of women filing their nomination papers in any election, national or State, is only a fraction of the corresponding number of men. Some withdraw at the last moment and the contesting candidates become fewer in number. Ultimately the number of women winning elections will be so small that their percentage in the legislative body will be nominal.

The percentage of winning candidates has been below ten in Parliament, in all the past elections, as shown in the chart. The State Assemblies too present a similar situation. No variation whatsoever has occurred in half-a-century! In the same period, Indian women have achieved commendable progress in literacy, education, and employment. They have achieved rights equal to that of men for parental assets. They have proved their ability to master science and technology. In the past we were under the impression that political empowerment will follow economic empowerment automatically, but we were utterly wrong. Under the circumstances it became obligatory for the women's organizations as well as the Government of India to search for remedial measures to improve the political status of women.

After prolonged deliberations, as a first step, the government made the provision in the *Panchayat* and Nagarpalika Bills of 1992 to reserve 33 per cent of candidature and constituencies in the local bodies- *panchayats*, municipalities and corporations- for women. There was widespread criticism that it will be difficult to find such a big number of eligible women candidates all of a sudden, and the newly elected members' performance may not be befitting to the dignity of the post etc. Two local body elections have taken place since then and twelve uneventful years have passed. Now nobody is bothered about the women members of the local bodies.

In 1995 the representatives of the Government of India reported at the Fourth World Conference on the Status of Women at Beijing that the government intended to reserve 33 per cent of candidature and constituencies in the legislative bodies- Parliament and State Assemblies- for women. In September 1996, the Constitution 81st Amendment Bill, 1996 was introduced in Parliament. However, following opposition, the bill was referred to the scrutiny of the Joint Select Committee of Parliament with late Ms Geeta Mukherjee as the chairperson. The report of the Committee was produced in the Rajya Sabha and the Lok Sabha in the winter session, presuming that the Bill could be reintroduced in the current session itself but nothing positive happened.

The main provisions of the Bill, as introduced in Parliament in September 1996, were: (1) not less than one-third seats have to be reserved in the Lok Sabha and Legislative Assemblies for women, and among these reserved seats, provision has to be made for reserved seats for women belonging to the Scheduled Castes and Scheduled Tribes, in the same proportion as provided in the Constitution for the SC and ST people in general; (2) in the States where there are less than three seats for the Lok Sabha, there will be no reservation. The original Bill made no mention of Rajya Sabha or the Legislative Councils of States.

Women's organizations all over the country went on protesting and in the end the Bill was reintroduced on May 16, 1997. Overtly and covertly coalition partners of the ruling as well as the Opposition groups put forward objections. Some members wanted the quantum of reserved seats for women to be reduced to 25 per cent. Leaders of the Other Backward Classes wanted to reserve special quota for the OBC women. There were suggestions that half the parliamentary/State Assembly constituencies could be given dual representation, a male and a female representative simultaneously. All these suggestions, which could be implemented only by further constitutional amendments, were intended to make matters more and more complicated and obstruct the Bill. Now and then a few more attempts were made to take up the Bill, but without success.

After all, reservation is a constitutional provision to improve the status of weaker sections of the society. It is only natural that the male dominated legislative bodies would try to find out any number of excuses to obstruct the Bill and maintain male domination in the legislative bodies. The system of reserving for women 33 per cent seats in Parliament already exists in Russia, the Philippines, Korea etc. In certain other countries- Norway, Sweden, France, Germany etc.- the political parties take initiative to reserve 33 per cent seats for women.

Both ways it has worked well. Unfortunately in India, no political party has come forward with the suggestion of reserving the candidature for women. Also the Indian political parties arriving at a consensus on the issue is remote.

In the majority of our States, women form a bigger vote-bank than men. Eyeing on the women's vote-bank, before every election, most national political parties, in their manifestos, do not fail to promise to make women's reservation a reality. They gather the votes and do nothing to make the Bill an Act of Parliament. "What is the root cause of the low representation of women in the elected bodies? I have had opportunity to discuss the matter with many eminent men and women including late Ms Geeta Mukherjee, the chairperson of the Joint Parliamentary Committee, for the scrutiny of the Women's Reservation Bill. The women put the blame on the patriarchal society. The men accept male domination to a certain extent, but place the main responsibility for thus vicious situation on the women themselves.

The crux of the matter is that in politics a person who is not a member of a political party is a lay person politically. The membership of women in the political parties is extremely low. The representation of women in the higher cadres of the political parties is lower still. The number of women at the top, policy-making executive bodies of the parties is absolutely nominal. In any political party, if there is a section without sufficient and effective presence in the executive bodies, the interests of that section will naturally be neglected. The male dominated political parties are interested only in the female vote-bank. They are not interested to promote female membership in the party beyond a certain limit so that men could hold maximum number of important positions.

In all the main national parties there are separate sub-sections for women- Mahila Congress of the Indian National Congress, Mahila Morcha of the Bharatiya Janata Party, National Federation of Indian Women of the Communist Party of India etc. The women's wings are eternally agitating against price rise, atrocities against women or such other topics, which any government should take up in the priority list and address, with the objective of resolving them. But in practice, the governments leave such issues unresolved, and women go on making a little noise now and again, and gain certain illusory gratification that they have performed some great political task. The poor women are not much aware of the mainstream activities of their respective parties at all. When the election comes they vote for the party's symbol and the matter ends there.

Obviously women have to change their mode of approach to political participation, if they aspire for substantial representation in the legislative bodies. Women from all strata of society should join political parties of their choice and correct the disparity in male-female ratio in the parties at the grass root level, as well as in the executive bodies. More and more women should take the primary membership of the parties and involve themselves in the local activities. Without improving the primary membership and the grass root level activities, not many people could go up in the cadres. Political status could be achieved only through hard and persistent work.

If you have your husband or father or brother to prop you up, you are extremely lucky. In general women may have to face a lot of obstacles- gender discriminations, petty jealousies, scandals, economic constraints, discord in the family and so on- which should be circumvented with grace and determination. However, it is easily said than done! Without proper representation of women in the legislative bodies and political participation of women at all levels, issues concerning women would remain neglected. According to the Indian Constitution women being the weaker section are eligible for reservation wherever necessary.

Till date, women's representation in the legislative bodies is literally being obstructed by male domination. Constitutional and political action has to play a positive roll to solve the problem. As an interim measure, reservation of 33 per cent seats in the legislative bodies for women, through an Act of Parliament, is only just, prim and proper.

LEGAL STATUS OF WOMEN

From the time of Independence in 1957, Malaysian women have had the right to vote and to hold office. Today women comprise one half of the registered voters and are active in political life. The trends of participation among women members of various political parties do not show significant differences among them. Women have continued being loyal supporters of political parties in Malaysia. Members of the Wanita UMNO in 1971 have continued to gain wide recognition for their prominent role amongst women's political organizations in Malaysia. These party members are regarded as the very backbone of the UMNO party. However, women have continued the trend of providing solid support for male leaders, and have engaged themselves primarily in raising financial support for the parties.

Women members turn out in full force during election campaigns, and carry out routine tasks related to daily campaigning and facilitating voter participation during the election process. While women provide strong support to their parties, the majority of women seem to have remained in their role as supporters of male leaders, and have, with important exceptions, retained traditional gender roles within contemporary political life. Despite the significant roles played by the Wanita UMNO and the other women's auxiliaries at the level of mass politics, the representation of women as branch or division heads is limited.

In UMNO, in 1993, 5 out of 30 members (17 percent) of the central committee were women, and out of 153 divisions only one is headed by a woman. None of the 14,784 branches is headed by a woman. For more than forty-five years, the women's auxiliary of UMNO has only three women heads of divisions. The discrepancy between women's participation as members of the UMNO and their representation at higher echelons of the party is reflected by a comparison of the above mentioned figures with the fact that women constitute 872,116 of the total 1.8 million total UMNO members. Within the central committee of the Malaysian Chinese Association

(MCA), of a total of 38 members, there are only 3 women (8 percent). In the Malaysian Indian Congress, (IMC), only one woman was in the central committee in 1995.

WOMEN IN LOCAL AND STATE GOVERNMENTS

The proportion of women gaining electoral office in local and state governments is limited. Gender inequalities still persist in this sphere, as is indicated by the extremely low percentages of women at all levels of political office. The proportions of women to men in the advisory board of the Kuala Lumpur City Hall, and local councils in five states of West Malaysia are extremely low. At the Kuala Lumpur City Hall, the ratio of women to men was 1:12 between 1985- 88 and 1:13 between 1989-91. From available data on local councils from five state governments in Peninsular Malaysia, (Selangor, Penang, Johor, Kelantan, and Terengganu), the number of women councilors for the period 1988-93 is insignificant in comparison to male councilors.

The representation of women in Selangor local councils is now lower than the pre 1991 period at seven percent of the total, as compared to eight percent in the earlier period. Women's representation in Penang local authorities has not changed significantly since 1988. On the basis of data analyzed from the states of Johore, Kelantan, Terengganu, similar trends are to be found. In 1993, women were even less visible in state assemblies. At the national level, women's representation is still relatively low. Women's participation in decision making positions in government ministries is similar. Since 1985 the number of women appointed as senators has remained at similar levels. In the period 1985-87, there were 11 women senators, with a decrease in the next period of 1988-90. In 1994 the number went up to 13.

Women's participation in the cabinet reflects the overall pattern of their roles in decision making positions in the political hierarchy. It was not until 1969 that the first woman member of the Malaysian cabinet was elected. In 1994-95, the female-male ratio in the cabinet was 1:12.5, and nothing has happened to increase women's representation. In this period there were three women deputy ministers. Women's participation in the diplomatic services is limited. The first woman ambassador was appointed in 1976. In 1994-95 there were three women ambassadors, as compared to 67 men. The current overall ratio of women to men serving as diplomats overseas is 1:22. The Ministry of Foreign Affairs does not impose any limitations when appointing women overseas. Gender stereotypes still prevail, with women themselves not preferring to go abroad on long postings, unless single or divorced.

WOMEN IN GOVERNMENT SERVICE

Trends in women's participation in the government sector are important insofar as government is still the single largest employer, although the share of the private sector is increasing rapidly. Government policies therefore directly and indirectly impact on policies and approaches of employers in the private sector. Government officers also develop policy advice for government and implement the same. The advancement of women, with gender sensitive policy making and program/ project design and implementation, is dependent upon their access to higher levels of policy agenda setting, and decision making, in politics and government. It is also dependent upon the creation of gender awareness and sensitization, among both men and women responsible for policy making, implementation of programs and projects, monitoring and evaluation.

Women's participation in government service has increased rapidly between 1980 and 1991, from 27 percent to 33.6 percent. Several factors are important in this regard, the most significant being women's increasing participation in education. It was also in part due to the expansion of the health and education sectors, and the increased opportunities in government service for teachers and health workers. There is a positive correlation between the educational attainments of women, and their labor force participation rates. Women have increasingly opted to join the government services. This has to do with the expansion of government employment from the 1960s until the 1980s, during which period, government extended its scope to include support services to provide for the rapid social and economic development of the nation.

Women's entry into government service also helps illustrate attitudinal changes among parents, who recognize that girls have educational and professional potential, which provides options for them outside of marriage. Only 8.9 percent of women were in this category of a total of 214,814 women in government employment by 1988. By 1993 there was an increase to 25.5 percent. In the Category B, there was a 51.6 percent increase. While the trends in women's participation in Categories A and B were favorable as compared to men between 1988-91, in absolute terms, the majority of women are in category C, and they account for 42.6 percent of total government employees in this category. Women are also concentrated here in traditional women's jobs such as in health, medical, and education services.

These are still in keeping with gender roles of women as providers of care, and child rearers. Also, within the medical and health services, women are still predominantly nurses, rather than doctors or hospital administrators. The under representation of women in the higher and middle echelons of government service is an area of concern, insofar as these positions are critical in terms of gender sensitive policy making, and program and project design and implementation.

WOMEN'S LEGAL STATUS

Women under the Federal Constitution

The State enacts laws which are meant on the one hand, to prevent any forms of discrimination among citizens, with regard to the laws and policies of government, and on the other, to create positive opportunities for vulnerable groups to be able to participate in development processes. In Malaysia, there are two sources of laws, written and unwritten laws.

The written laws comprise the Federal constitution,

legislation enacted by parliament, and subsidiary legislation prepared under powers conferred by Parliament and State Assemblies. Unwritten laws consist of English common law suitable to local circumstance, judicial decisions of the Supreme Court, and local customary laws. Since Independence in 1957, Malaysian women's rights as citizens to participate in the political and administrative life of the nation have been recognized and guaranteed by the Federal Constitution, which states under Article 8, clause 1, that "all persons are equal before the law and entitled to the equal protection of the law".

Clause 2 further provides that "except as expressly authorized by this Constitution, there shall be no discrimination against citizens on the ground only of religion, race, descent, or place of birth in any law or in the appointment to any office or employment under a public authority or in the administration of any law relating to the acquisition, holding or disposition of any property or the establishing or carrying on of any trade, business, profession, vocation, or employment".

The Federal Constitution thus contains no specific provision against gender-based discrimination, as opposed to other types of discrimination based upon religion, race, descent or place of birth, which are expressly stated in the Constitution. The omission of gender from among the categories is increasingly regarded as significant, and needing change, inasmuch as it allows for the existence of provisions that provide for protective discrimination against women in the Employment Act, and avoids elimination of alleged discrimination under Islamic laws.

WOMEN'S PARTICIPATION IN THE LEGAL SYSTEM

Within the legal system, women are well placed to support reforms to improve the legal status of women. In 1991, one-third of the registered lawyers were women. In 1993, one-half of the session court judges, 44 percent of the Magistrate judges, and 15 percent of the appointees to the Attorney-General

Chambers were women. In 1994, the first female Solicitor General was appointed.

LAWS AFFECTING WOMEN

Citizenship and Permanent Residence

Under the Federal Constitution, both men and women are equally competent to acquire citizenship by means of the law, through registration, or naturalization. Under Article 15 of the Constitution, no conditions were imposed upon foreign wives of citizens from applying for citizenship to the registering authority. However by a subsequent amendment made in 1962, conditions are imposed upon such acquisition of citizenship, including "good character". By another amendment in Clause (2) of Article 15, citizenship rights could be acquired by any child of a citizen.

This amendment put women on par with men as regards the automatic citizenship of children born to them. However, discrimination remains as regards acquisition of citizenship rights by foreign spouses of Malaysian women. This can be related to the view that upon marriage a woman should follow her husband and not vice versa. There is a growing demand among educated Malaysian women that the policy requires to be changed in order to reflect women's increasing participation in education, and in the economy, and their contribution to the advancement of the country.

It is feared that if the policy is not changed, highly skilled and educated women may leave the country in search of other opportunities simply as their foreign husbands cannot stay in the country. This would militate against the country's need for a highly skilled and increasingly technically competent labor force.

Education

In the area of education, there are written laws which categorically forbid discrimination against women and men with regard to education. An important legislation in this regard, is the Universities and University College Act of 1991 which stipulates open membership to all irrespective of sex.

Women's Status under Labor Legislation

While labor laws do not reflect inequalities on the surface, and apply to both the sexes equally, yet there are gender concerns related to provisions of laws that apply exclusively to women, and can be discriminatory.

The Employment Act, 1955

This Act covers both unionized and non-unionized labor and employers but it only applies to Peninsular Malaysia, while Sabah and Sarawak have their own labor ordinances. The Employment Act is more beneficial to workers than the latter, and there are ongoing debates to extend it to all of Malaysia. This is the major legislation which regulates all labor relations, and certain parts apply equally to men and women, such as contracts of service, wages, rest hours, hours of work, holidays, annual leave, sick leave, maternity benefits and termination and lay-off benefits. However, there are some aspects of these that can be detrimental to women workers.

There is no stipulation in the Act with regard to employers paying lower wages to their women employees, as compared to male workers, for doing the same amount of work. Women in the private sector are subject to wage discrimination as compared to their male counterparts. In the public sector, women are better placed as the norm of equal pay for equal work prevails. Women in the private sector do not at present have any legal redress against wage discrimination.

Prohibition against Night Work

Section 34 of the Act prohibits night work for women in the agricultural and industrial sector, subject to the proviso that empowers the Director General of Labor to exempt in writing, any female employees from the prohibition. Given the structural changes in the economy and in the labor market, the increasing employment of women in light industries, and for longer hours of work involving night work, is becoming more widespread.

The practical value of such prohibitions is now being called in question by women in today's conditions, and Malaysian women are asking for legislation to regulate the working conditions for women during night time employment, not by prohibition, but by employers being asked to provide suitable support facilities for women who opt to work during night shifts.

Maternity Benefits

Pregnant women under the Employment Act are entitled to maternity leave for 60 days during which they are to receive full pay. Recently, the Government has reviewed maternity leave allowed for public sector employees and extended the 42 days to 60 days after which the leave can be extended up to three months as unpaid leave. Women in Malaysia are entitled to full pay for five deliveries. It is important from the public viewpoint, that young Malaysian women who are increasingly entering the labor force, should gain full social protection benefits for themselves and their children.

Employees' Social Security Act, 1969, and Pensions Act, 1980

These Acts regulate social insurance and pension benefits for Malaysian workers. The Employers' Social Security Act provides social security protection for workers. It excludes certain categories of workers including domestic servants and self-employed persons. These Acts are based on the premise that the male is the breadwinner of the family, and hence, should not be dependent upon the benefits arising from the loss of a female worker belonging to the family. Both acts prescribe different entitlements for widows and widowers, in case of compenzation, and pension payments for employees suffering death or injury sustained during work.

While social security and income laws have been amended to meet the needs of working women to pay taxes and accumulate pensions, there are ongoing gender issues regarding differentials in laws, rules and regulations. Some ongoing issues are the following:

i. self employed women must pool their income and file in their husbands' names;

ii. women supporting families are not entitled to the same dependent allowances as men; and

iii. while tax reliefs are available for men claiming to have a "dependent" wife, no such provision is made for women who support their husbands.

These are important gender considerations for legal reform, especially given the increasing participation of women in the Malaysian labor force, and the situation of households which are female headed or primarily supported by women.

OTHER LAWS IMPACTING UPON WOMEN'S STATUS

Guardianship of Children

The Guardianship of Children Act of 1961 militates against women, as regards the legal recognition of their guardianship of their children, vis-à-vis their husbands. This poses a particular difficulty for women whose husbands desert their families, and who then have to apply to the courts for legal recognition as guardians of their children. Malaysian women have been advocating a change in the law to provide for equal rights to guardianship for both parents.

Inheritance

The Distribution Act also goes against the interests of women who die intestate in that, their property will be inherited by their husbands irrespective of whether they have children or not. This Act is also under review and amendment. For Muslims, the rule whereby the widow gets an eighth share of the husband's estate if there are children, and a fourth if there are none, is justified by the patriarchal ideology that the man is responsible for support to all the members of his family, whereas by implication women do not have such a responsibility. The provisions related to marriage and divorce for non-Muslims is governed by the Law Reform (Marriage and Divorce) Act 1976 (LRA). The law outlaws bigamous and polygamous marriages, and its implementation in 1982 represents a progressive step for the women of the country.

Secular Family Law

The LRA invalidated early marriages (below the minimum age of 18), and introduced compulsory registration of all marriages. The LRA provides for divorce by mutual consent after two years of marriage, which is easily effected. However, when the divorce is contested, the entire process is complicated and long. Women are disadvantaged on issues such as child custody, division of matrimonial assets, and maintenance payments. Although the LRA includes provision for the maintenance of the spouse, the real problem arises for women in the enforcement of the husbands' legal responsibility to provide maintenance. Women thereby suffer the most due to the breakdown of marriage. Guardianship of children is vested with the father under the Guardianship of Infants Act 1961. This law is in the process of amendment in the Attorney-General's Chambers.

The Islamic Family Law Enactment

Islamic Family Law is under the legislative authority of the States with the Sultan as the prime authority. In each state, the Islamic Religious Council takes care of all matters pertaining to Islam, and the Mufti presides over a legislative committee. Administrative matters are under state religious departments, while the judiciary is under the state Syariah Court system. A fundamental issue of contention is the problem of ensuring uniformity of laws across the different states. In the late 1970s, the federal government started a process of legal reform, which is still ongoing.

A Committee set up by the Department of Islamic Development in the Prime Minister's Office has drawn up a model statute which has been passed on to the states for adoption. Model statutes for family law, administration of the law, procedural law, Syariah Criminal Law, and laws of evidence have been submitted to the states. The problem that arises is that after adopting the model statutes of the Islamic Family Law, the states make their own amendments. The model statute of the Islamic Family Law provides for greater protection of women's rights, which are whittled away by state amendments. The lack of uniformity leads to errant husbands crossing state boundaries to escape court judgments, payments of maintenance, or in order to contract polygamous marriages.

Women's organizations recently presented two memoranda on legal and administrative reform to the Government, one on polygamy and the other on other aspects of Islamic Family Laws and the overall administrative system. Consent to marriage is required from both parties. However enactments in certain states allow the father or paternal grandfather to marry off an unmarried, virgin daughter/grand daughter without her consent. Change in this has been asked for by women, as all marriages should be based upon women's consent. Besides this, the consent of the father/guardian to the marriage has also to be obtained. In cases where such consent is not forthcoming, there is the possibility of women going to other States, or outside the country to escape the provision. This creates complications regarding "foreign marriages" and the registration of these under the local laws.

Violence against Women

The Domestic Violence Act of 1994 (DVA) implemented in 1996 was the "crowning achievement" of a campaign that began in 1985. It is administered by the Ministry of National Unity and Social Development, and enforced by social welfare officers and the police. The rules and regulations under this Act are still to be prepared. The main problems with the law are the difficulty and length of time needed to obtain police protection, which is very often ineffective due to the lack of adequate provisions, as well as the attitude of the law enforcement agencies, which tend to treat domestic violence against women as a private family matter. The rape laws were amended in 1989 as a result of a vigorous campaign, but there are still shortcomings.

There is no law specifically for incest, which is subsumed under rape. This is unsatisfactory, and proposals for a new law are under consideration. The Women and Girls Protection Act of 1975 (WGPA) contains provisions for prosecuting persons involved in prostitution and trafficking of women. The Act is very vaguely worded and can be liberally interpreted. As a result, any under-aged woman found in a questionable place or circumstance may be defined as "in need of protection" and detained. This law needs to be studied and its discriminatory aspects should be amended or repealed. The Government is currently reviewing all legislation that pertains to social matters. This is being undertaken by an inter-ministerial committee chaired by the Minister of Education. Recently, it was announced that a new law has been proposed to replace three existing Acts -the Juvenile Courts Act (1947), Child Protection Act (1991), and the WGPA (1975).

Sexual Harassment

At present, there are no laws against sexual harassment at the workplace. Women who wish to pursue the matter have to make a police report and rely on the police to prosecute the aggressor under criminal law. It is very difficult to prosecute harassers in the courts and at the workplace. The situation is complicated as the women's jobs may be at risk if they file a complaint against the aggressor(s). The Labor Department headquarters has set up a special division in its office to deal with problems of female employees at their workplace. There is clear need for specific legislation to deal with the problem of sexual harassment. It should also be addressed as an area of concern in the National Policy for Women.

POLITICAL POLICIES IN THE 1990s AND STATUS OF WOMEN IN INDIA

The principle of gender equality has been basic to Indian thinking for over a century; i.e., even in the pre-independence period a thought was given to this principle through various social reformers like Rajaram Mohan Roy, Vidhyasagar, Pandita Ramabai, Mahatma Phule, Agarkar, Ranade, Veeresalingam Pantalu, Sri Narayana Guru, etc. It was in 1931 that the Indian National Congress adopted gender equality as a guiding principle in the Fundamental Rights Resolution. The Constitution of India adopted in 1950, not only grants equality to women, but also empowers the State to adopt measures of affirmative discrimination in favor of women and it also imposes a fundamental duty on every citizen to uphold the dignity of women, which, in reality is still an illusion.

Despite the above provision within the Constitution it was not until 1971 that the Govt. of India gave much thought in actuality towards the principle of gender equality and even this, only after the request from the U.N. The Govt. of India appointed a Committee on the Status of Women in India (CSWI) to examine the position of women in the changing socio-economic context. The Committee in its report (1975) entitled "Towards Equality" recommended and stressed the need for special temporary measures to transform the *de-jure* equality guaranteed by India's Constitution into *de-facto* equality.

As a consequence one could see that the shift in recognition to women and the welfare measures regarding women were reflected in the VI Five Year Plan (1980-85). In 1985, under the Human Resource Development Ministry, a separate Department of Women and Child Welfare was set up. The year 1993 witnessed two constitutional amendments i.e., 73rd and 74th, which guaranteed 1/3rd representation to women at Local Self-Government (Rural as well as Urban). Despite the efforts of the Government in leading the women into the national development process, there are still many problems like marginal employment, low level of skill, problem of being excluded from decision making, poverty, lack of education, training and information, patriarchal impact etc.

With such challenges the women's movement has been asking for more space in the decision making process at all levels: economic, social as well as political. In this context it is important to highlight three important issues undertaken by the Government of India, i.e., (1) The new economic policy, highlighting the impact on women. (Economic status), (2) The Uniform Civil Code, discussing what is it that is being asked for? (Social status), (3) The proposal of 1/3 reservation for women in the House of People and State Legislative Assemblies, (Political status).

NEW ECONOMIC POLICY

The New Economic Policy (N.E.P) was introduced primarily due to the 1990's fiscal position of the Central Government which came under severe strain because of sustained borrowing over several years. The worsening fiscal deficits of 1980's had weakened the micro-economic situation, and the Gulf War of 1990 precipitated the balance of payment crisis. The growing political instability at the turn of the decade into the 1990's further contributed towards the collapse of international confidence in the ability of Government to manage the economy.

This led to a drying up of the market for external commercial loans in 1990/1991 and capital outflow of Non-Resident Indian (NRI) deposits. Despite emergency borrowing from Reserve Tranche and the compensatory contingency financing facility of the International Monetary Fund (IMF), the level of foreign exchange reserves dropped precipitously to a little over $4 billion in June 1991, barely sufficient to finance imports for a fortnight. All these factors compelled the Congress Ministry to formulate a new economic policy on 1st June 1991. With the introduction of new economic reforms the Government of India accepted liberalization, privatization and globalization.

Basically, in the reformed economic system, liberalization broadly meant reducing import duties, giving more scope for foreign investment, lessening the control, reducing the 'Quantitative' restrictions on the imports, privatization, lessening state intervention and making the economic system more free. Taking into consideration the period prior to the entry of the new economic policy, the State played an important role concerning the problems of women. Most of the gender issues pertained 'to oppression within the family or outside to which redress was sought through the intervention of the State. Legal reforms in criminal law, particularly against dowry, rape, domestic violence and of recent regarding the property rights along with laws for equal wages, maternity protection, etc. led to considerable progress.

Although the progress achieved was not up to the expectations of the women's movement, the very actual existence of the rights and guarantees meant that an appeal could be made to an enforcing authority. Thus prior to 1990 state intervention led to much progress in the status of women although not as anticipated. The pre-reform model of development, although supported by a number of policies, was too half-heartedly established, e.g., subsidies took care of the poorer but not always all the poor; eradication of poverty was never achieved, despite wide network of schools and Public Health Centres; basic health services remained unattended and complete literacy is miles away.

With the process of liberalization and privatization of the economy, it is argued by the feminist that the new policies will further marginalise the majority of women through reduction in their employment, reduction in their family resources, withdrawal of subsidized food, and abandonment of preferential and affirmative policies like lower interest rates for the unorganized sectors and poor women. Besides, with privatization of educational and health institutions, the high cost would deprive a large number of women and poor of education and health facilities. Female labour would be exploited by the free market economy in areas where women are at a disadvantageous position.

With such an economy, can a women avail herself of and afford education with the tremendous cost that goes along with it? Although the old policy was not so good either, from the point of view of the poor and women, it did achieve a few things for both of these categories. Securities and guarantees are given in the organized sectors where one can find only 6% of women working. The organized sector has done much to draw women out of the family and household circumstances. It has also given a sort of independence to women under this sector but they meet with problems regarding their future career advancement.

Further rapid changes in technology, automation and curtailment of employment has immensely reduced the opportunities of women to work in an organized sector. Transportation, communication, and financial services are areas, besides insurance, post-telegraph, tourism, industries, and banks, where women find opportunities. But here it seems to be open only to women with education. Women are also concentrating on information handling, secretarial and clerical jobs. This being a small group they do not enjoy the same status with their male counterparts in the trade unions or associations.

Most of the union or association movements have systematically neglected the women's interest e.g., the insensitivity of trade unions towards women problems has forced some of the activists to move and establish their own organizations like SEWA (Self Employed Women's Association) split from the textile labour association of Ahmedabad (Gujarat). Taking into consideration the above two areas, women had a ray of hope in the organized sector under the public enterprises with a definite scope for educated women to enter into the work force and be a part of national development in the economic front. In the unorganized sector, with a large number of women toiling in traditional roles, women are going to face acute insecurity in the era of privatization.

The 6% women workforce in the organized public sector under the old economic policy is going to face a sharp decrease under the New Economic Policy. With the free trade, particularly in the agricultural field as construed in the GATT, denial of freedom to small farmers follows as a natural concomitant, but it will also hit the women hard. The GATT policies are aimed at further marginalizing the household and domestic food economies in which women play a significant role. It also leads to setting up multilateral trade organizations with which World Bank and IMF (International Monetary Fund) will form the centre of world governance.

The GATT is the platform where the capitalist patriarchy's notion of freedom as the unrestrained right of men with economic power to own, control, and destroy life is articulated as 'free-trade.' But for the Third World, and for women, freedom has different meanings. In what seems the remote domain of international trade, these different meanings of freedom are a focus of contest and conflict. Free trade in food and agriculture is the concrete location of the most fundamental ethical and economic issues of human existence of the present times. It is here that Third World women have a unique contribution to make because in their daily lives they embody the three colonizations on which modern patriarchy is based, the colonization of nature, of women and of the Third World?

IMPACT ON EMPLOYMENT

The impact of N.E.P. on employment at rural as well as urban areas is clear enough from the data. The male unemployment as well as female unemployment rate seems to have increased in 1993-94 as compared to the status in 1990-91. This impact is seen at both levels i.e., at urban as well as rural. The percentage of women as per rate of employment in agriculture, mining and quarrying manufacturing, utilities, construction, and total non-agricultural areas, has been declining in the post-reform period, i.e., 1993-94 as compared to the 1987-88 pre-reform period, indicating the visible adverse impact of New Economic policy.

Even in case of overall employment during the period 1983-91, it increased by 1.6%, while during 1990-98 it increased only by 1.17 which clearly indicates a decrease in employment percentage in the post reform period.

Another important result that needs mention is women's reservation policy in the public sector undertaking. Owing to privatization, there is considerable cut in governmental expenditure in public sectors. A number of public undertakings have turned into sick units and this is going to make the reservation policy of 33% for women meaningless. There has already been a deep impact on Scheduled Caste and Scheduled Tribe reservation which shows decline in percentage share after 1991. The Govt. budget cuts on government programmes for women e.g., expenditure on DWCRA (Development of Women and Children in Rural Areas) was down by 21% while Nutrition Programme declined to 11% in post- reform period.

POVERTY AND N.E.P.

Poverty in the rural sector is another problem the N.E.P has failed to address effectively. There was a steady decrease in poverty rate from 56.4% in 1973 to 34.4% in 1989. But in the post reform period particularly in 1990-91 it decreased to 35% while in 1992-93 it increased again to 44%. Thus overall, the N.E.P. seems to have a negative impact on the developmental scope of women in India.

The massive increase in rural poverty, by over 60 millions during 1990-92 was, to a large extent, a direct result of stabilization and structural adjustment policies. Comparatively, if one considers the 1983-91 situation, the 'Below Poverty Line' percentage decreased by 3.1% while during 1990-98 it increased by 2.7%. The comparison between pre-reform and post-reform situation, clearly indicates the negative impact of the NEP on the status of women.

UNIFORM CIVIL CODE

The second major policy decision of the government is the uniform civil code, another political stunt which has a base of religious identity and gender bias. This is a major challenge to the women's movement today in the form of fundamentalism and communalism. The communal frenzy generated by the demolition of Babari Masjid on 6 December 1992 and the growth of fundamental values devalued the freedom of women. The right wings of the Indian political parties are reviving traditions in the name of protecting the nation. The traditions and customs of India being patrilineal, they all the more devalue women.

Dr. B.R. Ambedkar's speeches and writings at the time of his moving Hindu Code Bill (1947) have also had a bearing on the debate over Uniform Civil Code, especially among feminists. Even at the time the defenders of the Brahminical Hindu Social Order cried against the reform of Hindu Personal Laws protesting that the Muslims should be forced to adopt a Uniform Civil Code (UCC). Dr. Ambedkar was against this. Hindu fundamentalists tried to present the UCC as a necessity for the "modernization" of the Muslim community.

But Ambedkar was very clear in saying that unless the Hindu community adopted a code that included a cohesive set of principles for reducing case and gender-based inequalities in religious practice, it had no right to insist on imposing a UCC on Muslims. In India, being multi-religious, multi-cultural, multi-lingual, it is difficult for women groups to decide in the context of religious fundamentalism to either go for a universal gender agenda or go in for a set of laws recognising their separate identities. In fact, all the personal laws are discriminatory against women. On one hand, the Constitution declares that there would be no discrimination on sex basis while on the other hand it accepts personal laws as the right of the respective groups.

This seems to be ultravires of the Constitution but the Supreme Court rejected this stand. The personal laws do not incorporate the democratic values within themselves. In fact they carry the patriarchal power structures as they exist in the realm of religion. This is what is intended to be wiped out. Instead, the Uniform Civil Code has today become a major political issue and has been totally communalized. In particular it has become a tirade against the Muslim community. The stress on the Uniform Civil Code has hailed from certain political parties and others feel the demand is in the context of Muslims.

The delay in the implementation of Article 44 of the Constitution and the enactment of the Muslims protection on Divorce Law (1986) have been the areas of emphasis. It may appear that the Uniform Civil Code has the scope limited to just Hindu and Muslim personal laws and other personal laws are to be forgotten or are not of any concern. The Christian women insist on reforms, the voice of the Parsi women does not reach the ears of the concerned since they are numerically negligible. The Hindu Code is considered to be progressive and also beyond any religious bias. Since the Preamble of the Indian Constitution promises a secular approach with equal respect to every religion, evolving a Uniform Civil Code would definitely mean picking up the best of tradition that would not obstruct the development and progress of women.

The question that arises here is what should be the stand of women groups fighting for the cause of equality and empowerment? The debate has been perused at various women platforms and the question in the Indian context is - could we really put forth a secular, democratic, gender code without ignoring or keeping aside our cultural and social norms of the society? 'The Forum of Women Against Oppression' has taken a stand of just and secular law for all irrespective of their religion, caste and creed. It is working out in detail the modus operandi of the Uniform Civil Code. There has been a suggestion by the forum to the people to press for changes in the personal law, challenging the basis and bond of patriarchy.

The forum also takes a position that there has to be universal set of laws governing divorce, maintenance, custody and guardianship, inheritance and matrimonial property rights. These laws would serve as guidelines to reform the personal laws. Besides, it also gives a thought to the infrastructure required to translate the law into reality. As the 'Forum of Women Against Oppression' has worked out the details of the Uniform Civil Code, there is a need for the other women's organization s to take positions individually at first instance and later co-ordinate the various positions after in-depth discussion. This is necessary irrespective of the different ideological base of the women's organization s to eradicate the patriarchal domination existing in the personal laws that have suppressed women of all religions, castes and ideology.

RESERVATION POLICY FOR WOMEN IN LOK SABHA AND LEGISLATIVE ASSEMBLIES

The third most important question raised is regarding women empowerment by political participation which is expected to come through reservations, where opinions diverge. The delay in the acceptance of the proposal of 33.33% reservation for women in Lok Sabha, first presented in September 1966, is caused by various factors. The basic fears raised are (i) only elite women will get in, (ii) the proxy women i.e., wife, daughter, daughter-in-law, sister, sister in-law, etc. would be put up as candidates. But some believe positively that 33.33% of women's presence would definitely improve the state of affairs in the Government.

While such fears are raised and debated in the context of reservation for women in the Lok Sabha, why was there no such outcry over the 73rd and 74th Amendments to the Constitution, providing reservation at the level of Local Self-Government - both rural and urban? As the study points out most of the women elected at local levels i.e., urban and rural, could be easily dominated and handled by their male counterparts, which it is felt, may not be so easily done at the national level.

Moreover, one third means nearly 163 men losing their power position to women in the Lok Sabha considerable enough to effect the decisions made in the House. This points towards the patrilineal tendency of providing space to women in politics at the lower rungs of the ladder without any debate. The politics of reservation could be read in between the lines of the provision of Reserved Constituency by rotation. There has been an optimistic approach of many feminist analysts that reservation has helped at least to bring up a woman who never dreamt of contesting election. The fears raised today, in the case of Lok Sabha reservation, are true for Local Self-Government level, too.

The 'daughter, wife, sister, phenomena' has been working even in the third round of election of *Panchayats* (elected body for village administration) or Corporation due to the rotation proviso. A survey showed that only one percent of women were elected for the second time without reservation. The Woman Sarpanch (Head Woman of village by election) again, to the extent of 99% were proxy, governed by the male members within the family, caste and community. This raises a question as to whether women elected in such a manner really represent women issues and achieve the objectives of the reservation policy?

The feminists are confident of having a qualitative change in the system with the introduction of women in large numbers. This is a basis for them to argue that there would be less corruption, less criminalization and less of all those negative tendencies in the system. In doing so they neglect/contradict themselves on account of accepting the gynocentric thesis of equality and equal human traits. Further, the fear of elite women upper caste/class getting in political positions is also not unrealistic. This could be supported with the small survey that was conducted which showed that as large as 80% of working women in organized sector belonged to upper caste/class.

This is associated with the opportunity of education for women. It indicates that the 33% of reservation for women in job is carried away by the upper caste/class category. Hence the fear of female elite class domination cannot be ruled out. This leads to another question as to whether the women we elect under reservation really represent the middle class and the grass-root rural women. The argument regarding representation of women on caste basis particularly to Other Backward Community women being denied by the set of women politicians ticks the mind of an unbiased - nonpartisan analyst.

Although political parties by themselves are naturally not making any effort to increase the number of women membership or women candidates for election, it has been astonishing to see the very little effort expended by women members of almost all the parties to increase the women membership of their respective parties as well as to influence the party to allow women members contest. The 1998 election had just 292 women contesting, which was half of 1996 election where 547 women had contested. Reservation will definitely make a lot of difference but, again, as at the Local Self Government level, even if caste lines are accepted, there is still a doubt that the representatives really represent their women community from all strata.

Hence, it is obvious that reservation is necessary for women as an opportunity to achieve equal status by entering into the decision/policy making arena. But the above said discrepancies cannot be ruled out.

This is once again a major issue before the women's movement, which needs to be sorted out taking into consideration the socio-religious cultural implications on one hand, as well as the objective to be achieved, i.e., empowerment of women on the other. It is rather a delicate issue to be dealt with without providing fundamentalists/communalists as well as patriarchs the opportunity to divide women along caste/class lines. The caste-class factor, the traditional social hierarchical system which dominated the male politics, is bound to influence the set up of politics.

The women's movements today have to formulate a strategy within the socio-cultural framework without disintegrating the women community. It becomes necessary to create conditions so that women would be able to forge alliances and platforms cutting across party/caste/class barriers on issues concerning women. Unfortunately, although all political parties, despite being positively unanimous regarding the reservation positively, are not supporting it when it comes to the floor of the House in the Parliament. It is being opposed and delayed - delay means denial.

The above three areas that have been discussed show that the New Economic Policy, particularly the process of privatization and liberalization, has had a very negative impact on the developmental process of women, especially in agriculture and in the unorganized sector. The Government of India needs to bridge up the lacunas that are bound to widen if no conditions in private sector are laid down. The reservation policy needs to be extended to the private sectors to equal the facilities that women in public sector enjoy. The Uniform Civil Code, too, has become a political issue and since all personal laws are discriminatory against women it is doubtful as to whether changes within personal laws to the extent as expected by women, will be made.

This speaks of the inability to break out of the caste-community bondage that has been playing havoc in the society, and is reflected even in the case of political reservation for women in the Lok Sabha and State Legislative Assemblies. There has been a demand of Other Backward Communities reservation for women, which needs separate amendment to the Constitution. But then there seems a point in the political parties' (Male counterparts) argument that Other Backward Communities would not be adequately represented just by General or Scheduled Tribe/Scheduled Caste women. As there is a need for Scheduled Tribe/Scheduled Caste women, there is a demand for OBC women reservation, too. This is a new trend emerging within women's movement, reflecting the need to address women's identity as members of their community, class, caste or religious group with a growing sensitiveness to India's diversities within her unity.

Bibliography

Arneson, R., 1992, "Exploitation," in Lawrence C. Becker (ed.) *Encyclopedia of Ethics*, New York: Garland, pp. 350-52.

Benn, S., 1988, *A Theory of Freedom*, Cambridge: Cambridge University Press.

Bigwood, R, 2003 *Exploitative Contracts*, Oxford: Oxford University Press.

Brewer, J., 1987, "Exploitation in the New Marxism of Collective Action," *Sociological Review*, 35, pp. 84-96.

Buchanan, A., 1985, *Ethics, Efficiency, and the Market*, Totowa: N.J.: Rowman and Allanheld.

---, 1984, *Marx and Justice*, Totowa: N.J.: Rowman and Allanheld.

Chang, R. (ed.), 1997, *Incommensurability, Incomparability, and Practical Reason*, Cambridge: Harvard University Press.

Elster, J., 1983, "Exploitation, Freedom, and Justice," in J. Roland Pennock and John Chapman (eds.) *Nomos XXVI: Marxism*, New York: New York University Press, pp. 227-52.

--- (ed.), 1986, *Karl Marx: A Reader*, Cambridge: Cambridge University Press.

Emanuel, E. and Hawkins, J., 2008, *Exploitation in International Clinical Research*. Princeton: Princeton University Press.

Feinberg, J., 1988, *Harmless Wrongdoing*, Oxford: Oxford University Press.

Field, M., 1989, *Surrogate Motherhood*, Cambridge: Harvard University Press.

Goodin, R., 1988a, *Reasons for Welfare*, Princeton: Princeton University Press.

---, 1988b, "Reasons for Welfare: Economic, Sociological, and Political—But Ultimately Moral," in J. Donald Moon (ed.) *Responsibility, Rights, and Welfare*, Boulder, Co.: Westview Press, pp. 19-54.

Hill, J. L., 1994, "Exploitation," *Cornell Law Review*, 79, pp. 631-99.

Holsmstrom, N., 1997, "Exploitation," *Canadian Journal of Philosophy*, 7, pp. 353-69.

Kennedy, D., 1990, "So What if College Players Turn Pro Early?" *New York Times*, January 19, 1990, Section B, p. 7.

Korsgaard, C., 1993, "The Reasons We Can Share" *Social Philosophy and Policy*, 10, pp. 24-51.

Kymlicka, W., 1989, *Liberalism, Community and Culture*, Oxford: Clarendon Press.

Levine, A., 1988, *Arguing for Socialism*, London: Verso.

Moore, B., 1973, *Reflections on the Causes of Human Misery*, Boston: Beacon Press.

Munzer, S., 1990, *A Theory of Property*, Cambridge: Cambridge University Press.

Nagel, T., 1991, *Equality and Partiality*, New York: Oxford University Press.

Nozick, R., 1974, *Anarchy, State, and Utopia*, New York: Basic Books.

Okin, S., 1989, *Justice, Gender and the Family*, New York: Basic Books.

Rawls, J., 1971, *A Theory of Justice*, Cambridge: Harvard University Press.

Reiman, J., 1987, "Exploitation, Force, and the Moral Assessment of Capitalism: Thoughts on Roemer and Cohen," *Philosophy and Public Affairs*, 16, pp. 3-41.

Roemer, J., 1985, "Should Marxists Be Interested in

Exploitation?" *Philosophy and Public Affairs*, 14, pp. 30-65.

---, 1986, "An Historical Materialist Alternative to Welfarism," in J. Elster and A. Hylland (eds.), *Foundations of Social Choice Theory*, Cambridge: Cambridge University Press.

Sample, R, 2003, *Exploitation, What It Is and Why it is Wrong*, Lanham, Md.: Rowman and Littlefield.

Temkin, L., 1993, *Equality*, New York: Oxford University Press.

Tormey, J. F., 1974, "Exploitation, Oppression and Self-Sacrifice," *Philosophical Forum*, 5, pp. 206-21.

Wertheimer, A., 1987, *Coercion*, Princeton: Princeton University Press.

---, 1996, *Exploitation*, Princeton: Princeton University Press.

Wood, A., 1995, "Exploitation," *Social Philosophy and Policy*, 12, pp. 136-58

Index